STUDIES IN HISTORY, ECONOMICS
AND PUBLIC LAW

Edited by the
FACULTY OF POLITICAL SCIENCE OF
COLUMBIA UNIVERSITY

NUMBER 432

A FINANCIAL HISTORY OF MAINE

BY

FRED EUGENE JEWETT

A FINANCIAL HISTORY OF MAINE

BY

FRED EUGENE JEWETT, Ph.D.

PROFESSOR OF BUSINESS ADMINISTRATION
OKLAHOMA AGRICULTURAL
AND MECHANICAL COLLEGE

NEW YORK
COLUMBIA UNIVERSITY PRESS
LONDON: P. S. KING & SON, LTD.
1937

COPYRIGHT, 1937

BY

COLUMBIA UNIVERSITY PRESS

PRINTED IN THE UNITED STATES OF AMERICA

To

THE MEMORY OF
JUDGE FRED EMORY BEANE

PREFACE

This study is a detailed account of the financial history of the state of Maine. It was undertaken in the hope that such a history of a typical New England state might aid in formulating plans for the future by making available the lessons of the past.

The author is especially indebted to Robert Murray Haig, McVickar Professor of Political Economy at Columbia University, whose careful reading and detailed criticism of the manuscript has been of inestimable value. Carl S. Shoup, assistant professor in the School of Business at Columbia University, has also read the manuscript and offered many helpful suggestions. Mr. Elbert D. Hayford, state auditor of Maine and William A. Runnells, state controller, have been helpful in supplying material not otherwise obtainable. Ethel Davis Jewett, the author's wife, has rendered assistance in collecting and analyzing data. Appreciation is also expressed for the courtesy shown by the staff of the Maine state library.

F. E. J.

STILLWATER, OKLA.
MARCH 25, 1937.

CONTENTS

PART ONE

A General Account of the Finances of the State, 1820–1936

Chapter		Page
I	Formative Period, 1820–1835	15
II	Extravagance and Its Aftermath, 1836–1860	30
III	The Civil War Debt and Its Liquidation, 1861–1889	42
IV	Expanding Government Functions and Extinction of the Debt, 1890–1912	66
V	The Present Day Period, 1913-1936	78

PART TWO

Studies of Selected Aspects of the Finances of the State

VI	The Property Tax	107
VII	The Taxation of Financial Institutions	138
VIII	The Taxation of Public Service Corporations	159
IX	The Public Lands	184
X	The Trust Funds	201
XI	Financial Organization and Procedure	214
Chart I.	Organization prior to 1931	opp. 220
Chart II.	Organization after 1931	opp. 220
Appendix.	Revenues and Expenditures. Tables A, B, C, D, E.	opp. 228
Bibliography		229
Index		233

LIST OF TABLES

Table		Page
1	Summary of Revenues and Expenditures 1820-1835	21
2	Debt Incurred and Paid and Amounts Outstanding by Years 1820-1835	28
3	Summary of Revenues and Expenditures 1836-1860	31
4	Debt Incurred and Paid and Amounts Outstanding by Years 1836-1860	33
5	Expenditures Classified 1836-1860	36
6	Maturities of the Public Debt of the State of Maine as of December 1, 1842	38
7	Maturities of the Debt of the State of Maine as of December 1, 1860	40
8	Revenues and Expenditures 1861-1889	43
9	Expenditures, 1861-1870	46
10	War Expenditures 1861-1870	48
11	Funded Debt of the State of Maine Outstanding December 31 for the Years 1861-1870	54
12	Temporary Debt and Unpaid Claims of Maine, December 31, 1865	55
13	Expenditures 1871-1889	58
14	Maturities of the Debt of the State of Maine as of January 1, 1871	61
15	Maturities of the Debt of Maine as of December 31, 1876	63
16	Maturities of the Bonds of the State of Maine as of December 31, 1889	65
17	Revenues and Expenditures 1890-1912	67
18	Expenditures 1890-1912	69
19	Debt Incurred and Amount Outstanding by Years 1890-1912	75
20	Revenues and Expenditures 1913-1932	80
21	Expenditures Classified 1913-1932	81
22	Expenditures Classified for Health and Welfare Purposes 1933	89
23	Revenues and Expenditures 1933-1936	96
24	Revenues 1933-1936	97
25	Expenditures 1933-1936	97
26	Bonded Debt of the State of Maine as of the End of Each Fiscal Year 1913-1936	100
27	Property Tax Levied Segregated According to Governmental Jurisdictions 1900-1932	129
28	Trend of Property Taxes Levied	130
29	Total Property Tax Rates in Maine 1902-1932	131
30	Percentage of Assessed Value to Actual Cash Market Value as Determined from Lists of Specimen Properties Showing As-	

LIST OF TABLES

		PAGE
	sessed and Actual Cash Market Value Submitted by Local Assessors in 1930	134
31	Variation in Assessment of Farm Property in Maine	135
32	Number and Capital Stock of State Commercial Banks 1819-1880	140
33	Trust Companies, Number and Assets 1885-1936	146
34	Number of Saving Banks and Deposits 1855-1936	148
35	Excise Taxes and Gross Transportation Receipts for Steam Railroads in Maine 1923-1934	171
36	Bangor and Aroostook Railroad, Data Concerning Excise Taxes and Income 1923-1934	173
37	Maine Central Railroad, Data Concerning Excise Taxes and Income 1923-1934	174
38	Sales of Public Land in Maine 1824-1878	190
39	Minimum Price Set on Each Class of Public Land by the Law of 1832	192
40	Sales of Settling Lands in Maine 1840-1878	199
41	State Trust Funds 1932	212

PART ONE

A GENERAL ACCOUNT OF THE FINANCES OF THE STATE

CHAPTER I

FORMATIVE PERIOD, 1820-1835

FINANCIAL mechanisms and financial policies usually have deep roots which run far down among historical precedents. In this country particularly, perhaps because of its comparative youth and because of the rapidity of the pace of its economic evolution, this fact is often overlooked. Too often, in the formation of plans for change, are the issues weighed without an adequate appraisal of the worth of mechanisms and policies in the light of their history and without an adequate consideration of previous experiences. It is the hope that this detailed account of the financial history of a typical New England state may facilitate the task of making intelligent use of the lessons of the past in laying the financial plans of the future.

The first part of the study, chapters I-V, is primarily a chronological story of the fluctuations in the financial situation of the state of Maine, with a brief analysis of the important factors that operated to affect that situation in various periods of its history. There follows in Part II, a series of studies of special financial topics, in more detail than can conveniently be inserted in a general chronological account of the variations in the general financial fortunes of the state.

The "District of Maine" was separated from Massachusetts and admitted to the Union as a state in the year 1820. Prior to this date the region was governed as an integral part of Massachusetts and no separate history of the finances is possible.

Sentiment in favor of separation grew out of the geographical isolation of the region and from the particular economic and social conditions that existed there. Maine was physically separated from Massachusetts proper by the state of New Hampshire. Massachusetts was well settled while Maine was still largely in the early pioneering state of development. As early as 1784 and again in 1787 conventions were held looking toward separation, but they accomplished nothing.[1] A statement of the "evils and grievances under which the people of Maine labored," drawn up by a committee appointed by the convention of 1784, shows that irritation caused by taxation played an important role. In addition to complaints regarding the general lack of understanding, the inconvenience caused by the distance from the seat of government, the expense of contesting law suits at Boston, the trade regulations which, it was alleged, operated to depress lumber prices and the inadequate representation of Maine in the legislature, the following financial grievances were cited: (1) the Massachusetts method of taxing polls and estates was unjust; (2) an undue burden fell upon the inhabitants of Maine by reason of the excise and import acts; and (3) because of the smaller value of land conveyed and the more frequent conveyance, the tax on deeds involved discrimination against the territory.

In spite of the lack of success that attended these early efforts the agitation for separation continued. In 1816 the legislature of Massachusetts went so far as to authorize the people of Maine to vote on the question but the poll failed by a narrow margin to produce the required five-to-four majority.[2] However, three years later the legislature passed a law authorizing another vote [3] and this time the count was overwhelmingly in favor of it, 17,091 to 7,132. A Constitutional Convention was promptly held in Portland. This convention drafted a constitution and petitioned for admittance to the Union. On the granting of this, Maine became a state on March 3, 1820.

The separation involved two serious financial problems: first, the distribution of the public property and, second, the distribution of the public obligations. The act of June 19, 1819, which

[1] Edward Stanward, "The Separation of Maine from Massachusetts," *Proceedings of the Massachusetts Historical Society*, Series III, pp. 125-165.
[2] Stanward, *op. cit.*, p. 138.
[3] This law was incorporated in the constitution of Maine and may be found in the volume entitled *Laws of Maine 1820*.

authorized the vote on separation, also stipulated how these problems should be met and established a joint commission to carry out its provision.

The division of the public lands between the two states was by far the most important task of the commission and was not finally completed until the early Fifties. Nearly one-half the area of the state of Maine was public land. A great portion of it was unsurveyed and the available statements of its amount, quality and characteristics were rough and undependable. Moreover, the location of the northeast boundary was in dispute, as much as three or four million acres being involved in the long standing controversy with England. The act provided that all the public land, including the area in dispute, should be equally divided between the two states and that the land allotted to Massachusetts should be exempt from taxation so long as the state held title to it.

In approaching the public land problem the commission decided to ignore the area involved in the boundary controversy and to confine its immediate activities to the territory to which England could not possibly lay claim. In its report, submitted in 1821, it compiled estimates of the amount and value of the land. These estimates established the total area of the public land at 8,218,320 acres and valued it at from four to twenty-five cents per acre, or at an aggregate of $361,680. One-half of this, $180,840, represented the interest of Massachusetts. In addition, that state had a two-thirds' interest in $12,124 of unpaid purchase money notes.[4] The commission recommended that the interest of Massachusetts in the public land be purchased by Maine, not on the ground that the purchase would be of pecuniary interest to Maine, but for the reason that such action would eliminate a cause of possible controversy between the two states. The legislature of Maine approved this suggestion, but Massachusetts declined to accept it and it was not

[4] "Report of the Joint Committee of Maine and Massachusetts," found in *Resolves of Maine 1821*, p. 77.

until 1853 that Maine acquired full title to the unsold public land within her borders.

Massachusetts had a claim against the Federal government for money spent during the War of 1812. Under the Act of Separation, Maine was to receive one-third of the proceeds of this claim. Moreover, the act provided that all "productive property" owned at the time of separation should be used to settle any outstanding indebtedness and, should a surplus remain, Maine should receive one-third. After the outstanding indebtedness had been paid, there remained a surplus of $71,997.16. One-third of this was awarded to Maine by the commission, to be paid in the following manner: in cash out of the treasury of Massachusetts, $15,888.00 and one-third of the remaining securities.

There remained the Penobscot Indian annuity. On June 19, 1818, Massachusetts had made a treaty with the Penobscot Indians under the terms of which the Indians gave up title to all their lands except four townships located on the Penobscot River and Oldtown Island in the Penobscot, and Massachusetts agreed to purchase for the Indians two acres of land in the town of Brewer, to provide them with a man to instruct them in the arts of husbandry, to repair their church at Oldtown and to deliver to them annually the following articles: five hundred bushels of corn, fifteen barrels of flour, seven barrels of clear pork, one hogshead of molasses, one hundred yards of double-breadth broadcloth, fifty good blankets, one hundred pounds of powder, four hundred pounds of shot, six boxes of chocolate, one hundred and fifty pounds of tobacco and fifty dollars in silver.[5] The Act of Separation provided that in return for $30,000 from Massachusetts, Maine should assume the obligations of this treaty. This arrangement was completed by the treaty of August 17, 1820, between Maine and the Indians. The financial burden of the annuity amounted to about $1,200 annually.[6]

5 *Laws of Maine 1843*, p. 253.
6 *Public Documents of Maine 1843*.

Maine was now ready to enter her career as a state. When the first legislature met, May 31, 1820, it found its immediate task considerably simplified by a provision in the Act of Separation that continued in effect the laws of Massachusetts until they might be modified by the legislature of the new state. The taxes, licenses and fees for the year 1820 were imposed under this provision; estimated to yield $64,000,[7] they actually produced only $23,407.[8] No explanation of this disappointing yield has been found, but whatever the reason may have been, Maine took prompt steps to collect her future revenues under her own statutes rather than under the authority of the old Massachusetts laws. As early as June 27, 1820, an act of the legislature called for a new assessment of property. The assessors of each district, town and plantation were ordered to render a return of the estates and polls in their respective districts, towns or plantations to the Secretary of State before the first day of November, 1820.[9] On the base so established, the legislature, by a resolve passed the following spring, levied a property tax for the year 1821 of $50,000.[10] In the meantime, on January 23, 1821, the legislature established a semi-annual tax of one-half of one per cent on the par value of the capital stock of state banks,[11] this act being practically a re-enactment of the Massachusetts law of 1812.[12] Other minor sources of revenue were provided, such as licenses, fees, fines, etc.

Thus was framed the tax system that, with practically no important changes, was destined to serve the state of Maine until after the Civil War. During the period under consideration, between 1820 and 1835, the annual levy on estates and polls varied from $40,000 to $50,000, but the actual collections

[7] *Resolves of Maine 1820.*
[8] Derived from Table A in Appendix.
[9] *Public Laws of Maine 1820*, ch. 19, p. 22. For a detailed explanation of this act *cf. infra*, pp. 109-115.
[10] *Private and Special Laws of Maine 1821*, ch. 85.
[11] *Public Laws of Maine 1821*, ch. 144.
[12] W. D. Williamson, *History of the State of Maine 1603-1820* (Hallowell, 1839), vol. ii, p. 625.

often ran substantially below the amounts of the levies. The tax on bank stock which produced about $15,000 annually at first, gradually increased in yield and in 1835 brought $26,390.49 into the treasury. Non-tax receipts, particularly from land sales, played an important role in these early years. Indeed taxation was responsible for only slightly more than half of the revenues of the state.

The data of both revenues and expenditures for this period are set forth in detail in Table A of the appendix. A summary of the more important facts is set forth in Table I. It is important at this point to make certain comments and explanations regarding the items of income and out-go and the resulting financial condition of the state.

First, the large items of non-tax revenue require additional comment. It has been noted that income from public lands became an important item before the end of the period. In 1824, an act was passed providing for the administration and sale of the public land, in which it will be recalled Massachusetts had a half interest.[13] Because of a specification that the land must be sold in small parcels, little progress was made under this law. Moreover, previous to 1832, the practice was to divide the land and to assign a part to Massachusetts before sale. In that year an agreement was reached whereby the land held jointly by the two states could be sold and the proceeds divided after the sale.[14] This arrangement gave an added impetus to the sale of land. In the year 1835, when speculation in Maine timber lands reached fantastic heights, the amount received from the land office amounted to $133,567.55, almost double the amount received from taxes in that year.

Another interesting item of non-tax revenue was the income from lotteries.[15] It became common for the legislature to grant

13 *Public Laws of Maine 1824*, ch. 280.

14 *Resolves of Maine 1832*, ch. 119.

15 Money from this source can not properly be considered state revenue because the state acted merely as a collecting agency for the beneficiaries of the lotteries.

TABLE 1
SUMMARY OF REVENUES AND EXPENDITURES, 1820-1835 *
(Figures in thousands)

	Revenues						
Year	State tax on polls and estates	Tax on bank stock	Sale of public land	Other revenue	Total	Expenditures	Surplus or deficit for year
1820	$ 1	$15		$ 8	$ 24	$ 38	$ -14
1821	33	15		7	55	80	-25
1822	52	15		28	95	75	20
1823	37	13	$ 1	43	94	102	-8
1824	41	14	2	13	70	80	-10
1825	44	16	1	13	74	93	-19
1826	44	18	1	26	89	82	7
1827	50	20	13	15	98	98	0
1828	49	21	22	41	133	142	-9
1829	51	18	33	18	120	123	-3
1830	49	14	45	35	143	189	-46
1831	50	17	3	147 (a)	219	150 (b)	69
1832	53	15	31	26	125	113 (c)	12
1833	50	20	24	12	106	152	-46
1834	46	24	31	11	112	143	-31
1835	51	26	134	40	251	166	85
Total	701	281	341	498	1,808	1,826	-18

* Appendix Table A.

(a) Includes $132,000 received from Federal Government on account of War of 1812 Militia Claim, *Cf. supra*, p. 21.

(b) In addition $28,000 was invested in bank stock.

(c) In addition $1,000 was invested in bank stock.

the privilege of raising money by lottery to corporations which were engaged in some activity of direct advantage to the public. These grants were chiefly to canal companies and schools. The idea seems to have been to render aid to these undertakings without directly appropriating money raised by taxation. The first lottery authorized, that of the Oxford Canal Corporation in 1823, was fairly typical.[16] The governor and council were

[16] *Private and Special Laws of Maine 1823*, ch. 219.

directed to appoint managers of the lottery, to prescribe what their pay should be and to audit their books. The managers were required to pay into the treasury of the state all money taken in, within sixty days after its receipt. The governor and council were to examine the progress of construction of the canal and to pay the money to the corporation as fast as it was needed. It was the duty of the governor and council to see that the money was expended for the purpose for which the lottery was created. Numerous other lottery grants were made but in the early Thirties opposition to them on ethical grounds arose and they were discontinued.

Included in the " other revenues " in Table I, are two extraordinary items received as the result of the agreement under the Act of Separation. The first is the $30,000 received in 1823 in return for the assumption by Maine of the Penobscot Indian annuity,[17] and the second is the $132,200 received in 1831 as a payment on Maine's share of the War of 1812 claim against the Federal government.[18]

Turning now to expenditures,[19] it is of interest to note the manner in which the new state worked out the assignment of financial responsibilities for the functions of government as between the state and the local treasuries. The building and maintenance of highways was left entirely to the counties and towns. On the other hand, the expenses of the militia were assumed by the state.[20] In the case of education and the administration of justice, the responsibility was divided and the division was several times readjusted during the period under review.

At the outset, the entire expense of maintaining the common schools was placed on the towns,[21] no appropriation by the state

17 *Cf. supra*, p. 18.
18 *Cf. supra*, p. 18.
19 For details see Appendix Table A.
20 *Public Laws of Maine 1820*, ch. 30.
21 *Ibid., 1821*, ch. 117.

being made for this purpose prior to 1828. However, small appropriations were made by the state to Bowdoin College and to certain academies. The year 1828 saw the founding of what has come to be known as the common school fund. In that year an act was passed instructing the land agent to sell twenty townships of the public land for the benefit of the primary schools.[22] This fund was " to be put out at interest, in such manner as a future legislature may determine, and the interest annually distributed among the several towns and plantations in the state according to the number of scholars." The same act directed that any money received from the Federal government on account of the claims for the War of 1812, greater than the amount the public debt might then be, should be placed in the common school fund.[23] On March 4, 1833, the legislature passed an act providing that in the future the money received from the bank tax should be apportioned to the towns and plantations for the benefit of the common schools.[24] The basis of apportionment was the number of pupils in each school district. This was the first direct appropriation of money made by the state for the benefit of the common schools and marked the beginning of a policy which recognized that common school education could not be left entirely to the towns. In 1834 another act was passed providing for the sale of twenty additional townships, the proceeds to be used in the same way as those of the act of 1828. The sale of this land was not completed for many years.

One of the very first acts of the legislature had as its object the establishment of a supreme judicial court, which was financed from the state treasury.[25] The court consisted of one chief justice and two associate justices and sat in each county on certain months of the year. The compensation of the justices

22 *Ibid., 1828*, ch. 403.

23 In 1831 this section of the act was repealed and consequently no part of the $132,200 received from this source in that year accrued to the common school fund.

24 *Public Laws of Maine 1833*, ch. 82.

25 *Ibid., 1820*, ch. 17.

was three dollars per day while attending court and one dollar for every ten miles traveled. Courts of common sessions, financed by the counties, were established to serve as local courts.

The housing of prisoners was the occasion for the state's first venture in the financing of the construction of public buildings. A very early law had directed that state prisoners be lodged in the jails of the counties in which the offense was committed.[26] The prisoners were to be provided with tools and materials and the proceeds of their labor sold, the money being applied toward the expenses incurred by the counties in caring for the prisoners. The wording of the act reveals the hope, if not the expectation, that the sale of the product of the prisoners' labor would pay all expenses, and until 1823 no payments from the state treasury for the maintenance of state prisoners is recorded. The plan, however, did not prove permanently successful and in 1823 an appropriation of $30,000 for the erection of a state prison was made.[27] Governor Paris in his message to the legislature in 1823, stated that the county jails were too small to take care of the prisoners of the state and that it would be necessary either to enlarge them or build a state prison. He advocated the building of a state prison on the ground that proceeds from the sale of the product of prisoners' labor would make the prison self-supporting. He said, " In the adjoining state the whole expense, including clothing, superintendents, guards and every other charge, averages to between fifty and sixty dollars only for each convict, annually, and this the prisoner fully pays for by his own labor."[28] A committee appointed by the legislature, reporting on January 13, 1823, did not concur with Governor Paris in regard to operating expenses, but justified their recommendation that a prison

---

[26] *Ibid.,* ch. 22.

[27] The $30,000 received from Massachusetts on account of the Penobscot Indian annuity was available for this purpose. *Cf. supra,* p. 5.

[28] "Annual Message of the Governor, 1823," found in *Resolves of Maine 1823.*

should be built on the ground that prisoners could be better cared for in a state prison. The idea that the state prison should be self-supporting persisted for some years. Although the sales of prison-made products did contribute materially to the expenses of operation, they were never sufficient to liquidate all the expense.

It was during this period, also, that the state capitol and the state insane asylum were built and the financing of these two ventures were interesting episodes. From 1820 to 1832 the administrative offices and the legislative branch of the government had been housed in the county courthouse and temporary buildings in Portland. The erection of a state capitol had been delayed by difficulties in selecting a city as the permanent seat of government. Augusta was finally chosen and on February 24, 1827, the legislature authorized the governor and council to procure a lot in that city on which public buildings could be erected, providing the lot could be obtained without cost to the state.[29] In June, 1828, the governor and council met at Augusta, selected a lot and accepted title to it as a gift to the state from citizens of Augusta.[30] A commissioner of public buildings was appointed to obtain plans for and to erect a state capitol building. The land agent was instructed to sell public land to the extent of ten and one-half townships in order to raise a maximum of $80,000. Construction began in 1829, $26,405.12 being expended in that year and $58,652.66 in 1830. In 1830, a committee of the legislature estimated that $25,000 more would be needed to complete the building and this amount was appropriated.[31] However, in 1831 it developed that an additional appropriation would be necessary to complete the building. When the matter was taken up in the legislature, a movement of considerable strength appeared calling for abandonment of

29 *Public Laws of Maine 1828*, ch. 366.

30 Report of the committee of the legislature. Found in *Resolves of Maine 1828*, p. 640.

31 *Resolves of Maine 1830*, ch. 23 and p. 113.

the project and locating the capital at some other place. It was intimated that some other city, probably Portland, would provide sufficient funds to erect a state capitol. The question was settled by the passage of an act appropriating a final $25,000 on condition that the citizens of Augusta agree to provide whatever remaining money might prove necessary to finish the building.[32] A group of Augusta citizens gave bond for $50,000 to protect the state in the performance of this agreement. Ruel Williams, an able Augusta lawyer and business man, was appointed commissioner of public buildings and the project was completed in 1832, the legislature meeting in Augusta for the first time that year. A joint committee of the legislature reported that cost of the building exceeded appropriations by $11,466.75, which was collected from the bondsmen.[33]

The next institution for which need was felt was an insane asylum. Governor Dunlap, in his annual message to the legislature in 1834, recommended that one be built.[34] A joint committee of the legislature studied the situation and reported favorably on the undertaking, stating that there existed in Maine 560 insane for whom no adequate provision had been made. It also stated that there had long been an active movement in Maine toward this end and private aid might be available.[35] The legislature appropriated $20,000 for this purpose, under the condition that a like amount should be contributed by private individuals.[36] On March 4, 1835, Benjamin Brown, of Vassalboro, offered a farm of two hundred acres, located partly in Augusta and partly in Vassalboro, and $6,000 in money provided the asylum be erected either on the farm or in Augusta. On the same date Ruel Williams offered an additional $10,000 subject to the same conditions.[37] By a resolve of March 31,

[32] *Ibid., 1831*, ch. 44.
[33] *Ibid., 1833*, ch. 98 and p. 538.
[34] *Ibid., 1834*, p. 601.
[35] *Ibid., 1834*, p. 637.
[36] *Ibid.*, ch. 53.
[37] *Public Documents 1835.*

1835, the legislature directed the treasurer to accept these gifts and to dispose of the farm and credit the proceeds to the asylum fund.[38]

Another interesting episode in this period was the venture of the state into banking. When the legislature convened on January 1, 1831, hopes were entertained that the state would soon receive a large amount of money on account of the claim against the Federal government for expenses of the militia in the War of 1812.[39] Although in 1828 a law had been passed which provided that money received from this source, in excess of the amount of the public debt, should go to the common school fund, the idea now (1831) seemed to be prevalent that this money should be invested. The charters of all the state banks expired this year and there was a strong feeling that it would be financially advantageous to the state to take advantage of this situation and enter the banking field. Thus, the investment of the money from the militia claim became connected with rechartering the banks. Governor Hunton in his annual message to the legislature said, " As it is important that provision should be made for the safe and profitable investment of the amount expected to be received from the militia claim, it has been suggested that our banking system should be arranged in reference to this object." [40] A law was passed providing that the state should have the right to purchase ten per cent of the stock of any bank and to have one member on the board of directors.[41] The act also provided that money from the militia claim should be used either to pay the public debt or to buy bank stock. Under the authority of this act, the state invested $28,000 in 1831 and $1,000 in 1832 in bank stock. No further purchases of bank stock were made and in the Forties the stock was sold and the proceeds applied on the payment of the public debt.

38 *Resolves of Maine 1835*, ch. 53.
39 *Cf. supra*, p. 18.
40 "Annual Message of the Governor, 1831." *Found in Resolves of Maine 1831*, p. 148.
41 *Public Laws of Maine 1831*, ch. dxix.

Viewing the period as a whole, it is apparent that during these early years of small beginnings and of modest undertakings, the revenues of the state fell short of its expenditures by the small sum of $18,000, as shown in Table 1. However, the results of the financial operations year by year varied widely, substantial deficits occurring in some years and substantial surpluses in others. The lack of articulation between annual income and out-go necessitated considerable resort to borrowing. The credit operations are summarized in Table 2:

TABLE 2

Debt Incurred and Paid and Amounts Outstanding by Years, 1820-1835 *

Year	Debt incurred during year	Debt paid during year	Net increase or decrease during year	Debt outstanding at end of year
1820	$ 25,300		$ 25,300	$ 25,300
1821	22,500	$ 1,000	21,500	46,800
1822	40,000	46,800	–6,800	40,000
1823				40,000
1824				40,000
1825				40,000
1826	25,000	10,000	15,000	55,000
1827	29,073	26,173	2,900	57,900
1828	27,050	39,950	–12,900	45,000
1829	7,800	7,800		45,000
1830	50,900		50,900	95,900
1831	33,434	76,334	–49,900	53,000
1832	20,000	30,000	–10,000	43,000
1833	50,466	1,500	48,966	91,966
1834	70,000	27,500	42,500	134,466
1835	59,000	138,466	–79,466	55,000

* "Special Report of Treasurer, 1835," found in *Public Documents, 1835*.

During the first decade there was some temporary borrowing but it was small in amount and soon repaid. On January 1, 1830, the state debt amounted to only $45,000. During the rest of this period, expenditures were relatively heavy and had it not been for large receipts of an unusual nature in two years the state would have been deeply involved in debt by the end of 1835. In 1830, $50,900 was borrowed and nothing paid on the debt. In 1831, $33,434 was borrowed, but because of the receipt of $132,200 from the Federal government on account of the claim for militia expenses during the War of 1812, the state was able to pay $76,334. As a result of this unusual receipt, the state was also able to invest $28,000 in bank stock in 1831 and $1,000 in 1832. In 1832, receipts exceeded expenditures slightly, but in 1833 the debt was again increased by $50,466 and in 1834 by $70,000.

The treasurer in his annual report for 1834 called attention to the financial condition of the state in the following words:

> By the foregoing exhibit it is apparent that the expenditures of the state exceed the revenues. Some recent enactments, permanent in character, such as the appropriation of the bank tax to the primary schools, the remissions of the duties for entries in action in the Judicial Courts, and the increase in expense in the military department withdraw from forty to fifty thousand dollars annually from the operative funds of the state, and no systematic provision has yet been made for this deficiency thereby created.

The legislature took no action to relieve this situation but levied only the usual state tax of $50,000. In 1835, $59,000 was borrowed but with the aid of very large receipts from the sale of public lands, $138,466 was paid on the debt, reducing it to $55,000. However, against this $55,000 debt should be offset an investment of $29,000 in bank stock and $6,000 of cash in the treasury, thereby reducing the net debt to $20,000.

In summarizing this period, it may be said that during the first decade the government was conducted economically and the legislature showed a willingness to levy taxes sufficient to meet the expenditures. During the next six years expenditures increased, largely because of the building program but also in part because of more liberal provisions for education, the administration of justice and the militia. The legislature did not adjust the tax system so as to increase its productivity and the state was saved from becoming involved in considerable debt only by the receipt of two unusual items of revenue.

CHAPTER II
EXTRAVAGANCE AND ITS AFTERMATH
1836-1860

THE year 1836 ushered in a remarkable episode in the financial history of Maine. As has been pointed out in the preceding chapter, the state treasury began the year quite unprepared for heavy financial weather. Expenditures had reached a level where the regular taxes were inadequate to finance them and to achieve a budget balance great dependence was placed on the highly sensitive and unstable item of receipts from land sales. The receipts from this source in the year 1835 had reached a figure that was destined not to be achieved again for fifteen years.[1] So great was the confidence in the continued productivity of this source that the dependable state tax on estates and polls was abandoned for a period of four years early in this period. At the same time the speculative optimism which was sweeping the country during the early years of this period was felt in Maine and expenditures for various purposes were authorized on a scale previously unheard of. The great business crisis and depression of 1837 soon began to affect the revenues from land sales. The net result was a series of annual deficiencies extending over seven years that aggregated about one and one-half million dollars and that was terminated only with a collapse of the state's power to borrow on any but ruinous terms. As a consequence of this plunge into unsound financial practice, the state found it necessary to retrench sharply and to reintroduce the state tax on property at a substantial rate. For nine years the task of liquidating the debt occupied the energies of those responsible for the state finances and only after this extended period were calm financial waters reached once more.

Most of the significant facts regarding the state's financial operations during the years of this period are summarized in

1 The fiscal year 1849-50. During the fiscal period 1845-46 the figure was exceeded but this period covered 16 months.

TABLE 3
Summary of Revenues and Expenditures, 1836-1860 *
(Figures in thousands)

Year	State tax on polls and estates	Tax on bank stock	Sale of public lands	From Federal government	Other revenues	Total	Expenditures	Surplus or deficit for year
1836	$ 49	$ 36	$ 45		$ 16	$ 150	$ 207	$ –57
1837	1	49	12	$ 22	19	102	229	–127
1838 [a]								
1839		45	30		15	90	514	–424
1840	3	41	3		5	52	654	–602
1841	99	34	69		10	212	352	–140
1842	198	30	22		9	259	299	–40
1843	204	28	55	434	10	731	289	442
1844	215	26	107		22	370	292	78
1845-1846 [b]	220	39	157	162	34	612	317	295
1846-1847	155	26	68	20	16	285	278	76
1847-1848	165	25	103		39	332	273	59
1848-1849	123	26	90		37	276	267	9
1849-1850	191	27	136		42 [e]	396	273	123
1850-1851	208	28	142	3	45	426	279	147
1851-1852 [c]	338	51	158	176	21	744	470	275
1853	191	41	106		23	361	424	–62
1854	206	57	75		22	360	314	46
1855	201	70	28		8	307	355	–48
1856	211	76	106		17	410	348	62
1857	193	75	54		6	328	427	–99
1858	199	75	51	10	8	343	315	28
1859 [a]								
1860 [d]	222	75	30	8	63	398	478	–80

* Appendix Table B.
[a] No reports found.
[b] Period of 16 months, January 1, 1845 to April 30, 1846.
[c] Period of 20 months May 31, 1851 to December 31, 1852.
[d] Because data are lacking for 1838 and 1859 no totals are given.
[e] In addition during this year the treasurer received $130,000 from sale of United States bonds which had been purchased previously from surplus revenues.

Table 3.[2] The story of the revenues and expenditures of the state year by year can be traced in these figures. For the credit operations the reader is referred to Table 4.

The large sales of public lands in the year 1835 formed the foundation for the most extravagant hopes regarding the role which this resource would play in the future finances of the state. In a report of the committee on finance of the house of representatives, submitted April 1, 1836, the following remarkable passage occurs:

> Sales of 229,986 acres of the public land have been made by the Land Agent during the past year, for which cash and notes have been received to the amount of $335,478.62 and the sum of $133,567 has been paid into the treasury; and your committee are of the opinion that the interest at six per cent on the present value of the public lands now owned by the state would be amply sufficient to meet all of the necessary expenditures.
>
> The operations of the financial department of the last year fully confirm your committee in the opinion heretofore expressed that a State tax in the future will not be necessary.[3]

The legislature was quick to accept this view and levied no state tax in 1836 or in any of the succeeding years until 1840.

Disillusionment came almost at once. Receipts from the land office for 1836, estimated at $120,000, amounted to only $44,591.66. To meet the expenses of 1836, the treasurer was obliged to borrow $80,000. One might think that the experience of 1836 should have led the treasurer to demand that the legislature levy a state tax for 1837. However, his position, as revealed in his annual report dated December 31, 1836[4] was distinctly antagonistic to direct taxation. Referring to the public lands as a source of revenue, he said:

> Though these lands are of great value and will ultimately yield great revenue to the state, the present income from them can but

[2] For details see Appendix Table B.
[3] *Resolves of Maine 1836*, p. 117.
[4] "Annual Report of the Treasurer, 1836," *Public Documents 1837*.

TABLE 4

Debt Incurred and Paid and Amounts Outstanding by Years, 1836-1860
(Figures in thousands)

Year	Debt incurred during period (a) 1	Debt paid during period (a) 2	Net increase or decrease during period 3	Debt outstanding at end of each year (b) 4
1836	$ 80		$ 80	$ 135
1837	181	$ 35	146	281
1838 (c)				584
1839	647	225	422	1,187
1840	1,280	603	677	1,619
1841	134	20	114	1,734
1842		9	−9	1,725
1843		62	−62	1,663
1844		73	−73	1,590
1845-46		317	−317	1,247
1846-47		132	−132	1,143
1847-48	137	162	−25	1,117
1848-49		56	−56	1,061
1849-50		206	−206	855
1850-51		228	−228	627
1851-52		155	−155	472
1853	250 (d)	10	240	712
1854		30	−30	682
1855	218	242	−24	658
1856	180	138	42	700
1857	30	30		700
1858	30	30		700
1859 (c)				
1860	51	51		700

(a) Derived from Table B in Appendix.

(b) Column 4 derived from columns 1, 2, and 3 except for years 1838, 1839, 1840, and 1841 which were taken from *Annual Report of Treasurer, 1867*, p. 12. Figures in columns 1, 2, and 3 for the years 1839, 1840 and 1841 do not reconcile with column 4 for those years because figures in column 4 include unpaid claims which do not appear in Table B of Appendix as borrowing or debt payment.

(c) No reports found.

(d) Bonds issued to Massachusetts in payment of public land.

partially supply the current needs of the Treasury: and it may be many years before this source of revenue shall be equal to the public expenditures. It is therefore necessary that for several years to come a system of ways and means shall be provided from other sources for a portion of the public disbursements.

He then continued: " Direct taxation is the most odious and the most expensive way of sustaining the government. It should be avoided if possible." He pointed out that a state tax in 1837 would not relieve the treasury for that year because the tax could not be collected until 1838, and also that a state tax would be very unjust because the state valuation which had been made in 1830 did not represent the true value of property. As a way out of the difficulty he recommended that the bank tax be diverted from the common schools to the general use of the treasury and that the funds expected from the distribution of the Federal surplus [5] be invested and the interest used for the general expenses. The legislature ignored his specific recommendations and did nothing to provide for the expected deficiency. For the year 1837, in spite of the windfall from the Federal government, the expenditures exceeded the revenues by $127,000. Land sales produced only a meager $12,000.

When the legislature met in 1838, the condition of the finances was recognized as serious. Governor Kent, in his annual message to the legislature in January, 1838, estimated that the expenditures for the year would exceed the revenues by $85,717.09, but still he felt that " in the present pressure and difficulty in the community it would be unjust and oppressive to meet all the demands of the treasury by a direct tax the present year." [6] His only suggestion was further borrowing. Again the legislature levied no state tax and provided no additional revenue. No record of expenditures for 1838 could be

[5] The payment was the result of a law passed by Congress in 1836 providing that the surplus in the Federal treasury should be deposited with the states. Maine received $22,180.91 from this source in 1837.

[6] "Annual Message of the Governor, 1838," *Public Documents 1839.*

EXTRAVAGANCE AND ITS AFTERMATH

found but it is known that the state debt increased $303,690.97 during the year.[7]

In 1839 the revenues decreased to $90,000 while expenditures, largely as the result of military operations in connection with the border dispute with England, rose to $514,000. The treasurer, by the end of the year, was deeply alarmed and in his annual report made December 31, 1839, he said:

> Since 1835 the state has been involving itself deeper and deeper in debt, exclusive of the great expenses of the quasi border war of 1839. No longer pursue this downward course; curtail all expenses not imperiously necessary; withhold grants and gratuities which were liberally bestowed by the last legislature; and above all let a fixed certain amount of revenue be established to meet the current necessary expenses of the government. Nothing short of this will revive and sustain the credit of the state at home and abroad.
>
> Therefore, levy a State tax for 1840, of sufficient magnitude to pay all expenses, including interest on the State debt. This tax will not be available until the commencement of 1841. To meet the claims on the Treasury for 1840 . . . further loans must be resorted to.[8]

The treasurer had reason for concern. The treasury was empty and there remained unpaid claims amounting to $199,192.39. Toward the end of the year the treasurer had been unable to borrow except at a discount of from fifteen to twenty per cent. He chose to let the claims go unpaid rather than borrow under these conditions. During the year 1839 the net increase in the debt, exclusive of unpaid claims, was $422,023.

Expenditures were heavy during the period 1836-1841. Attention is called to the figures in Table 5 and to the Appendix Table B-II. It will be observed that all items of expense rose somewhat but the greater portion of the increase is accounted for by new activities and by certain emergency items.

[7] *Annual Report of the Treasurer 1867*, p. 12.
[8] "Annual Report of the Treasurer, 1839," *Public Documents 1840.*

TABLE 5

EXPENDITURES CLASSIFIED, 1836-1860 *

(Figures in thousands)

Year	General	Education	Interest	Developmental	Defectives	Taxes collected and paid to towns	All others	Total
1836	$ 81	$29	$ 3	$ 18	$ 14		$ 62	$207
1837	91	36	7	10	39		46	229 (e)
1838 (a)								
1839	96	7	31	17	21		341 (c)	514
1840	152	42	90	202 (b)	22		146 (c)	654
1841	143	46	98	4	13		48	352
1842	111	36	103	2	9	$ 2	35	299
1843	124	29	100	2	8	11	15	289
1844	115	29	98	2	17	10	21	292
1845-46 ...	113	27	138	2	10	12	16	317
1846-47 ...	102	27	79	3	21	9	38 (d)	278
1847-48 ...	96	29	73	3	23	27	21	273
1848-49 ...	109	28	69	4	21	23	12	267
1849-50 ...	120	29	62	3	20	24	14	273
1850-51 ...	139	36	52	8	15	1	28	279
1851-52 ...	190	65	51	9	122	5	27	470
1853	136	44	42	4	60	6	132 (f)	424
1854	148	51	39	6	50	3	19	314
1855	144	69	38	7	67	6	24	355
1856	141	85	38	7	51	3	23	348
1857	199	83	39	10	59	4	33	427
1858	151	41	39	9	55	3	18	315
1859 (a)								
1860	121	96	41	11	42	4	161	478

* Derived from Table B in Appendix.

(a) No reports found.

(b) Includes payments of back claims for 1839.

(c) Includes expenses for boundary dispute.

(d) There was also purchased $150,000 of United States Government bonds out of surplus funds.

(e) Discrepancies in last digit of Total column due to rounding figures.

(f) Includes payment of $112,000 to Massachusetts for public land. Bonds amounting to $250,000 were also given directly to Massachusetts as additional payment for the land. Since this did not involve a cash outlay at this time this amount was not included in the expenditures.

EXTRAVAGANCE AND ITS AFTERMATH

The mania for internal improvements which swept the country at this time and brought financial disaster to so many states, left Maine's finances relatively unscathed. In 1836, it is true, a board of internal improvements was created, the purpose of which was to make surveys and to acquire information about the state. Its activities, however, were confined to making surveys for the routes of two proposed railroads and a geologic survey, the cost of which was only about $30,000 a year.

Much more serious in its effect upon the state treasury was an early experiment in farm relief. In 1837, an act was passed granting a bounty to each wheat producer of $2.00 for the first twenty bushels produced and six cents for each additional bushel.[9] This bounty cost the state $76,945.65 in 1838.[10] The next year, the bounty for amounts of wheat in excess of 200 bushels was reduced to three cents and the following bounty was granted on corn: $2.00 for the first thirty bushels of "sound husked ears of Indian corn," for the next thirty bushels $1.00, and two cents per bushel for all over sixty bushels.[11] These bounties cost the state $153,981.75 in 1839.

Most important of all for the immediate financial problem was the border episode of 1839. In that year, the Northeastern Boundary Dispute became acute and troops were sent to defend the territory. This activity cost the state $316,337 in 1839 and additional claims were paid in 1840. In its ultimate effects, this episode was not serious because the Federal government reimbursed Maine for all of its disbursements and paid an indemnity of $125,000 in addition. But these Federal payments did not arrive until years later after the most acute stage of the state's financial trouble had been passed.

In 1840, the legislature was at last forced to face the fact that the state's treasury was empty and her borrowing power at least temporarily exhausted. The bounty laws were repealed

9 *Public Laws of Maine 1837*, ch. 295.
10 *Resolves of Maine 1838*, p. 295.
11 *Public Laws of Maine 1838*, ch. 334.

and appropriations were brought down to a minimum. A new property valuation was ordered, to be completed by November 1, 1840,[12] and a state tax was levied on it, estimated to produce over $100,000 early in 1841.[13] The calendar year of 1840 shows the worst record of any year during the period, with $654,000 of expenditures and only $52,000 of revenue. With an improvement in the outlook, borrowing again became possible and the unpaid bills of 1839 were liquidated.

TABLE 6

MATURITIES OF THE PUBLIC DEBT OF THE STATE OF MAINE AS OF DECEMBER 1, 1842 *

1842	$ 731	1851	$450,685
1843	17,000	1852	134,000
1845	262,146	1854	10,000
1846	1,500	1855	282,000
1847	55,800	1856	133,000
1848	283,000	1860	63,500
1850	31,500		

* *Annual Report of the Treasurer, 1842, p. 4.*

Although retrenchment in expenditures was pushed still further during the next year and the amount of the property tax was doubled, the year 1841 brought an operating deficit of $140,000 and a net increase in the outstanding debt of $114,000. In six years the debt had risen from $55,000 to $1,734,000 and the state now began to reduce it.

Table 3 shows that after 1842 for a period of nine years receipts exceeded expenditures and permitted a reduction of the outstanding debt. By 1852 it had been brought within manageable limits. In 1842 the problem of paying the state debt was complicated by its irregular maturities and by certain irregular receipts. How unevenly the maturities fell will be apparent from Table 6.

12 *Public Laws of Maine 1840*, ch. 71.
13 *Ibid.*, ch. 72.

EXTRAVAGANCE AND ITS AFTERMATH 39

Very large receipts came from the Federal government on account of the Northeastern Boundary Claim, $434,000 in 1843 and $162,000 in 1845, and caused cash to accumulate in the treasury in much greater amount than the maturing public debt. This cash balance was a constant temptation for the legislature to reduce the annual $200,000 state tax which had been levied since 1842. As a means of reducing this temptation, the treasurer, in 1843 and 1844,[14] persuaded the legislature to pass laws allowing him to purchase state bonds when they could be obtained without paying too great a premium. Few bonds were purchased in these years, however, because the bonds commanded too high a price. Conditions changed in 1846 so that state bonds could be purchased at par and a policy was adopted of buying bonds in the open market as fast as funds became available. Receipts from the sale of public land were unusually large from 1848 to 1852 and in the latter year another large payment ($176,000) was received from the Federal government on account of the Northeastern Boundary Claim. These funds made possible the reduction of the debt to $472,000 by the end of 1852.

In 1853, the state purchased the remaining public lands owned by Massachusetts, giving in payment $112,000 in cash and serial bonds amounting to $250,000. As a result of this operation, the state debt increased to $712,000 in 1853. Following 1853, receipts from the sale of public lands decreased and little was paid on the debt. From 1855 to the end of the period the debt was refunded as it matured. Table 7 presents the maturities of the debt as of December 31, 1860.

No extended treatment of the tax revenues is necessary because on the whole they remained relatively constant and there were no important changes in the laws. In all but three years the state tax on property was approximately $200,000. To produce $200,000, a rate of approximately three mills was needed on the valuation of 1840. This rate was levied in all but two

14 *Resolves of Maine 1843*, ch. 203; *1844*, ch. 234.

TABLE 7
MATURITIES OF THE DEBT OF THE STATE OF MAINE AS OF DECEMBER 31, 1860 *

1861	$30,000	1870	$30,000
1862	30,000	1871	40,000
1863	50,000	1872	40,000
1864	50,000	1873	54,000
1865	37,000	1874	50,000
1866	37,000	1875	30,000
1867	37,000	1876	60,000
1868	37,000	1877	51,000
1869	37,000		

* *Annual Report of the Treasurer, 1860, p. 9.*

years until 1850. In 1845, the rate was cut to 2.18 mills, while in 1847 it was cut to one and one-half mills.[15] In 1850, a new valuation was taken which amounted to $100,157,573. On this valuation a rate of two mills was necessary to produce approximately $200,000 and this rate was levied each year until 1860.[16] The valuation in 1860 amounted to $164,714,168 and on this valuation it was necessary to levy only a rate of one and one-fourth mills for 1860.[17]

The bank tax increased from $29,590 in 1842 to $75,000 in 1860. This increase was caused by the growth in the number and capitalization of banks. The law was not changed.

The business recovery which began in the early Forties resulted in increased sales of timber land. Fluctuations in receipts from this source from 1843 to 1856 were largely the results of changing conditions in the lumber market. By 1856 the most valuable of the timber lands had been sold and receipts from this source declined and soon became negligible.

Expenditures for the period 1842-1860 are presented in Table 5. For a more detailed treatment, the reader is referred to Table B-II in the appendix. The general expenditures, which included those for the executive, the departments and the judiciary, were $111,000 in 1842 and increased gradually. Educa-

[15] *Annual Report of the State Board of Assessors, 1928*, p. 300.
[16] *Ibid.*
[17] *Ibid.*

tional expenditures increased because of the increased yield of the tax on the capital stock of banks which was annually appropriated for the support of the common schools. Interest payments decreased from $103,000 in 1842 to $41,000 in 1860 because of a reduction in the outstanding indebtedness. The greatest increase occurred in the item "Defectives," which included the state prison, state insane asylum and the reform school for boys. In 1849, the construction of a reform school for boys at South Portland was started which was completed in 1852 at a cost of $52,000. In 1852, new construction at the state prison cost $18,000 and a new wing was built on the insane asylum at Augusta, which cost $24,000, replacing damage by fire which had occurred in both of these institutions in 1851. After this year there were no unusual items of expenditure for defectives, but the increase which took place was caused by the opening of the reform school and the enlargement of the insane asylum. An additional large item of expenditure occurred in 1852 when Maine purchased the remaining public lands owned by Massachusetts, for $362,000. Bonds were given in payment to the extent of $250,000, while the remainder was paid in cash.

In summarizing the period from 1842 to 1860, it can be said that it was a commendable one in the history of the state. From 1842 to 1855 revenues exceeded expenditures in all but two years and the debt was reduced to manageable proportions. From this year to the end of the period expenditures exceeded revenues by a small amount and the debt was refunded as it matured. Sound finance called for the continuance in the Fifties of the three-mill state tax which had been levied in the Forties, thus providing funds for payment of the debt as it matured. Nevertheless, at the end of the period the state was in a strong financial position. On the valuation of 1860, a state tax rate of one and one-quarter mills produced revenue enough to meet the ordinary expenditures. The debt amounted to only $700,000 or about $1.15 per capita and, as will appear from Table 7, offered no particular difficulties.

CHAPTER III
THE CIVIL WAR DEBT AND ITS LIQUIDATION

THE year 1861 saw the beginning of the Civil War, which involved the state so heavily in debt that it was twenty-four years after the close of the war before the debt could be reduced to manageable proportions. As has been pointed out in the preceding chapter, the state treasury, at the beginning of the year, was in a strong financial position, but by the beginning of 1865 expenditures and debt had increased to such an extent that the state credit was temporarily impaired and it was only restored by the levy of a state property tax at the hitherto unheard of rate of fifteen mills. In 1870 the Civil War financing was completed and from that time until 1889 it was necessary to hold the operating expenses of the government to a minimum and for those responsible for the financial management of the treasury to devote their energies to the reduction of the debt. A revision of the tax system was also necessary. In 1860 nearly half of the state revenues came from sources other than the state property tax but by 1870 the state property tax had become nearly the sole source of receipts and, consequently, from 1870 to the end of the century, strenuous efforts were made to find other sources of revenue in order that part of the burden of supporting the state government might be lifted from property.

Most of the significant facts regarding the financial operations of the state are summarized in Tables 8, 9, 10, and 11.[1] The story year by year can be traced in these figures.[2]

[1] For details see Appendix Table C.

[2] Because of the complicated operations of the sinking funds, for which data are lacking, it has not been possible to construct a table showing the yearly debt increase or decrease.

REVENUES AND EXPENDITURES, 1861–1889 *
(Figures in thousands)

	Revenues						Expenditures	Surplus or deficit for year
	State tax on property	Bank taxes (a)	Taxes on public service corporations	From Federal government	Other revenues	Total		
1861	$ 227	$ 78		$200	$ 54	$ 559	$1,327	−$768
1862	264	79		251	66	660	607	53
1863	423	60		429	48	960	1,741	−781
1864	829	35		204	64	1,132	4,321	−3,189
1865	1,279	19		51	31	1,380	2,201	−821
1866	2,156	5			70	2,231	1,185	1,046
1867	1,345	4		209	46	1,605	1,305	300
1868	816	1		248	84	1,149	862	287
1869	889				51	940	805	135
1870	1,176			678	48	1,902	1,753 (b)	149
1871	2,096				46	2,142	975	1,167
1872	1,152	120			52	1,324	917	407
1873	1,244	140			35	1,419	1,148	271
1874	1,168	143	$ 14		98	1,423	1,299	124
1875	1,050	372	51		95	1,568	1,286	282
1876	899	279	54		79	1,311	1,184	127
1877	872	246	29		61	1,208	1,244	−36
1878				No reports found				
1879	819	167	70		47	1,103	1,086	17
1880	941	167	19		37	1,164	1,104	60
1881	1,092	178	59		68	1,397	1,073	324
1882	1,055	206	124		44	1,429	968	461
1883	1,062	175	100		51	1,388	1,259	129
1884	969	192	102		55	1,318	1,069	249
1885	1,084	210	100		54	1,448	1,195	253
1886	856	235	94		61	1,246	1,106	140
1887				No reports found				
1888	638	272	100		77	1,087	1,127	−40
1889	683	296	109		1,478 (c)	2,566	1,487	1,079

* Source: Appendix Table C.
(a) From 1861 to 1869 composed of tax on capital stock of state banks. After 1872 composed of tax on deposits of savings banks.
(b) Includes payment of $678,000 as subsidy to European and North American Railroad.
(c) Includes $1,235,674 received from sale of bonds in sinking fund.

The receipts from 1861 to 1870 do not call for an extended treatment. Table 8 shows that the state property tax greatly increased and that in 1870 it was almost the sole source of tax revenue. During the first three years of this period the belief was common that the war would soon be over and that the excess of expenditures over receipts could safely be met by borrowing instead of by increased taxation. By the end of 1863, this belief was dissipated and a higher state property tax was levied for 1864 but this proved inadequate. Before the end of the year 1865, the condition of the treasury became serious; many unpaid claims were outstanding, which the treasurer had no money to pay, and it had been found impossible to borrow except at a discount of from fifteen to twenty per cent. The situation was well described by the treasurer in his annual report.

Among the questions engaging the attention of the legislature, none were more pressing than that of finance. To continue to sell its bonds must from very weight endanger the financial integrity. The policy of the past was changed. The resolution was taken to tax the people, but not only for the current expenses and for the debt maturing during the year, but for a sinking fund, looking to the ultimate extinction of the debt.[3]

The change of policy referred to by the treasurer resulted in the levying of a fifteen-mill property tax due January 1, 1866, which produced sufficient revenue to pay all back claims and current expenses for the year 1866 and to start a sinking fund for the retirement of the funded debt. From this time until 1870, the rate was gradually reduced until in that year it amounted to five mills.

Between 1861 and 1870, receipts from the tax on the capital stock of state banks ceased and those from the sale of public lands became negligible, leaving the state property tax as almost the sole source of revenue. Conversion of state banks to national

[3] *Annual Report of the Treasurer 1865*, p. 10.

banks and the passage of an act which permitted state banks to offset federal taxes on banks against state bank taxes caused the cessation of revenue from this source,[4] while receipts from the sale of public lands became negligible because by 1861 the most valuable of the public land had been sold.

Receipts from the Federal government during these years were, for all except 1868 and 1870, on account of equipping soldiers for the United States army and soldiers' allotments.[5] Those for 1868 and 1870 were partially on account of the War of 1812 militia claims and the claims arising from the settlement of the Northeastern Boundary Dispute.

Expenditures from 1861 to 1870 were dominated by the cost of the Civil War. During this period, as shown in Table 9, the ordinary operating expenses were held to a minimum, being little more than sufficient to offset rising prices, the payment of pensions and a railroad subsidy. In 1866, a pension was granted to disabled soldiers and seamen and to the widows and orphans of soldiers and seamen of eight dollars per month,[6] which, in 1867 and years immediately following, cost the state approximately $125,000 a year. In 1868 and 1870, payments were made to the European and North American Railroad to aid in the construction of a railroad from Bangor to St. John. Maine and Massachusetts had a claim on the Federal government for expenses during the War of 1812 which they agreed to give to the railroad company as a subsidy when collected. The Federal government paid $146,593.75 in 1868 and $678,000 in 1870 on account of this claim and these amounts were paid to the railroad company in the years received. Maine also made a large grant of land to the railroad company for the same purpose.[7]

[4] *Cf. infra*, p. 138.
[5] *Cf. infra*, p. 47.
[6] *Public Laws of Maine 1866*, ch. 48.
[7] *Cf. infra*, p. 188.

TABLE 9
EXPENDITURES, 1861–1870 *
(Figures in thousands)

Year	General	Education	Interest	Defectives	Health and Charity	Taxes collected for county, city, and town	Other (a)	Total
1861 ...	$ 82	$ 72	$ 40	$ 52		$ 5	$1,076	$1,324
1862 ...	89	81	84	45		3	305	607
1863 ...	99	90	100	54		6	1,392	1,739
1864 ...	102	82	226	53		4	3,854	4,321
1865 ...	92	48	323	74		4	1,660	2,201
1866 ...	113	40	325	81		4	622	1,186
1867 ...	125	63	349	80		5	683	1,305
1868 ...	112	35	296	80		5	332 (b)	862
1869 ...	120	46	313	118	$ 30	5	173	805
1870 ...	155	126	473	129	34	6	830 (c)	1,753

* Appendix Table C.

(a) Includes expenditures for war purposes. For details of war expenditures see Table 10.

(b) Includes payment of $146,593 to European and North American Railroad as subsidy.

(c) Includes payment of $678,000 to European and North American Railroad as subsidy.

Most of the important facts concerning the war expenditures are summarized in Table 10. On April 22, 1861, the legislature convened in special session on the call of the governor to consider the exigencies which had arisen as a result of the opening of hostilities. The President had called for one regiment of the militia to be mustered into the service of the United States and it was expected that additional calls would soon be made.[8] The condition of the militia was such, as shown by the following quotation, that quick action was necessary to fit it for active service.

[8] *Message of Governor Washburn to the Extra Session of the Legislature 1861.*

CIVIL WAR DEBT AND LIQUIDATION 47

With an enrolled but unarmed Militia of some 60,000 men, not more than 1,200 were in condition to respond to the call for ordinary duty within the state, ... while uniforms, equipment and camp equipage were of a character totally unfitted for service in the field. With full knowledge of this state of things, and apprehending the embarrassment under which the general government would labor ... our legislature determined upon furnishing the government, at the earliest possible moment, with ten regiments, fully armed and equipped, to serve under a two year enlistment.[9]

The legislature acted promptly to meet the emergency by passing an act authorizing the governor and council to enlist and equip ten regiments for the United States service, pay bounties to non-commissioned officers and enlisted men equal to two months' pay as an incentive to enlistment, and appropriated $1,000,000 for these purposes. The governor and council were also authorized to take such action as should be thought necessary for the protection of the coast and $300,000 was appropriated for this purpose. The treasurer was instructed to borrow as much of $1,300,000 as might be needed to provide for these appropriations.[10] Another act provided that the militia should be reorganized in such a manner as would best fit the needs of the war.[11] The first regiment was mustered into the service of the United States on May 7, seven days after the passage of the authorizing act, and during the year a total of 16,345 men entered the Federal army. The first ten regiments, as planned, were enlisted and equipped by the state while the remainder were enlisted and equipped by the Federal government.[12]

In Table 10, war expenditures have been classified in order to show for what purposes they were made. The item " Gen-

[9] *Report of the Adjutant General 1861*, p. 1.
[10] *Public Laws of Maine 1861*, chapters 60 and 63; *Resolves of Maine 1861*, ch. 96.
[11] *Public Laws of Maine 1861*, ch. 64.
[12] *Annual Message of the Governor 1862*.

eral" was largely made up of the expenses of the Adjutant General's department except in the years 1861 and 1862 when the expenses of enlisting and equipping the first ten regiments were included.

TABLE 10

WAR EXPENDITURES, 1861-1870 *

(Figures in thousands)

Year	General	Bounties	Aid to families	Allotments	Total
1861	$ 813	$ 195			$ 1,008
1862	125			$ 109	234
1863	64	636	$ 223	410	1,332 (a)
1864	74	2,988	532	186	3,780
1865	70	748	670	96	1,584
1866	19	46	462	14	541
1867	3	416	75	1	495
1870 (b) .		3,105			3,105
Total	1,167 (a)	8,134	1,963 (a)	816	12,080 (a) (c)

* Annual reports of the treasurer.
(a) Discrepancies in last digit accounted for by omission of thousands.
(b) Municipal bounties assumed by the state.
(c) Total war expenditures, exclusive of allotments, $11,254,046.25.

The largest item in the direct cost of the war was payments of bounties to soldiers for the purpose of encouraging enlistments. These payments amounted to 72.2 per cent of the direct cost of the war. The bounty system developed as a result of the method used by the Federal government in securing soldiers for the United States army. When additional soldiers were needed, the President called for a certain number and apportioned this number among the states according to population, allowing the states to secure this number in any way they saw fit. The states usually followed the same procedure and apportioned the number among the cities and towns according to population. Both the state and cities and towns offered bounties, attempting thereby to facilitate the fulfilling of their quotas. The passage of the draft act in 1862 did not, as might have been supposed, eliminate the bounty system, because of the practice of allowing a drafted man to furnish a substitute and because of the competition between the states and among cities and towns in attempting to enlist one another's citizens. The result of the practice of allowing drafted men to furnish substitutes was that wealthy men could buy free of the draft while poor men could not. Actuated by a spirit of justice, many cities and towns attempted to offer bounties sufficiently large to enable every drafted man to hire a substitute. Competition among the states and among cities and towns in the payment of bounties grew out of the regulation which permitted an enlistment to be counted toward filling the draft quota of the city or town where the enlistment took place instead of at the residence of the enlisted man. Large bounties were offered in the hopes of attracting men from other places or for the purpose of counteracting such offers. A contemporary view of the bounty system was well presented by the Adjutant General in his annual report for 1862, from which the following quotation is taken.

But the wealthier New England states, having set the example of paying exorbitant bounties, thereby inducing our citizens to enter service in other states, the same system was adopted almost universally throughout this state, and bounties varying from twenty to four hundred dollars were offered for single enlistments by our cities, towns and plantations.

More than a million and a half dollars have been distributed by our cities and towns, to volunteers to fill the quotas. . . . The payment of this vast sum has been prolific of evil. . . . Many of the recipients, unaccustomed to the possession of so large amounts of money at one time . . . regarded them as a gift, of which they were obliged to rid themselves at the earliest possible moment. Some of these volunteers were members of our earlier regiments, who reentered the army at this time only to secure the enormous gratuities so insanely proffered. . . . A large amount of the money has gone into the pockets of agents and brokers. . . . Deceptions and frauds in all forms . . . characterized the details of so much of this work.[13]

The legislature, in 1861, as previously noted, authorized a bounty of two months' pay to enlisted men as encouragement for enlistment in the first ten regiments, which cost the state $195,000 in 1861. Authority to pay bounties expired with the completion of the enlistment of the first ten regiments, but when the legislature met in January, 1863, it was informed by the governor that during the preceding year his predecessor, with the approval of the council, had authorized the payment of bounties to the extent of $340,000 and had borrowed the money from banks to make these payments, forty dollars having been paid for enlistments in new regiments and fifty-five for regiments in the field.[14] This was illegal because no legislative authority existed for the payment of these bounties and because the governor and council had no authority to borrow without authorization by the legislature. The legislature, however, authorized the governor to pay the bank loans and to continue to pay such bounties as long as he saw fit.[15] No payments for bounties appear in the expenditures for 1862 because the procedure followed was for banks to advance the money directly to the paymaster general who made the payments to the soldiers. An act was passed later in the year providing that a bounty of $100 should be paid to every drafted man,[16] previous bounties having been payable only to men who had voluntarily enlisted. In 1864, bounty payments by the state were increased to $300.00, but the amount which cities and towns could pay was limited to $25.00. The treasurer was also authorized to pay these bounties in script instead of cash, should the condition of the

13 *Report of the Adjutant General 1862*, pp. 6, 7.
14 *Annual Message of the Governor 1863*.
15 *Resolves of Maine 1863*, ch. 199.
16 *Public Laws of Maine 1862*, ch. 218.

treasury necessitate it.[17] These laws remained in effect until the end of the war. The last script was not redeemed until 1867.

One other feature of bounty payments remains to be considered, which is the assumption by the state of debts incurred by the municipalities as a result of paying bounties. In 1868, the legislature instructed the governor to appoint a committee to study the question of the state's assuming the municipal bounty debts.[18] The committee reported favorably, giving as its reasons: that the burden of the bounties was one which was common to the whole state, but because of the disparities in the population and wealth of the cities and towns the burden bore very unequally. The committee recommended that the basis of the assumption of the debt should be that of paying each city and town $100.00 for every man furnished for three years of service, and in the same proportion for shorter periods of time, providing that the city or town had spent that much for bounties.[19] Governor Chamberlain, in commenting on this report, said " The report of the Committee on the Assumption of the Municipal War Debt will show how unequally the municipal war debt has been borne. Their facts, arguments and conclusions seem to me irresistible." [20] The legislature approved the recommendations of the committee and authorized the treasurer to secure a loan of as much of $3,500,000 as might be needed for this purpose. The same act provided that a constitutional amendment should be submitted to the people, giving constitutional authority to the government to borrow this much. This was necessary because the borrowing power of the government was limited to $300,000 except for war purposes and this evidently was not considered as borrowing for war purposes. This act also provided for a sinking fund for the ultimate payment

17 *Ibid., 1864*, chs. 221, 227.
18 *Resolves of Maine 1868*, ch. 174.
19 *Message of the Governor 1868*.
20 *Ibid.*

of this debt.[21] The amendment was adopted in 1869 [22] and the legislature included in the state property tax for that year a levy of one-half mill for the sinking fund.[23] The treasurer in his annual report of 1869 stated that the commissioners who had been appointed to adjudicate upon the claims presented by the several cities and towns had completed their work and that they had reported the claims as $3,105,183.33. Bonds were issued and claims paid in 1870.

The item in Table 10, entitled "Aid to families" represented payments made to dependents of soldiers. An act was passed in 1862 which provided that a wife, mother or sister of a soldier dependent on him for support should receive seventy-five cents a week, and that every child under fourteen should receive fifty cents a week, but that no family should receive more than $10.00 a month. The treasurers of cities and towns were ordered to pay these claims weekly and to present records of the amounts paid to the state on January 1 of the following year, when the state would reimburse the cities and towns.[24]

Payments of soldiers' allotments were not a financial burden for the state government, the state acting merely as a distributing agent for the Federal government. Soldiers were permitted by the Federal government to assign part of their pay to persons at home, and the Federal government agreed to pay the money so assigned to those persons. An agreement was reached whereby the Federal government paid this money to the state government, which distributed it to the assignees.

The foregoing discussion shows that the greatest part of the financial burden of the Civil War was caused by the payment of bounties. Of the total direct war expenditures, excluding allotments, 72.2 per cent was for bounties, 10.4 per cent for general expenses and 17.4 per cent for aid to families of

21 *Public Laws of Maine 1868*, ch. 225.
22 *Revised Statutes of Maine 1871*, p. 73.
23 *Private and Special Laws of Maine 1869*, ch. 274.
24 *Annual Report of the Treasurer 1862*.

CIVIL WAR DEBT AND LIQUIDATION 53

soldiers. In later years the Federal government reimbursed the state for the expenses of enlisting and equipping the first ten regiments.

The amount of the state debt at the opening of the Civil War as stated in the preceding chapter, was $700,000 which amounted to $1.15 per capita. It was arranged in small annual maturities running to 1877 and was paid as it came due. The history of the debt for the years 1861 to 1870, consequently, is limited to presenting the facts concerning the borrowing for the purpose of financing the war and the methods adopted for the payment of this debt.[25] There was considerable temporary borrowing, accumulation of unpaid claims, and issuance of script during the first five years of this period, but records are not available which permit following these operations through in detail. Prior to 1865 temporary borrowings were soon paid off from the proceeds of sale of bonds. In 1866, all unpaid claims were liquidated from the receipts of the fifteen-mill state property tax levied for that year but it was not possible to separate payments made on account of current expenses for that year from payments made on account of unpaid claims. The last of the script was paid in 1867.

The funded debt, as it stood on December 31 of each year from 1861 to 1870, is presented in Table 11. The first sale of bonds occurred in 1861 for the purpose of providing funds to enlist and equip the first ten regiments, and to reorganize the militia. This issue amounted to $800,000. No funded debt was issued in 1862, but certain events occurred which materially contributed to the necessity of borrowing the next year. An act was passed granting aid to families of soldiers but this aid was paid by cities and towns which were not reimbursed until

[25] It has not been possible to construct a table showing the annual net increase or decrease of the debt because of the complicated operations of the sinking funds, concerning which little information is available, and because unpaid claims in some years were in later years paid as current expenses. Tables presented have been taken from summary tables found in treasury reports.

TABLE 11*
FUNDED DEBT OF THE STATE OF MAINE OUTSTANDING DECEMBER 31 FOR THE YEARS 1861-1870

1861	$1,499,000
1862	1,472,000
1863	2,422,000
1864	5,137,000
1865	5,164,500
1866	5,127,500
1867	5,090,500
1868	5,053,500
1869	8,100,000
1870	8,067,900

*Compiled from the annual reports of the treasurer.

the next year. The governor and council, as previously stated, illegally paid bounties to the extent of $340,000 and borrowed the money from banks to do it. These accumulated obligations and the continuance of bounties and aid to soldiers' families made necessary the issuance of $1,000,000 of bonds in 1863, making the debt oustanding at the end of the year, $2,422,000. In 1864, the funded debt further increased to $5,137,000 at the end of the year and there was a temporary loan of $200,000 outstanding.

The climax of the borrowing program came in 1865. The treasurer was instructed to sell bonds to the extent of $1,000,000 but the credit of the state had become so impaired that he was able to sell only $67,000 worth. At the end of the year the treasury was empty and there was a large amount of temporary loans and unpaid claims outstanding, as shown in Table 12.

The legislature became alarmed and the financial policy was reversed. A state tax of $2,449,122 at the rate of fifteen mills, due January 1, 1866, was levied and a sinking fund to take care of the funded debt was provided. This tax was sufficient to pay the unpaid claims, temporary loans, and current expenses of 1866, while the last of the bounty script was redeemed in

CIVIL WAR DEBT AND LIQUIDATION 55

1867. The act creating the sinking fund, which became officially known as the Sinking Fund of 1865, provided that an annual property tax of three-fourths of a mill should be levied on the valuation of 1860 and that the proceeds of this tax should be paid into a fund to be used to retire the funded debt, outstanding on December 31, 1865, as it matured. It was also provided that this fund might be invested in State of Maine bonds or bonds of the United States Government.[26] The proceeds of this tax amounted to approximately $130,000 annually. In 1866, the legislature passed a law providing that all payments received from the Federal government on account of Civil War claims should be added to this fund.[27] Under this authority $209,144.35 was added to the fund in 1867 and $124,685 in 1868.

TABLE 12 *

TEMPORARY DEBT AND UNPAID CLAIMS OF STATE OF MAINE,
DECEMBER 31, 1865

Soldiers' Bounty Script	$355,600
Temporary Loans	944,151
Due Towns for Aid to Families	500,000

* *Annual Report of the Treasurer, 1865.*

In 1868, provision was made for the assumption by the state of municipal bounty debts and the creation of a sinking fund to retire the issue of bonds which this assumption made necessary.[28] Bonds were issued to the amount of $3,084,400. The provisions of the sinking fund, which became officially known as the Sinking Fund of 1868, were that an annual property tax of one-half mill on the valuation of 1860 should be levied and the proceeds of this tax paid into the fund. It was also provided, as in the case of the sinking fund of 1865, that this fund should be invested in bonds of the state of Maine or bonds of

26 *Annual Report of the Treasurer 1865*, p. 11.
27 *Public Laws of Maine 1866*, ch. 14.
28 *Cf. supra*, pp. 51-52.

the United States Government. Interest received from bonds held in both these funds was added to the principal and profit or loss caused by the buying and selling of bonds was debited or credited to the fund. State bonds acquired by the funds were not cancelled but left outstanding and the state paid interest on them to the funds.

On December 31, 1870, as shown in Table 11, the funded debt outstanding was $8,067,900. The value of the sinking fund of 1865 was $1,178,677 while that of the sinking fund of 1868 was $92,048, leaving the net debt of the state $6,797,174.[29]

From 1871 to 1889, when the last of the debt matured, the chief energies of those responsible for the management of the state's finances were directed toward liquidating the debt. Operating expenses of the government were rigidly curtailed with the result, as shown in Table 8, that in all but two of these years, surplus revenues were available to apply on debt reduction. Also, the revenue system was changed during this period from one, which in 1871 relied almost wholly on property taxes, to one which in 1889 produced nearly half the receipts from sources other than property taxes.

The important facts concerning the receipts for the years 1871-1889 are presented in Table 8,[30] which shows the development of new sources of revenue and the balance between receipts and expenditures for the operation of the government. No detailed treatment of changes in the tax laws will be given here because they are treated elsewhere.[31]

The first change in the tax laws occurred in 1872 when a tax was levied on the deposits of savings banks.[32] Following the decline of state commercial banks, there had been a great increase in the number and in the deposits of savings banks, and

29 *Annual Report of the Treasurer 1870*, p. 14.
30 For a more detailed treatment, see Appendix Table C.
31 *Cf. infra*, chapters vi, vii and viii.
32 *Public Laws of Maine 1872*, ch. 74.

CIVIL WAR DEBT AND LIQUIDATION 57

it was but natural that people who had been accustomed to bank taxation for over half a century should turn to this new source. Further impetus to the search for new sources of revenue was given by the panic of 1873, which caused the state property tax to become a heavy burden on the people. Governor Dingley, in his annual message to the legislature in 1874, called attention to the fact that the state government was being almost entirely supported by property taxes, and urged the development of other sources.

I most earnestly urge, however, that you should consider whether it is not advisable to devise some method other than direct taxation to secure part of the revenue required for state expenditures; so that the rate of taxation may further be reduced.... Without indicating more in detail what sources of revenue may be made available to this state, I desire to call your attention to the subject, and to suggest a careful inquiry and investigation, with a view to lifting some portion of the burden of taxation from real estate.[33]

In 1874, a law was passed levying a tax on railroads; in 1875, insurance companies were taxed; in 1880, telegraph companies; and in 1883, telephone and express companies.[34] The result of this legislation was that by 1889, nearly one-half the state revenue came from sources other than the state property tax.

From 1871 to 1889, the operating expenditures of the state were held to a minimum and efforts were directed toward liquidating the debt, with the result that by 1889, it was sufficiently reduced to enable a refunding operation to be carried through which reduced the interest rate and so distributed the maturities that the burden was not again heavy in any one year. The facts concerning the expenditures from 1871 to 1889 have been summarized in Table 13.[35] Table 8 shows that in all but

33 *Annual Message of the Governor 1874.*
34 *Cf. infra,* chs. vi, vii and viii.
35 For details, see Appendix, Table C.

TABLE 13
EXPENDITURES, 1871-1889 *
(Figures in thousands)

Year	General	Education	Interest	Defectives	Health and Charity	Taxes collected for county, city and towns	Other	Total
1871	$160	$ 66	$480	$ 94	$26	$ 6	$143	$ 975
1872	132	94	433	82	21	7	148	917
1873	133	343	431	63	29	8	141	1,148
1874	140	424	432	119	41	8	135	1,299
1875	138	439	424	111	28	9	137	1,286
1876	71	451	358	85	34	11	174	1,184
1877	91	500	354	90	33	12	164	1,244
1878				No reports found				
1879	69	405	353	79	27	11	142	1,086
1880	101	353	349	84	30	29	158	1,104
1881	104	338	339	134	16	13	129	1,073
1882	91	356	327	68	30	24	72	968
1883	128	394	363	165	31	38	140	1,259
1884	119	393	316	82	32	37	90	1,069
1885	107	414	317	123	39	34	161	1,195
1886	116	411	313	68	44	34	120	1,106
1887				No reports found				
1888	145	444	243	88	48	43	111	1,127
1889	174	466	229	191	58	76	293	1,487

* Appendix, Table C.

two years the receipts exceeded the expenditures and that large surpluses were available to apply on the debt.

The item " General ", in Table 13, which includes the expenses of the governor and council, the legislature and the administrative departments, shows no marked change during this period.

The item which showed the greatest increase during this period was " Education." It will be recalled that before the Civil War the receipts from the tax on the capital stock of state banks was annually appropriated for the support of the common

CIVIL WAR DEBT AND LIQUIDATION 59

schools.[36] After the disappearance of these banks, the only money available for the common schools was the interest on the common school funds,[37] which, in 1871, amounted to $19,156. Small annual appropriations were also made by the legislature for colleges and academies. Shortly after the close of the Civil War a movement developed demanding that the state provide greater support for the common schools, with the result that in 1872 a law was passed levying an annual state property tax of one mill for this purpose, and in 1873, another law was passed levying an annual tax of one and one-half per cent on the deposits of savings banks for the same purpose.[38] The money received from these taxes was apportioned to the cities and towns in proportion to the number of pupils in each. In 1873, another act was passed granting state aid to cities and towns for the establishing of free high schools, which in a short time cost the state approximately $50,000 annually. As a result of these laws, expenditures for education, which in 1871 amounted to $66,000, increased by 1877 to $500,000. Comments by state officials indicate that such an increase in expenditures for education had not been expected or desired. Consequently, in 1877 the amount of the savings bank tax appropriated to the common schools was reduced to one half.[39] This change in the law and the decrease in savings bank deposits, caused by the depression of the Seventies, resulted in the beginning of a downward trend in expenditures for education which lasted until 1881. Following that year, savings bank deposits began to increase, with a consequent increase in money going to the common schools.

The gradual decline in the payments for interest, as shown in Table 13, was brought about by retirement of the debt. Expenditures for defectives were held to a low point, but the

36 *Cf. supra*, p. 23.
37 *Ibid.*
38 *Public Laws of Maine 1872*, ch. 43; *1873*, ch. 74.
39 *Ibid., 1877*, ch. 218.

institutions became overcrowded, and in the case of the insane there were many in the state who could not be admitted to the insane asylum at Augusta. The item " Health and Charity " included expenditures for care of state paupers, insane, and small appropriations for hospitals. There was a considerable growth in the item " Taxes collected for cities and towns." In the early years of the period, this item was composed of dog taxes. In the later years part of the money collected from taxes on railroads and telegraph and telephone companies were paid to cities and towns. Also, the duty of collecting the county taxes on wild lands was placed on the state. The growth in the item " Other " was caused by the assumption of new governmental functions, none of which alone amounted to any considerable sum. The departments of agriculture and health, the fish and game, and the forestry commissions were created during the later years of this period, and expenditures for them had reached significant amounts.

On December 31, 1870, the amount of the funded debt outstanding, as previously stated, was $8,067,900, while the value of the sinking funds was $1,270,725, leaving a net debt of $6,797,174.[40] Table 14 presents the maturities of the funded debt as of January 1, each year from 1871 to 1889. This debt was provided for by the sinking funds of 1865 and 1868, which, if continued, would supply ample funds to pay the debt as it matured.[41]

The debt was paid as it matured and the payments to the sinking funds were continued until 1875, when the sinking fund of 1865 was discontinued. The reasons which motivated the discontinuance of the sinking fund of 1865 were stated by Gov-

[40] It has not been possible to reconcile for this period debt payments and debt incurred as they appear in Appendix Table C, with statements of the funded debt as they appear in the annual reports of the treasurer. These discrepancies, which are not great, may be accounted for by the complicated operations of the sinking funds, concerning which little data are available. The writer has chosen to use the figures given by the treasurers.

[41] Cf. supra, pp. 54-55.

TABLE 14
Maturities of the Debt of the State of Maine as of January 1, 1871 *

Year	Amount
1871	$ 40,000
1871 war loan	800,000
1872	40,000
1873	50,000
1874	50,000
1875	30,000
1876	60,000
1877	51,000
1878	30,000
1880 bounty loan	475,000
1883 war loan	525,000
1889 war loan	2,832,500
1889 municipal war debt loan	3,084,400
Total	8,067,900

* *Annual Report of the Treasurer, 1871.*

ernor Dingley in his message to the legislature in 1875 as follows:

Thus, in ten years, nearly seven million dollars have been paid by the people of Maine on account of the state debt . . . nearly three millions being for reduction of the principal and four millions for interest. Should the present rate of taxation be continued, the balance of this immense war debt would be extinguished in fourteen years from this date. Thus, the generation which met the personal responsibilities of the terrible contest to preserve the national existence, would also be called on to bear the financial burdens which it imposed on the state . . . surely others who are to share in the fruits of a struggle, which has scarcely a parallel in history, though they can not participate in the terrible sacrifice of blood, will esteem it a privilege, as well as a duty, to aid in discharging the pecuniary liabilities which it entailed on the country.

So long as business was conducted on the speculative basis it assumed during and immediately following the war, and profits were supposed to be unusually large, it was wise to take advantage of the opportunity to rapidly reduce the debt. But in the present financial condition of the country and indeed in the near future when business shall have resumed its normal state, so large an annual assessment as is required by existing laws, cannot but be severely felt.[42]

The legislature acted on the suggestion of the governor and abolished the sinking fund of 1865, which provided for the liquidation of all the debt except the municipal war debt loan maturing in 1889; bonds of the state of Maine held in the sinking fund were cancelled; United States bonds and cash were transferred to the sinking fund of 1868; and the treasurer was instructed to exchange new six per cent bonds for bonds outstanding. The maturities of the new bonds were to be arranged so that $200,000 of them would mature annually beginning in 1890.[43] On December 7, 1875, the day when the sinking fund of 1865 was closed, there was in that fund $1,112,900 in Maine bonds, $100,000 in United States bonds and $1,524 in cash. In accordance with the act abolishing the sinking fund, the Maine bonds were cancelled and the United States bonds and cash were transferred to the sinking fund of 1868. Through the elimination of the three-quarter-mill tax, which had been levied for the sinking fund of 1865, and the saving of interest on the bonds cancelled, the annual debt service charge of the state was reduced by $190,000. The maturities of the bonds left outstanding after this operation was completed are shown in Table 15.

The treasurer during the year 1875 was not in sympathy with the movement to refund the debt. He said in his annual report made at the end of the year:

The State will undoubtedly adhere to the policy of paying its indebtedness as it matures, and I trust will raise by taxation each year a sum sufficient to meet all of its expenditures, avoiding tem-

[42] *Annual Message of the Governor 1875.*
[43] *Public Laws of Maine 1875*, ch. 48.

CIVIL WAR DEBT AND LIQUIDATION

TABLE 15
MATURITIES OF THE PUBLIC DEBT OF MAINE
AS OF DECEMBER 31, 1876 *

1876	$ 29,000
1877	46,500
1878	25,000
1880	307,000
1883	385,000
1889	2,330,000 war loan
1889	2,827,000 municipal war loan

* *Annual Report of the Treasurer, 1875.*

porary loans or an increase of the permanent debt of the state. If the people are taxed for all appropriations of money, there will be but little danger of extravagant legislation.[44]

The treasurer went on to say that he had not prepared or issued any of the bonds which the law provided should be exchanged for war loan bonds, because he did not deem it " important or necessary to do so." He pointed out that no large maturity of the debt came due until 1880, and proposed that the $307,000 which matured then be provided for by using the $100,000 of United States bonds which had been transferred to the sinking fund of 1868, and raising by taxation $100,000 in each of the years 1879 and 1880. As a means of paying the $385,000, which came due in 1883, he proposed that $100,000 be raised by taxation in 1882 and a like amount be levied for 1883, 1884 and 1885, and the receipts of these last three years be anticipated by temporary loans. Governor Connor, in his message to the legislature in 1876, approved this plan. The debt was paid as it matured until the end of 1878, but in 1879 and 1880, instead of levying taxes to pay the maturity of 1880, it was necessary to resort to temporary loans to pay the operating expenses of the government. The debt maturing in 1880 was refunded, the maturities being so arranged that $50,000 fell due each year beginning in 1881 and continuing

[44] *Annual Report of the Treasurer 1875*, p. 34.

until 1886 when $57,000 fell due. The temporary loan of 1879 was paid in 1880 and the temporary loan of 1880 was paid in 1881. From 1880 until 1889, no further borrowing was necessary.

In 1881 and subsequent years, revenues increased partly because of the increased decennial property valuation made in 1880, and partly because of increased yield from taxes on corporations, while expenditures did not increase. This permitted the payment of the debt as it matured until 1889. The treasurer, in his annual report dated December 31, 1886, and the governor, in his message to the legislature dated January 7, 1887, recommended that the sinking fund of 1868 be discontinued, giving as reasons that the sinking fund nearly equalled the debt for which it was created and that the high price of bonds, in which the sinking fund could legally be invested, made it difficult to invest the annual accretions to the fund without loss. The legislature, acting on these recommendations, authorized the suspension of payments to the sinking fund, the cancelling of the state bonds held in the fund, and instructed that the other bonds held in the fund be sold and that such state bonds as could not be paid be refunded.[45] The market value of the securities held in the sinking fund at this time was $2,357,650, of which sum $1,161,500 was invested in state bonds.[46] The state bonds were cancelled, but nothing was done about selling the other bonds or issuing new bonds until 1889.

On January 1, 1889, the debt amounted to $3,967,400. The bonds in the sinking fund were sold for $1,235,674.04. Bonds held in trust for the agricultural college, amounting to $118,000, were renewed. From the estate of ex-Governor Coburn was received $100,000, to be held in trust for the agricultural college, and $50,000 to be held in trust for the state insane asylum. This money was used to pay maturing bonds and

[45] *Public Laws of Maine 1887*, ch. 43.
[46] *Annual Report of the Treasurer 1887*, p. 17.

TABLE 16
Maturities of the Bonds of the State of Maine as of December 31, 1889 *

1890-1901, inclusive	$50,000 each year
1902-1911, "	70,000 " "
1912-1921, "	78,000 " "
1922-1929 "	60,000 " "

* *Annual Report of the Treasurer, 1889.*

new bonds were given to these institutions. Subtracting these amounts from the amount of the debt to be paid, there remained to be raised by a new bond issue, $2,463,725.96. The treasurer sold three per cent serial bonds, the par value of which amounted to $2,374,000, for $2,643,900.[47] The maturities of the bonds are shown in Table 16.

47 *Annual Report of the Treasurer 1889*, p. 38.

CHAPTER IV
EXPANDING GOVERNMENT FUNCTIONS AND EXTINCTION OF THE PUBLIC DEBT, 1890-1912

IN the year 1890, the finances of the state government entered a new phase. The refunding operation of 1889 had reduced the annual burden of debt and interest to a relatively small amount. Operating expenses of the government, which because of the Civil War debt had been held low during the preceding three decades, began to increase; enlargement of institutions, which had long been postponed, was undertaken; new functions of government were added to those already performed; and most extraordinary was the extinction of the public debt in 1912, nearly twenty years before the last of it came due.[1] Expenditures quadrupled during the period, but the revenue system was so adjusted that the state found itself at the end of 1912 without any public debt and with a large amount of cash in the treasury.

The facts concerning the state finances for this period have been summarized in Tables 17, 18 and 19.[2] From 1890 to 1900 both revenues and expenditures, as shown in Table 17, increased by approximately one-half. The increase in receipts was due more to increases in the tax bases than to changes in the tax laws, although certain changes in the tax laws did result in increased revenues. In 1893, the rate of the railroad gross receipts tax was increased.[3] In the same year an estate tax law was passed, but the revenue received from it was not great for a number of years.[4] Also, in 1893 the tax on the deposits of

---

[1] Bonds and coupons amounting to $269,000 remained outstanding at the end of 1912, but $268,300 were held by state trust funds and were not redeemable, while $700 were coupons held by persons unknown.

[2] For details see Appendix Table D.

[3] *Public Laws of Maine 1893*, ch. 166. *Cf. infra*, ch. viii, p. 190.

[4] *Ibid.*, ch. 146.

Revenues and Expenditures, 1890–1912 *
(Figures in thousands)

Year	State property tax	Railroad tax	Telephone and telegraph tax	Insurance tax	Inheritance tax	Trust company tax	Savings bank tax	Corporation franchise tax and fees	Other	Total	Expenditures	Surplus or deficit for year
1890	$ 661	$106	$ 8	$ 25			$324	$ 21	$ 53	$1,198	$1,251	–$ 53
1891	522	101	8	27			347	21	424 (a)	1,450	1,365	85
1892	829	103	9	32			368	28	110	1,479	1,321	158
1893	827	280	10	31	$ 1		402	24	163	1,738	1,459	279
1894	886	170	13	29	12		402	21	120	1,653	1,378	275
1895	775	145	11	33	42		388	26	114	1,534	1,651	–117
1896	840	153	14	36	23		381	25	104	1,576	1,613	–37
1897	782	164	15	38	29		382	29	111	1,550	1,751	–201
1898	902	170	14	59	23		394	26	114	1,702	1,602	100
1899	923	160	15	62	36		403	42	147	1,788	1,895	–107
1900	916	176	17	69	18		449	34	134	1,813	1,765	48
1901	929	292	17	73	39	$ 21	501	87	182	2,141	1,892	249
1902	862	327	20	79	40	24	538	132	295 (b)	2,317	1,850	467
1903	941	365	23	90	31	37	485	156	422 (c)	2,550	2,283	267
1904	954	404	25	97	74	44	409	134	167	2,308	2,189	119
1905	983	520	28	105	69	51	425	164	262	2,607	2,403	204
1906	936	494	35	111	71	58	442	251	284	2,682	2,231	451
1907	1,152	606	42	113	89	75	463	301	267	3,108	2,846	262
1908	987	658	47	114	99	88	471	243	286	2,993	2,887	106
1909	1,307	615	44	118	78	95	471	286	384	3,398	3,889	–491
1910	1,392	717	58	126	93	101	463	265	515	3,730	3,970	–286
1911	2,142	851	62	137	147	108	461	276	401	4,585	4,196	389
1912	2,553	888	90	151	276	124	466	311	462	5,321	4,662	659
Total..										55,221	52,349	2,872(d)

* Appendix Table D.
(a) Includes $358,000 received from Federal government for Civil War claims.
(b) Includes $132,000 received from Federal government for Civil War claims.
(c) Includes $228,000 received from Federal government for Civil War claims.
(d) The cash balance was $394,000 larger at the end of the period than at the beginning, which accounts for the excess of receipts over net reduction of the debt for the period.

savings banks was changed to a tax on the value of the franchise, the value being determined by making certain deductions from the average deposits. The evident purpose of this law was to encourage investment of savings in Maine.[5] In 1897, the tax on insurance premiums was changed, so that less deductions were allowed from gross premiums in determining the net premiums which were subject to the tax.[6] While these changes in the tax laws and the growth in the tax bases resulted in the collection of greater revenues, the increase was not sufficient between 1890 and 1900 to provide for the operating expenses of the government and the retirement of the debt as it came due.

Expenditures, as shown in Table 18, increased by approximately one-half from 1890 to 1900. It was pointed out in the preceding chapter that because of the heavy burden of the Civil War debt, the operating expenses of the government were rigidly curtailed from the end of the war until 1889. The cancellation of the state bonds in the sinking fund and the refunding of the remaining outstanding bonds in that year reduced payments for debt service to such an extent that it appeared as if surplus funds would be available in the treasury. It was but natural that departments and institutions, which had for so long been denied what seemed to them adequate support, should become insistent that their appropriations be increased. It was this situation that determined the character of increased expenditures during the next decade, which was that of more liberal provision for functions of government already performed rather than acquiring new ones. This increase was general and needs little additional comment.

When in 1889 it became apparent that surplus funds would be available, the legislature responded quickly to the demands of departments and institutions and increased appropriations for that year and also for 1890 by approximately $250,000,

[5] *Ibid.*, ch. 244. *Cf. infra*, pp. 149-150.
[6] *Cf. infra*, p. 156.

TABLE 18
EXPENDITURES, 1890-1912*
(Figures in thousands)

Year	General	Education	Highway	Interest	Defectives	Health and welfare	Conservation and developmental	Taxes collected and paid to cities and towns	Other	Total
1890	$207	$461		$94	$146	$56	$31	$56	$200	$1,251
1891	283	499		102	154	68	48	57	154	1,365
1892	226	570		92	126	56	47	57	147	1,321
1893	302	593		91	141	66	51	64	151	1,459
1894	249	600		81	109	61	51	106	121	1,378
1895	311	651		75	195	92	63	113	101	1,651
1896	254	647		74	225	88	67	110	148	1,613
1897	349	677		77	160	104	82	110	192	1,751
1898	277	656		77	141	90	77	122	162	1,602
1899	422 (a)	634		76	268	114	84	123	174	1,895
1900	302	663		79	256	118	90	117	140	1,765
1901	382	644		78	302	97	103	118	168	1,892
1902	333	702	$8	69	166	121	96	165	190	1,850
1903	409	775	8	63	300	127	153	170	278	2,283
1904	383	814	30	60	235	135	158	176	198	2,189
1905	433	770	73	55	296	162	185	206	223	2,403
1906	387	783	75	54	191	161	194	196	190	2,231
1907	493	910	93	29	450	202	241	245	183	2,846
1908	427	861	197	26	375	262	256	330	153	2,887
1909	544	1,266	184	25	516	469	395	304	186	3,889
1910	367	1,288	309	38	538	205	374	233	618	3,970
1911	418	1,973	226	35	533	283	342	167	219	4,196
1912	396	2,177	429	28	437	369	305	316	205	4,662

* Appendix Table D.
(a) Includes approximately $100,000 expenses of Spanish American War.

which would have resulted in a deficit in 1889 had it not been for the fact that not all of the bonds maturing in that year were presented for payment. As it was, the cash in the treasury was reduced to a dangerously low level. In 1890, although interest payments decreased $135,000, there was an operating deficit, and in order to meet this deficit and pay the maturing debt, the state was obliged to secure a temporary loan of $300,000. The legislature of 1891 made still larger appropriations and had it not been for the receipt of $358,000 from the Federal government on account of a Civil War claim, the state finances would have been seriously involved. Even with this extraordinary receipt the treasury was unable to retire the temporary loan of the previous year. The legislature did, however, increase the rate of the state property tax for the next two years and this, with enlarged tax collections which resulted from the changes in tax laws previously mentioned, enabled the state to finish liquidating the temporary debt in 1894. In 1897, expenditures again began to exceed revenues and by the end of 1900 the state had a temporary debt of $350,000.

The items "Education" and "Defectives" merit special consideration. Money which was distributed to the cities and towns for the support of the common schools was provided by the permanent allocation of one-half the receipts from the tax on savings banks and by the levy of a one-mill property tax,[7] while appropriations for normal schools, academies, free high schools, and the agricultural college were made out of the general fund. The major part of the increase in expenditures for education was the result of increased collections from the savings bank tax and the school mill tax, although there was some increase in appropriations from the general fund.

The increase in the item "Defectives" was the result of over-crowded conditions in the state prison, insane asylum and reformatories, which had come to exist during the preceding period when appropriations were restricted. The condition of

[7] *Cf. supra*, p. 59.

the insane was particularly critical. The insane asylum at Augusta was so crowded that no more patients could be received and there were many insane in the state uncared for. The enlargement of these institutions was now undertaken and in 1895 the construction of a new insane asylum was started at Bangor. The enlargement of these institutions resulted in a permanent increase in expenditures for maintenance.

The interesting features of the state finances between 1901 and 1912 were the rapid increase in expenditures and the extinction of the public debt years before it came due. Expenditures, which in 1901 amounted to $1,892,000, increased by the end of 1912 to $4,662,000. It was in these years that the ground-work was laid for the much greater increase which took place in the next period; old functions of government were extended and new ones were added, which in later years were to be the dominating features of the state finances. Adequate revenue was provided to take care of this large increase in expenditures and for the retirement of the debt, but this was achieved principally by increasing the rates of existing taxes rather than by drawing on new sources; the framework of the tax system remained much the same.

At the beginning of 1901, the finances of the state were in poor condition. The revenue since 1897 had not been sufficient to pay the expenses of the government and to retire the debt as it matured, with the result that at the beginning of 1901 there was a temporary debt of $350,000 outstanding. In order to meet this situation the legislature revised the tax system in 1901. The rate of the railroad tax was increased, which, together with increased gross receipts, brought about materially larger collections from this source.[8] The taxes on telephone and telegraph companies were changed to gross receipt taxes, although this change did not result in increased revenue at that time.[9] A tax was levied on trust companies similar to that on

8 *Cf. infra*, p. 169.
9 *Cf. infra*, p. 180.

savings banks.[10] Also, an annual franchise tax, which was in future years to produce large revenues, was levied on corporations incorporated under Maine laws. These changes, as shown in Table 17, resulted in a sufficient increase in revenue to pay the expenses of 1901 and to reduce the temporary debt. In 1902, the treasury, aided by the receipt of $132,000 from the Federal government on account of a Civil War claim, was able to meet all expenses and pay the remainder of the temporary debt. From this time until 1909, revenue was not only sufficient to meet expenses, but was large enough to make possible payments on the public debt in advance of maturity. Between 1903 and 1909, the increase in revenue required by the growing expenditures was provided by the growth of tax bases and by an increase in the state property tax rate in 1907 of one-quarter mill.

In 1909, expenditures increased by $1,000,000 with no corresponding increase in revenue, with the result that there was a deficit of almost $500,000.[11] In 1910, another deficit occurred. To meet this situation, the rate of the state property tax was increased from three to five mills for 1911, and again to six mills in 1912. This increase was sufficient to pay all claims, retire the temporary indebtedness which had been incurred in 1910, and to pay off the remaining bonded debt, as well as to leave a cash balance in the treasury at the end of 1912 of $457,000.

Expenditures for the years 1901 to 1912, as shown in Table 18, increased from $1,892,000 to $4,662,000. This increase, while general in all items,[12] was particularly marked in " Education " and " Highways." Expenditures for education, which in 1901 amounted to $644,000, increased by 1912 to $2,177,000. This increase was caused by the allocation of the collections from new taxes to the funds distributed to the cities and towns

10 *Cf. infra*, p. 145.

11 This situation was handled by allowing the claims on the state to go unpaid. No temporary loan was secured nor any non-payable warrants issued.

12 For a detailed explanation of expenditures included in the various items of Table 18, see chapter v.

for the support of the common schools and by the increase in the assessed valuation of the state. It will be recalled that prior to 1901, funds for the support of the common schools came from the Permanent School Fund, which had been created by setting aside proceeds of the sales of certain public lands; the School Mill Fund, which was supported by a one-mill property tax; and one-half the savings bank tax.[13] In 1903, one-half the proceeds on the new tax on trust companies was appropriated to the common schools.[14] In 1907, the rate of the School Mill Fund tax was increased to one and one-half mills.[15] In 1909, a new fund, known as the Common School Fund, devoted to the use of the common schools, was created and a property tax of one and one-half mills levied for its support.[16] Thus, at the end of 1909, the state was levying a three-mill property tax for the benefit of the common schools.

The first permanent participation by the state in the building of highways was undertaken in 1901. Prior to that time appropriations by the state were by special resolves for some particular project and were sporadic and of very limited amount. This activity, which in 1902 cost only $8,000, increased by 1912 to $429,000 and by 1932 amounted to over one-half the total expenditures of the state.

The first highway law of a permanent nature was passed in 1901. This law provided that on the petition of a city or town the county commissioners were to designate the main thoroughfare running through a town as a state highway, and that for the permanent improvement of this road, the state would match any amount appropriated by the town up to $100.00.[17] An appropriation of $15,000 was made by the state for this purpose, but only $8,000 of it was used.

13 *Cf. supra*, pp. 58-59.
14 *Public Laws of Maine 1903*, ch. 228.
15 *Ibid., 1907*, ch. 3.
16 *Ibid., 1909*, ch. 177.
17 *Ibid., 1901*, ch. 285.

In 1905, a law was passed providing for the appointment of a state highway commissioner, whose duties were to assemble data concerning the highways of the state and to give advice to county and local highway officials.[18] In 1907, a law was passed making it compulsory for cities and towns to designate the main roads through the towns as state highways and to appropriate certain amounts of money for improving them. The state was to aid in this work and the state highway commissioner was given authority to supervise and to require that a certain quality and type of work be done.[19] Under this authority, state participation in highway building increased rapidly, until in 1912 almost ten per cent of total expenditures were for that purpose.

Another interesting feature of this period was the creation of the Maine Forestry District for the purpose of controlling forest fires in the wild lands of the state. The large amount of unsettled land in the northern part of the state, which was valuable chiefly for the lumber it produced, was continually subject to great loss from forest fires. It was recognized by both the state and the landowners that the state was the only authority which could successfully handle this problem and that it would be unjust to compel the rest of the state to pay for this protection. Consequently, in 1909 the legislature passed a law creating the Maine Forestry District, in which was included 9,500,000 acres of forests or approximately one-half the area of the state. A property tax of one and one-half mills was levied on the assessed value of this land, the proceeds of which were to be used for fire control purposes. The administration of this work was given to the forest commissioner. From this beginning, which in 1910 cost $63,000, an efficient fire control service has been created.

The history of the funded debt from 1890 to 1912 is an interesting episode in that all the bonds in the hands of the public were retired a number of years before the last matured.

18 *Ibid.*, 1905, ch. 146.
19 *Ibid.*, *1907*, ch. 112.

TABLE 19
Debt Incurred and Paid and Amount Outstanding by Years, 1890–1912 *
(Figures in thousands)

Year	Debt incurred during period	Debt paid during period	Net increase or decrease during period	Debt outstanding at end of each year
1889		Debt outstanding December 31		$2,747 (a)
1890	$ 300	$ 130	$ 170	2,917
1891	287	348	–61	2,856
1892	100	152	–52	2,804
1893	125	377	–252	2,552
1894		150	–150	2,402
1895		50	–50	2,352
1896		50	–50	2,302
1897	200	50	150	2,452
1898	150	250	–100	2,352
1899	350	200	150	2,502
1900	200	250	–50	2,452
1901	250	400	–150	2,302
1902	100	420	–320	1,982
1903		70	–70	1,912
1904		510	–510	1,402
1905		23	–23	1,379
1906		287	–287	1,192
1907	200	580	–380	712
1908		15	–15	697
1909				697
1910	300		300	997
1911	300	322	–22	975
1912		706	–706	269
Total	2,862	5,340	–2,478	

* Appendix Table D.

(a) Ninety-five thousand dollars of this was bonds which matured in 1889, but which was not all paid until the end of 1893.

On January 1, 1890, the outstanding debt of the state, as shown in Table 19, amounted to $2,747,000. Of this amount, $95,000 was in bonds which had matured in 1889, but which had not been presented for payment. These old bonds were paid as they were presented, the last in 1893. The maturities of the bonds issued in 1889 were as follows: $50,000 each year for the years 1890 to 1901, inclusive; $70,000 each year for the years 1902 to 1911, inclusive; $78,000 in the years 1912 to 1921; and $70,000 for each of the years 1922 to 1929.

From 1890 to 1894, the financial condition of the state was not strong. The legislature of 1889, acting on the belief that the refunding operation of 1889 would result in surplus funds in the treasury, had increased appropriations to such an extent that in 1890 it was necessary to negotiate a temporary loan of $300,000. The receipt of $358,000 from the Federal government in 1891 and adjustments of the tax system made possible the retirement of the temporary debt by the end of 1893. In 1897, another period of temporary borrowing began, which was not terminated until 1902. Adjustment of the tax system in 1901 and receipts from the Federal government in 1901 and 1902, on account of Civil War claims, again placed the finances of the state in sound condition, and at the end of the latter year, there was a cash balance in the treasury of $439,000. The funded debt during these years was paid as it matured and no new debt created.

Governor Hill, in his message to the legislature in 1903, made the following suggestion concerning the payment of the funded debt.

From time to time an opportunity is offered for the purchase of State bonds of various maturities, and I believe that it would be sound business policy, and for the interest of the state, to give the Treasurer authority to buy such bonds whenever funds are available for the purpose. We should take advantage of these opportunities to more rapidly reduce our funded debt, which otherwise only can be paid as it matures.[20]

The legislature acted on this suggestion and authorized the treasurer, acting on the advice of the governor and council, to

20 *Message of the Governor 1903.*

EXPANDING GOVERNMENT FUNCTIONS

purchase bonds of the state, whenever there were surplus funds in the treasury and when it seemed for the best interests of the state to do so.[21] During most of the years from 1903 to 1912, revenues exceeded expenditures and there were surplus funds to apply on the debt. The policy of buying state bonds in the open market was followed with the result, as shown in Table 19, that by the end of 1912 all but $269,000 of the debt was retired. State trust funds held $268,300 of this amount which was not redeemable. The remaining $700.00 was old bond coupons held by persons unknown.

21 *Private and Special Laws of Maine 1903*, ch. 6.

CHAPTER V
THE PRESENT-DAY PERIOD, 1913-1936

IN Maine, as in many other states, the period following 1912 was one of greatly increased government spending. Every state service shared in the liberality in appropriations which characterized this period. Expenditures, which in 1913 amounted to $4,890,000, had by 1933 increased to $29,460,000. In 1933, the legislature, frightened by a decrease in revenues and by the general depression hysteria prevalent at that time, reversed the policy of prodigality and decreased appropriations by one-third. This reversal, however, was but short-lived, and the trend turned upward again in 1935, continuing into 1936, with the result that the legislature of 1937 is faced with the choice of again restricting appropriations or extracting several millions additional money from an already overtaxed people.

It would be natural to suppose, in view of the greatly increased expenditures, that a thorough-going revision of the tax system would have taken place. Such was not the case. With the exception of the gasoline tax and the motor vehicle license, no new sources of revenue of importance were developed. Resort was had to increasing the rates of old taxes and to borrowing. The debt, which in 1913 amounted to only $269,000, had by 1936 increased to $29,740,500. Tax administration, notwithstanding a reorganization in 1932, still remained archaic.

While collections from all important sources of revenue increased, with the exception of the taxes on banks, a significant change in the relative importance of each source occurred. The state property tax, which in 1913 produced thirty-seven per cent of the state revenue, in 1930 accounted for twenty-eight per cent and in 1936 only nineteen per cent. On the other hand, the motor vehicle license and receipts from the highway department, which in 1913 produced less than three per cent of the total receipts, in 1930, with the addition of the gasoline tax, accounted for forty-two per cent of the total.[1] It is interesting to observe that while highway expenditures increased from eleven per cent of the total in 1913 to fifty-five per cent in 1930 and then declined to thirty-five in 1936, a good portion of the funds required for this purpose came from sources which would not have existed had not the coming of the automobile necessitated the development of the present highway system.

It has been found desirable in treating this period to break it into two divisions: 1913-1932 and 1933-1936. The extensive reorganization which took place in 1932[2] and the increasing amount of receipts and expenditures for relief purposes seemed to set the years 1933-1936 off as a unit which could best be treated separately.

The facts concerning the revenues and expenditures for the years 1913-1932 have been summarized in Tables 20 and 21,[3] while for information concerning the funded debt the reader is referred to Table 26. A summary classification of revenues and the balance between revenues and expenditures for the years 1913-1932 are presented in Table 20. Expenditures, which in 1913 amounted to $4,890,000, increased by 1932 to $29,460,000. In each year to 1920, with the exception of 1914, revenues exceeded expenditures, but notwithstanding this there was a net increase in the funded debt by the end of 1919 of nearly $3,000,000. Payments on the debt during these years were small and the surplus funds were allowed to accumulate in the treasury. Following 1919 expenditures increased rapidly and exceeded receipts in all but two years, the annual deficits being met by borrowing. As a result of the increasing expenditures, the state was faced continually with the problem of providing additional revenue.

[1] It has not been possible to segregate receipts from the highway department after 1930, because of changed methods of making reports.
[2] *Cf. infra*, ch. xi.
[3] For more detailed figures see Appendix Table E.

TABLE 20

REVENUES AND EXPENDITURES, 1913–1932 *

(Figures in thousands)

Year	State property tax	Rail-road tax	Inheritance tax	Bank taxes	Corporation franchise tax and fees	Gasoline tax	Automobile registration	Highway	Other	Total	Expenditures	Surplus or deficit for year
1913	$1,871	$ 978	$ 170	$ 616	$289		$ 138	$ 9	$ 709	$ 5,082	$ 4,890	$ 192
1914	2,387	1,051	284	632	250		193	151	903	5,851	6,215	-364
1915	4,294	1,089	179	633	276		268	173	908	8,324	7,901	423
1916	2,253	998	224	621	280		363	215	1,410	6,864	6,513	351
1917	2,877	1,092	216	571	284		488	436	1,511	8,185	7,743	442
1918	2,786	1,292	274	508	242		570	520	1,312	8,323	8,121	202
1919	3,897	1,529	412	409	293		790	713	1,625	9,785	9,479	306
1920	3,684	1,671	594	386	317		833	1,089	2,034	10,608	13,057	-2,449
1921 (a)	88	410	213	203	32		747	470	935	3,098	6,543	-3,445
1922	3,148	2,273	564	535	287		1,342	1,500	3,190	12,839	15,350	-2,511
1923	3,404	2,305	1,119	687	298		1,612	2,075	2,132	13,632	14,653	-1,021
1924	4,405	2,386	556	642	305	$ 389	1,925	2,748	2,353	15,709	15,601	108
1925	4,053	1,847	1,373	607	405	537	2,170	2,080	2,351	15,423	16,080	-657
1926	4,483	1,626	688	698	505	1,464	2,258	2,655	2,511	16,888	16,071	817
1927	4,407	2,087	800	716	550	2,051	2,572	5,061	2,693	20,937	21,410	-473
1928	4,263	1,997	1,693	739	586	2,624	2,699	1,639	2,802	19,042	20,647	-1,605
1929	4,222	1,682	925	552	606	3,114	2,917	2,100	2,936	19,054	22,395	-3,341
1930	5,059	1,635	1,013	1,003	619	3,945	3,164	1,767	3,230	21,435	24,871	-3,436
1931 (b)											29,138	
1932 (b)											29,460	

* Appendix Table E.
(a) Six months ending June 30. Fiscal year change.
(b) Because of the confusion caused by the change in agencies making financial reports, provided for by the administrative reorganization of 1932, no reports were made for the biennium ending June 30, 1932 from which it was possible to draw a correct statement of revenues for those years.

TABLE 21
Expenditures Classified, 1913-32*
(Figures in thousands)

Year	General government	Health and welfare	Education	Highway	Interest	Taxes collected and paid to towns	Conservation and development	Defectives	Other	Total
1913	$497	$263	$2,072	$553	$12	$265	$416	$621	$191	$4,890
1914	415	297	2,283	1,395	24	270	473	879	179	6,215
1915	591	468	3,745	1,312	54	401	415	696	219	7,901
1916	788	535	2,279	1,159	69	290	389	774	230	6,513
1917	891	552	2,352	1,511	93	315	510	1,208	311	7,743
1918	847	670	2,256	2,139	107	292	446	1,113	251	8,121
1919	1,390	618	2,497	2,352	125	293	568	1,300	336	9,479
1920	1,634	1,145	2,689	4,416	215	262	940	1,523	233	13,057
1921 (a)	2,639	529	450	1,511	192	4	338	735	145	6,543
1922	896	1,300	2,939	6,364	467	236	1,168	1,649	331	15,350
1923	932	1,275	2,880	5,334	570	474	1,389	1,420	379	14,653
1924	788	1,307	3,147	6,083	656	505	961	1,783	370	15,601
1925	1,045	1,430	3,119	7,112	147	517	797	1,650	263	16,080
1926	785	1,429	3,194	7,358	225	533	911	1,363	273	16,071
1927	1,011	1,449	3,217	11,867	752	539	876	1,421	278	21,410
1928	887	1,526	3,476	10,112	878	571	1,014	1,763	420	20,647
1929	1,332	1,698	3,488	11,501	858	565	1,037	1,450	466	22,395
1930	953	1,972	3,683	13,647	879	566	1,107	1,529	535	24,871
1931	1,430	2,095	3,894	16,506	939	685	1,318	1,750	521	29,138
1932	1,384	2,072	3,115	17,476	1,049	492	1,393	1,301	1,178	29,460

* Appendix Table E.
(a) Six months ending June 30. Fiscal year changed.

State revenues increased from $5,082,000 in 1913 to $21,435,000 in 1930.[4] This increase, as previously stated, was obtained by increasing rates of old taxes and by the growth of tax bases, rather than by development of new sources of revenue, the gasoline tax and motor vehicle license being notable exceptions. No extensive treatment of the revenue system is attempted here because an excellent study is available elsewhere.[5] The increased collections from the state property tax were the result of both higher rates and growth of the assessed valuation, the rate increasing from five mills in 1913 to seven and one-half mills in 1932, while the assessed valuation increased from $478,192,044 to $757,289,579 during the same years. The only important change in the taxation of railroads was the change from the gross-receipts to the gross-net method in 1929,[6] which resulted in a decrease in receipts from this source.

The item "Bank Taxes," which appears in Table 20, is composed of taxes on savings banks, trust companies, and on bank stock. During this period the taxes on savings banks and trust companies decreased, but this loss of revenue was offset by the imposition of a state tax on bank stock in 1923.[7] The state, however, acted only as a collecting agency in the case of the bank stock tax, returning the receipts from it to the cities and towns in which the stock was owned.

Collections from the corporation franchise tax and corporation fees increased from $289,000 in 1913 to $619,000 in 1930. The corporation franchise tax is an annual tax levied on corporations chartered under laws of Maine. The situation concerning the taxation of corporation franchises in Maine is

[4] It has not been possible to obtain from published reports a correct statement of receipts for the years 1931 and 1932.

[5] H. L. Lutz, *The System of Taxation in Maine*, 1934. "Report of the Recess Commission on Taxation of the 86th Legislature." Also, *cf. infra*, chapters vi, vii, viii.

[6] *Cf. infra*, pp. 171-177.

[7] *Cf. infra*, pp. 142-143.

unusual because it applies to all corporations chartered under laws of Maine regardless of whether or not they do any business in the state. Maine has come to be what is sometimes called a " charter mongering " state. For over fifty years the policy of Maine has been to make her incorporation laws so liberal that business from all states would be encouraged to incorporate under Maine laws. That Maine has been successful in this policy is attested by the fact that Maine ranks near the top among the states in the number of corporations chartered. This tax is an annual tax on the capital stock outstanding. It should not be considered as a business tax because by far the greater number of these corporations do no business in the state. It should be considered as a charge for the privilege of doing business under a Maine corporate charter.

The important new sources of revenue, as previously stated, were those which came into existence as a result of the coming of the automobile. In 1913, the motor vehicle license produced $138,000, while by 1930, it had increased to $3,164,000. The first gasoline tax law went into effect in 1924, and by 1930 the yield of this tax had increased to $3,945,000. The item " Highways " shown in Table 20 is composed of money received from the Federal government and cities and towns to match state funds expended for highways.

Expenditures for the years 1913-1932, have been summarized in Table 21.[8] An examination of these figures will enable one to see the great increase which took place and also the change in the relative importance of the various items. The item " General Government " includes the expenditures of the administrative departments, such as the executive, treasury and state; expenditures of regulative commissions, such as the public utilities and banking commissions; cost of courts and the attorney general's department; expenses of the legislature and the adjutant general's department. The amount of work of all these departments has greatly increased and, consequently, in-

8 *Cf.* Appendix Table E for more detailed figures.

creased expenditures have been necessary. It has been necessary to increase salaries because of a rising price level. New regulative commissions have been established and the work of old ones expanded.

The state government has always been liberal in support of the common schools but never liberal in the support of higher education. A glance at Table 21 will show that in 1913, expenditures for education were $2,072,000, while in 1931 they had increased to $3,984,000, falling off in 1932 to $3,115,000. A greater portion of this fund was distributed to the cities and towns in aid of common schools, which in 1932 received $2,293,841, the remainder of the fund going to normal schools, the University of Maine, academies, and teachers pensions. The cities and towns in that year raised by taxation $9,391,465 to support the common schools of the state. Thus it is seen that the state government contributed nearly one-fifth of the money spent in maintaining the common schools.[9]

In 1913 funds for the support of the common schools came from the Permanent School Fund, the School Mill Fund, the Common School Fund, and one-half the annual tax on savings banks and trust companies. Money was appropriated out of the general revenue fund for normal schools, academies, the University of Maine, and teachers' pensions.

The Permanent School Fund had been created by setting aside the proceeds of the sales of certain public lands in 1828 and subsequent years. It was required that the principal of this fund be kept intact and the income used for the support of the common schools.[10] The School Mill Fund, created in 1873, and the Common School Fund, created in 1909, were each supported by an annual one and one-half mill state property tax. Thus, in 1913, the state government was levying a three-mill property tax for the benefit of the common schools.

9 *Annual Report of the Commissioner of Education 1932*, p. 100.
10 *Cf. infra*, p. 23.

THE PRESENT-DAY PERIOD, 1913-1936   85

In 1917, a new fund, known as the School Equalization Fund, was created and the annual income of the Reserved Lands Fund was appropriated to it.[11] Prior to this time the income from the Reserved Lands Fund had been added to the principal.[12] In 1921, the financing of education was reorganized. The School Mill Fund, the Common School Fund and the School Equalization Fund were abolished and in their place a new fund, known as the State School Fund, was created. For the support of this fund, a state property tax of three and one-third mills was levied; the income from the Permanent School Fund and the income from the Reserved Lands Fund, as well as one-half the tax on savings banks and trust companies, were appropriated to it.[13] In 1929, an annual property tax of one mill was levied for the support of the University of Maine. This tax was to be in lieu of all other appropriations.

As a result of these changes, the state property tax, which in 1913 had been three mills for school purposes, increased by 1929 to four and one-third mills, and at the same time the assessed valuation of the state increased from $478,192,044 to $743,688,259. The taxes on savings banks and trust companies decreased during this period and consequently the increase in state school funds is accounted for by the increase in the rate of the property tax and the increase of the assessed valuation.

Expenditures for education increased from $2,072,000 in 1913 to $3,683,000 in 1930, or seventy-seven per cent. This increase, however does not indicate that the state government of Maine is spending excessive amounts on education. Only eight states in the Union spend for education as small a share of the state tax dollar as the state of Maine. The average percentage, which expenditures for education for all states was of total expenditures in 1930, amounted to twenty-eight per cent, while in Maine it was only eighteen per cent, yet Maine's

11 *Public Laws of Maine 1917*, ch. 26.
12 *Cf. infra*, pp. 208-209.
13 *Public Laws of Maine 1921*, ch. 173.

ability to support education is not far from the national average.[14] In regard to the adequacy of both state and local expenditures for education, the Maine School Finance Commission, in 1934, had the following to say:

The evidence, while not altogether conclusive, points strongly to the conclusion that Maine has not been extravagant in its support of public schools. It is quite safe to say that Maine could increase its expenditures from one-fifth to one-fourth, without exceeding the rate of expenditures of states in its class.[15]

From the foregoing it appears that Maine is not spending so large a percentage of its state funds as many other states do. Moreover, the percentage which expenditure for education is of the total, as shown in Table 21, has been decreasing in recent years.

Health and welfare activities expanded to a greater extent than any other except highways, expenditures for this purpose increasing from $263,000 in 1913 to $2,072,000 in 1932, an increase of nearly 800 per cent. In 1913, expenditures for health and welfare were largely composed of appropriations for the State Bureau of Health, support of state paupers and private hospitals. The acquisition of new functions has been responsible for a major portion of the increased expenditures since that date. A brief history of the acquisition of these new functions and a statement of the amount expended on the most important of them will now be given.

The State Board of Health was established in 1885. Its functions were chiefly those of collecting vital statistics, disseminating information and giving advice.[16] The activities of this board were very limited until 1917 when it was made a Depart-

---

14 *The Financing of the Public Schools in Maine*, 1934, "Report of the Maine School Finance Commission," pp. 48-57.

15 *Ibid.*, p. 57.

16 *Public Laws of Maine 1885*, ch. 286.

THE PRESENT-DAY PERIOD, 1913-1936   87

ment of Health, with increased duties and enlarged appropriations. From that time on its activities increased rapidly.[17]

The Department of Charities and Corrections was established in 1913, the duties of which were to investigate and supervise state institutions and make studies concerning social welfare.[18] As the state acquired additional social welfare functions, the administration of them was given to this department. In 1927 the name of the department was changed to that of the Department of Public Welfare, but no changes were made in its functions or duties.[19]

In 1915, the state began to assume the responsibilities of providing for tubercular patients. In that year it took over a private sanitorium which became known as the Central Maine Sanitorium. In 1919, another private institution was acquired, the Western Maine Sanitorium, and the Northern Maine Sanitorium was established.[20]

Aid to mothers with dependent children was provided in 1917. This law was to apply when the father was dead or unable to support the home, its purpose being to enable the children to stay at home under the mother's care rather than have the family broken up and the children placed in institutions or with strangers. The administration of this law was placed jointly with town officials and the State Department of Charities and Corrections. The amount of aid was left to the discretion of the administrators, and the cost of it was to be borne jointly by the towns and the state, each to pay one-half.[21]

The care of delinquent and destitute children was assumed by the state in 1919.[22] Prior to this time, these children had been under the care of the courts and the expense of providing

17 *Ibid.*, *1917*, ch. 197.
18 *Ibid.*, *1913*, ch. 196.
19 *Ibid.*, *1927*, ch. 48.
20 *Report of the State Auditor 1932*, pp. 22-28.
21 *Public Laws of Maine 1917*, ch. 222; *1919*, ch. 17.
22 *Ibid.*, *1919*, ch. 172.

for them had rested on the cities and towns, but this method had proved unsatisfactory. The State Board of Charities and Corrections was made the administrative agency. Children of good habits and character were to be placed in private homes. Incorrigible children were to be sent to state reformatories. The state maintains but one small children's home and it is contended that the policy of placing children in private homes is more satisfactory than putting them in institutions. The cost is borne jointly by the state and cities or towns from which the children come, the state collecting from the cities and towns one-half the cost, but in no case more than two and one-half dollars a week per child. The result of this division of the cost is that the state pays far more than the cities and towns.

The state had for many years made appropriations for private and municipal hospitals as recompense of free treatment given. In 1929, this policy was changed and an appropriation was made to the Department of Public Welfare for the purpose of paying hospitals for treatment given people unable to pay.[23] Appropriations for each of the years 1930 and 1931 for this purpose were $160,000, which was approximately the same amount formerly made to hospitals.

Table 22 is presented for the purpose of showing the cost of the various Health and Welfare activities.

While the increase in expenditures for Health and Welfare has been great, it is by no means excessive, and further increases may be expected.[24]

The causes of increasing highway expenditures are so similar in all states and so well known that there is little need for giving an extended treatment of them here. The period of great highway expansion in Maine did not begin until 1913, when the first comprehensive program was established. Expenditures for this purpose, which were $553,000 in 1913, in-

23 *Ibid., 1929*, ch. 33.
24 *State Administrative Consolidation in Maine*, 1930, chs. v and vi, National Institute of Public Administration.

TABLE 22

EXPENDITURES FOR HEALTH AND WELFARE PURPOSES, 1933 *

Bureau of Health	$ 151,950.85
Aid to Mothers	262,528.60
Hospital Care	164,811.68
Support of World War Veterans	70,265.75
Maternity and Child Welfare	29,770.72
Support of State Paupers	570,830.27
Support and Education of Blind	151,616.43
Tubercular Sanitoriums	392,087.74
Aid and Care of Children	332,402.29
Other	309,735.64
Total	2,470,000.00

* Data secured from the state controller.

creased to $17,476,000 in 1932. In the latter year, they amounted to more than one-half the total expenditures.

In order that the expansion which has taken place since 1913 may be better understood, a brief history of the preceding development will be given. The first highway law of a permanent nature was passed in 1901, which provided that on the petition of a city or town, the county commissioners were to designate the main thoroughfare running through the city or town as a state highway, and that for the permanent improvement of this road, the state would match any amount appropriated by the local government up to $100.00. An appropriation of $15,000 was made by the state for this purpose, but only $8,000 of it was used.[25]

In 1905, a state highway commissioner was appointed, whose duties were to assemble data concerning the highways of the state and give advice to county and local highway officials.[26] In 1907, it was made compulsory for cities and towns to designate the main roads through them as state highways and to appropriate a certain amount of money for improving them.

25 *Public Laws of Maine 1901*, ch. 285.
26 *Ibid., 1905*, ch. 146.

State aid for this work was granted and the state highway commissioner was given authority to supervise the work and to require that a certain quality of work be done.[27]

The first real effective highway legislation was passed in 1913. A state highway commission was created. The highways were divided into three classes: state highways, which were to be the main highways of the state, were to be built and maintained by the state; state-aid highways, which were to be built and maintained by the state and towns jointly, were to be roads of secondary importance, acting as feeders to the state highways; all other roads were to be classed as third class highways and the expense of building and maintaining them was placed on the cities and towns.[28]

To finance this program, a $2,000,000 bond issue was authorized, but no more than $500,000 worth of these bonds was to be sold in any one year.[29] Loans in increasing amounts were granted until in 1932 the highway debt amounted to $21,475,500. In addition to loans, highway funds were provided by a one-mill property tax, motor vehicle licenses, the gasoline tax, federal grants in aid, money from cities and towns to match state funds, and small appropriations for special projects.

Expenditures for highway purposes, as previously stated, amounted to over one-half the total state expenditures in 1932. A study of the efficiency with which this money has been spent and the peculiar problems faced by Maine in developing its highway system is beyond the scope of this work, but such a study is available elsewhere.[30] The burden of support of this program has been heavy and it is clear that the state is rapidly approaching the point beyond which it would not be wise to extend its public debt. It should be borne in mind, however, that a con-

27 *Ibid., 1907*, ch. 112.
28 *Ibid., 1913*, ch. 130.
29 *Cf. infra*, pp. 99-101, for an account of borrowing for highway purposes.
30 *State Administrative Consolidation in Maine*, 1930, ch. ix, National Institute of Public Administration.

siderable portion of the expense has been defrayed by sources of revenue which would not exist today, to any great extent, if the highways had not been built. Motor vehicle licenses and the gasoline tax produced $7,341,245.55 in 1932. In the years following 1932, it was necessary for the state to decrease drastically its highway expenditures. Considering the mounting state debt and the increasing competition of social welfare activities for state funds, it seems doubtful if the state will, in the immediate future, be able to support highway activities on the scale they attained in 1932.

The item "Taxes Collected and Paid to Cities and Towns" is composed of taxes on railroads, telegraph and telephone companies, bank stock, wild lands, and dogs. In the case of the railroads, telegraph and telephone companies, the state had recognized that they could not be taxed successfully by local authority and consequently undertook the administration of this tax, paying to the cities and towns an amount equal to one per cent of the par value of the stock owned in them.[31] For a like reason, the state took over the collection of the tax on bank stock in 1923, but in this case the state paid all the tax to the cities and towns in which the stock was owned. The state received dog taxes which were collected by the treasurers of the cities and towns. Damages done by dogs were paid for by the state and if a balance remained after paying these damages. it was returned. In some counties there was a great deal of wild land which experience had shown could not be successfully taxed by the counties. Because of this, the state assessed and collected the county property taxes and paid them to the counties. The increase in this item, as shown in Table 21, is accounted for by the state's undertaking to collect the tax on bank stock in 1923.

The item "Conservation and Development" includes expenditures for the Maine Development Commission, Geologic Survey, Departments of Agriculture, Forestry, Inland Fish

31 *Cf. infra*, ch. viii.

and Game, Sea Shore and Fisheries, and several items of minor importance. In some instances, the activities are of a purely developmental nature, such as those of the Maine Development Commission, while in others, such as the Departments of Forestry and Agriculture, conservation and development are combined. Expansion of the activities of these, while not so great as that of some others, is significant.

The expenditures of the Department of Agriculture were $141,000 in 1913, while by 1932, they had increased to $324,000, the increase having been caused by the performance of new functions and an increase in educational and promotional work. In 1932, the Division of Inspection was engaged in inspecting seeds, feeds, fertilizers, foods and drugs, and in packing and grading apples and potatoes. The Division of Animal Industry was chiefly engaged in eradication of tuberculosis from dairy cattle. The Division of Plant Industry was engaged in the certification of seeds, inspection of nurseries, insect eradication and enforcing quarantine regulations. The Division of Markets and Marketing was engaged in inspection work at shipping points and endeavoring to improve the marketing of farm products.

The chief cause of the increase in the expenditures of the Department of Forestry was for the purpose of controlling forest fires. The problem of controlling forest fires in Maine is of particular importance because such a large part of the area of the state is forest land and because the production of lumber is one of the most important industries. In order to meet this problem, the legislature, in 1909, established the Maine Forestry District, designating 9,500,000 acres, which should be included in the district, and levied a state property tax of one and one-half mills on the assessed value of this land, the funds thus collected to be used to control forest fires in this district. The administration of this work was given to the Forest Commissioner. The expenditures of the Department of Forestry in 1913 were $97,000, while by 1932 they had increased to $353,000. Of this latter amount $241,000 was spent for control of forest fires, leaving $112,000 for the other functions of this department. The other duties of the department were to manage the Reserved Lands,[32] control disease of trees and plants, study problems in entomology peculiar to the state, and encourage reforestation. The rate of the tax on the forestry district was increased to one and three-quarters mills in 1919 and again increased to two and one-quarter mills in 1921.[33]

Another activity in which a large increase in expenditures took place was the work of the departments of Inland Fish and Game and Sea Shore and Fisheries. The work of these departments consisted of enforcing the fish and game laws and stocking the streams and lakes of the state with fish. While more was done in enforcing the fish and game laws, the greater part of the increased expenditure can be accounted for by the developing of fish hatcheries and feeding stations for the purpose of providing fish for stocking. In recent years, Maine has developed rapidly as a pleasure resort and it has been thought good policy for the state to do what it could to aid in this development. While the expense of these departments has been heavy, it probably can be justified by the fact that a large part of it has been met by receipts from hunting and fishing licenses.

Expenditures for "Defectives," which about doubled during this period, include those for penal institutions, reformatories, insane asylums, and other activities necessitated by defective persons. New institutions were added during these years, the State Reformatory for Women at Skowhegan and the State Reformatory for Men at Windam. In addition to the expense of these two institutions, more adequate provision was made for the others, but even with this additional provision, the standard of service in these institutions was not particularly high.[34]

[32] *Cf. infra*, pp. 202-206 for a description of the Reserved Lands.

[33] *Public Laws of Maine 1919*, ch. 104; *1921*, ch. 4.

[34] *State Administrative Consolidation in Maine*, ch. vii. National Institute of Public Administration, 1930.

The era of prodigality in expenditures reached its highest point in Maine in 1932, when the full effects of the depression began to be felt. Although the ability of the people to pay taxes had been steadily decreasing since 1929, the legislature and state officials seemed to have been singularly blind to this fact and continued the policy of extravagant spending. The years which followed 1932 may be characterized as years of retrenchment, with the chief energies of the government directed toward providing relief for the depression victims. The history of these years will now be presented.

The securing and presenting of data for the years 1933-1936 has been made difficult by the reorganization of the state government in 1932,[35] the summary nature of financial reports published since the reorganization, and the large amounts of federal money received and spent for relief purposes. Because of these difficulties, it has not been possible to extend Tables 20 and 21 beyond 1932. Tables 23, 24, and 25 summarize the revenues and expenditures for the years 1933-1936.[36] Table 23 presents the balance between receipts and expenditures in two different forms, varying as receipts from loans are excluded or included. Table 24 presents the receipts classified, while Table 25 presents expenditures classified.

The year 1933 brought the realization that the state could not, under depression conditions, continue to support expenditures at the high level which had prevailed during the past few years. In the early months of the year, large amounts of the state property tax became delinquent, receipts from other taxes showed signs of sharply decreasing, and in the spring, two large chain banks, as well as many unit banks, failed. Moreover, the constitutional debt limit had been nearly reached. The legislature, as a result of these factors, became alarmed and reversed

[35] *Cf. infra*, ch. xi, for an explanation of the reorganization.

[36] Total expenditures as given for the years 1933-1936 are not comparable to totals given in previous years, because in the latter years debt payments were included, while prior to 1933 they were excluded. It was not possible from reports available to segregate debt payments in the last four years.

the financial policy, giving the governor and council authority to reduce expenditures for the remainder of the year 1933 wherever possible, and drastically decreased appropriations for the next biennium. In addition, the policy of borrowing to provide funds for highway construction was stopped.

For the year 1933, as shown in Table 23, there was an operating deficit of $8,074,000, which by borrowing, was reduced to a treasury deficit of $1,580,000. The full effect of the economy program appeared in 1934, when state expenditures decreased to $20,053,000, while at the same time receipts increased by $1,300,000, leaving a surplus of receipts over expenditures of $1,473,000. The only borrowing this year was the renewal of a temporary loan of $796,000. When the legislature met again in 1935, it was thought that the legislature of 1933 had been unduly alarmed about the state finances and a more liberal policy of appropriations was adopted. Constitutional authority was successfully sought for additional borrowing for highway purposes and for construction of state buildings, the " make work argument " being used to justify borrowing for additional highway and building expenditures. At the same time, expenditures for relief increased rapidly. As a result of this greater liberality in appropriations, there was an operating deficit for 1935 of $1,119,000, which, by borrowing, was converted to a treasury surplus of $68,000. In 1936, the operating deficit was $3,375,000 but this was reduced by borrowing to $25,000.

Having traced the balance between the revenues and expenditures for these four years, it will now be interesting to see how the large reduction in expenditures was accomplished. Examination of Table 25 shows that the major portion of the reduction occurred in expenditures for highways, this item alone accounting for $6,947,000 of the $9,247,000 decrease which took place in 1934. A considerable reduction took place in the item of general government in 1934, but this can largely be accounted for by the fact that the legislature was not in session that year. Expenditures for health and welfare, which include those for relief purposes, increased from $2,470,000 in 1933 to $4,082,000 in 1936.

No important changes in the revenue system took place during these years, increase of receipts being largely due to recovery from the depression. The increase in receipts from the state property tax in 1934 was the result of collection of delinquent 1933 taxes. Bank failures, which reduced the capital stock and deposits of banks, were responsible for smaller collections of bank taxes.

TABLE 23

REVENUES AND EXPENDITURES, 1933–36 *

(Figures in thousands)

| | Revenues excluding loans, and expenditures (a) ||| Revenues including loans, and expenditures (a) |||
Year	Revenues	Expenditures (b)	Surplus or deficit for year	Revenues	Expenditures (b)	Surplus or deficit for year
1933	$20,226	$29,300	− $8,074	$27,720	$29,300	− $1,580
1934	21,526	20,053	1,473	22,322	20,053	2,269
1935	22,228	23,347	−1,119	23,279	23,347	68
1936	23,551	26,926	−3,375	26,901	26,926	−25

Biennial Reports Department of Finance.

(a) Federal Emergency Receipts and Expenditures, and Receipts and Expenditures of the Maine Liquor Commission have been eliminated.

(b) Includes debt payments.

The history of the state finances having been brought down to the end of the fiscal year 1936, it now remains to see what the financial condition of the state government is at present and what fiscal problems it is faced with. The budget, which had been balanced in 1934, in the fiscal year ended June 30, 1936, was again out of balance to the extent of $3,375,000. The funded debt on that date stood at $29,740,500, which is sufficiently large, considering the resources of Maine, to raise the question of the wisdom of further borrowing. Moreover,

TABLE 24
REVENUES, 1933–1936 *
(Figures in thousands)

Year	State property tax	Railroad tax	Inheritance tax	Bank tax	Corporation franchise tax and fees	Gasoline tax	Automobile registration	Other	Total excluding loans	Loans	Total including loans
1933	$4,223	$ 992	$696	$498	$259	$4,199	$2,713	$6,646	$20,226	$7,494	$27,720
1934	5,017	956	542	405	259	4,126	3,151	7,070	21,526	796	22,322
1935 (a)	4,520	990	493	424	238	5,056	3,160	7,347	22,228	1,051	23,279
1936 (a)	4,514	1,025	563	373	236	4,763	3,407	8,671	23,551	3,350	26,901

* *Biennial Reports Department of Finance.*
(a) Receipts of the State Liquor Commission and Federal Emergency receipts eliminated.

TABLE 25
EXPENDITURES, 1933–36 *
(Figures in thousands)

Year	General government	Health and welfare	Education	Conservation and development	Defectives	Highway	Treasury disbursements (b)	Other	Total
1933	$1,628	$2,470	$3,731	$1,039	$1,252	$13,984	$4,900	$296	$29,300
1934	1,237	2,683	3,143	969	1,249	7,037	3,370	365	20,053
1935 (a)	1,729	3,170	3,062	1,059	1,365	9,108	3,528	326	23,347
1936 (a)	1,522	4,082	3,254	1,154	2,068	9,384	4,685	777	26,926

* *Biennial Reports Department of Finance.*
(a) Expenditures of the State Liquor Commission eliminated because it is a commercial undertaking.
(b) Includes debt payments.

the state is faced with the problem of old age pensions. In 1936, the governor and council, acting under authority of an old law which authorized the governor and council to pay old age pensions of $30.00 a month when surplus funds should be available, started to pay them. In view of the facts concerning the finances which have been presented, it is hard to see by what processes of reasoning the governor and council arrived at the conclusion that surplus funds were available. This policy, however, was started so late in the year that payments for this purpose in 1936 were not large. The present legislature is faced with the demand, not only to continue these pensions but also to provide funds to match all the money offered for other welfare services by the Federal Social Security Act. If it grants these requests and maintains other expenditures on the same level as in 1936, it will be faced with the necessity of providing several million dollars of additional revenue. How this amount of new revenue can be provided is a serious problem. Professor Lutz, in his study of the tax system in 1934, estimated that new tax legislation, principally sales and income taxes, could provide a maximum of $5,000,000 for tax equalization purposes without the necessity of excessive rates in any of the new taxes.[37] It should be noted, however, that this estimate was predicated on the assumption that the new revenue would be used for tax equalization purposes and not to provide for additional expenditures. It is quite possible that the imposing of the taxes proposed by Professor Lutz and not using the proceeds for tax equalization might result in excessive strain at some other points in the revenue system.

The history of the public debt during this period is interesting for a number of reasons. The story is here revealed of how a state which owed nothing became, in a little more than twenty years, heavily involved in debt through its enthusiasm for highway building. Also, the futility of restricting state in-

---

37 *The System of Taxation in Maine 1934*, ch. v. Report of the Recess Commission on Taxation of the 86th Legislature.

debtedness by constitutional limitations is demonstrated. In addition, the result of an experiment in self-liquidating projects is shown.

At the beginning of 1913, the state of Maine was in the unusual condition of being out of debt, with the exception of $268,300 of bonds held by state trust funds and $700.00 of coupons due and uncalled for. In 1913, a new era of debt expansion began which reached its peak in 1933, when the debt amounted to $31,445,000. Following that year, small reductions were made, which reduced the debt to $29,740,500 on June 30, 1936. The greatest part of this debt was incurred for the purpose of building highways and bridges.

Table 26 shows the amount of the debt at the end of each fiscal year and the purposes for which it was created. Each one of these purposes will be considered. At the beginning of 1913, the authority of the legislature to authorize borrowing for purposes other than war was limited to $300,000.[38] This limit, which with one exception had been observed since 1847, was again and again increased during this period by submission of constitutional amendments to the people.

Maine began her present highway program in 1913. This program has been largely dependent upon securing constitutional amendments, permitting increased borrowing. The bond issues have been so numerous that no attempt will be made to treat each issue separately. Reference to Table 26 will show the growth of the highway debt year by year. In 1913, an amendment was approved which authorized the issuance of highway bonds to the extent of $2,000,000, but with the provision that not more than $500,000 of them could be sold in any one year.[39] In 1919, constitutional authority for borrowing for highway purposes was increased to $10,000,000;[40] in 1925, the highway debt limit was increased to $16,000,000, with the

[38] Constitution of Maine, article vi; *Revised Statutes of Maine 1856*, p. 49.
[39] Amendment xxxv, *Revised Statutes of Maine 1930*, p. 42.
[40] Amendment xliii, *Revised Statutes of Maine 1930*, p. 46.

TABLE 26
Bonded Debt of the State of Maine as of the End of Each Fiscal Year, 1913–1936 *
(Figures in thousands)

Year	Highway	Trust funds (a)	War loan	Soldiers' bonus	State pier	Kennebec bridge	Waldow-Hancock bridge	State of Maine improvement	Total
1913	$ 300	$269							$ 569
1914	793	269							1,062
1915	1,253	269							1,522
1916	1,715	269							1,983
1917	1,861	269	$ 500						2,629
1918	2,000	269	1,000						3,269
1919	1,921	269	1,000						3,190
1920	4,634	269	1,000	$3,000					8,902
1921					Fiscal year changed				
1922	6,175	269	1,000	2,700	$1,150				11,283
1923	7,296	269	1,000	2,700	1,150				12,414
1924	8,777	269	1,000	2,400	1,150				13,545
1925	9,663	269	900	2,100	1,150				14,081
1926	11,982	269	850	1,801	1,150				16,052
1927	13,385	269	800	1,501	1,150	$3,000			20,104
1928	12,919	269	750	1,200	1,500	3,000			19,287
1929	14,313	269	619	900	1,500	3,000			20,250
1930	15,138	269	565	602	1,150	3,000			20,723
1931	17,557	269	514	301	1,150	3,000	$700		23,491
1932	21,476		464	300	1,150	2,950	900		27,240
1933	26,152		439	3	1,052	2,900	900		31,445
1934	25,299		414		920	2,850	900		30,382
1935	24,609		414	2	815	2,800	900	$475	29,540
1936	24,472		414		730	2,750	900		29,740

* Compiled from annual reports of state auditor, 1913–1931; from treasurer's office 1932–1934; and Biennial Report of the Department of Finance 1935–36. End of fiscal year December 31 for years 1913–20; June 30 for years 1921–36.
(a) Non-negotiable bonds issued to University of Maine Trust Fund ($218,300) and to Augusta State Hospital ($50,000). Uncalled for coupons of Municipal War Debt Loan $700 for years 1913–15; $500 for years 1916–20 and 1922–31.

THE PRESENT-DAY PERIOD, 1913-1936   101

provision that bonds issued after that date should not be reissued after having been retired;[41] and in 1929, the creation of $15,000,000 additional debt for highway purposes was authorized.[42] Under the authority of these amendments, the legislature increased the highway debt until on June 30, 1933 it amounted to $26,151,500. On that date, authority to issue only $2,000,000 remained. As a result of the economy program of 1934, no bonds were sold in that year, but in 1935 borrowing was again resumed. Also in that year the constitutional debt limit for highway purposes was increased by $5,000,000, with the provision that none of these bonds could be reissued after having been retired. The amount of highway bonds outstanding on June 30, 1936 was $24,425,500. These are serial bonds, approximately $1,500,000 of them maturing each year until 1943, after which annual maturities will amount to approximately $1,100,000 until the last are paid in 1958.

When the war broke out in 1917 the legislature appropriated $1,000,000 for war purposes and authorized the governor and council to borrow as much of that sum as was needed.[43] In 1917, $500,000 was borrowed and another $500,000 in 1918. The last of these bonds matures in 1937.

The legislature, in 1919, authorized the payment of a bonus to soldiers and sailors of the World War and proposed an amendment to the constitution authorizing the issuance of $3,000,000 bonds for this purpose.[44] The amendment was approved by the people and the bonds sold in 1920.[45] These bonds have all been retired.

The first self-liquidating project which the state engaged in was the construction of the Maine State Pier at Portland harbor in 1922. The primary object of this project was to aid in the

[41] Amendment xlix, *Revised Statutes of Maine 1930*, p. 53.
[42] Amendment lii, *Revised Statutes of Maine 1930*, p. 52.
[43] *Public Laws of Maine 1917*, ch. 187.
[44] *Resolves of Maine Special Session 1919*, ch. 264.
[45] Amendment xlv, *Revised Statutes of Maine 1930*, p. 48.

development of the harbor, it being hoped that if adequate wharfage was provided, the winter commerce between Canada and Europe might move through the port of Portland. It was also hoped that the income from the pier might pay the operating expenses and interest, and amortize the debt. These hopes have not been realized in full. Operating expenses have been paid and by June 30, 1935, a surplus of $65,478.70 had been built up but nothing had been paid on interest or principal of the bonds out of income from the pier. Up to that date the state had paid $588,200 interest and $335,000 principal of the bonds.[46] Bonds amounting to $1,150,000 were sold in 1922, under constitutional authority granted in that year. On June 30, 1936 there were $730,000 of them outstanding, maturing at the rate of $115,000 a year until 1942, when the last of them will be paid.

A more succesful undertaking was that of the Kennebec Bridge. The legislature in 1925 provided for the building of a bridge across the Kennebec River at Bath and proposed an amendment to the constitution authorizing the issuance of $3,000,000 of bonds for this purpose. The amendment was approved [47] and bonds for that amount were sold in 1927. The law also provided that contracts should be entered into with the Maine Central Railroad and public utilities for the use of the bridge, and that motor vehicles should pay tolls.[48] This project has been successful financially. Up to June 30, 1936 income had been sufficient to pay not only operating expenses, interest and amortization of the bonds, but to accumulate a reserve for maintenance amounting to $54,022.98. On June 30, 1936 there was $2,750,000 of these bonds outstanding. They are serial bonds, with annual maturities ranging from $40,000 to $70,000 in different years, the last maturing in 1978.

46 *Sixteenth Report of the Department of Audit*, p. 15.
47 Amendment xlviii, *Revised Statutes of Maine 1930*, p. 49.
48 *Private and Special Laws of Maine 1925*, ch. 89.

THE PRESENT-DAY PERIOD, 1913-1936

Another successful self-liquidating project was the Waldo-Hancock Bridge, across the Penobscot River. This bridge was authorized in 1929 under the same plan as had been used for the Kennebec Bridge. An amendment approved in 1930 granted authority for the issuance of bonds amounting to $1,100,000 [49] but only $900,000 of them were sold. The law provided that contracts should be entered into with public utility companies for the use of the bridge and that motor vehicles should pay tolls. Up to the present, income has been sufficient to pay all expenses.

One other issue of bonds remains to be considered, the State of Maine Improvement Bonds. These bonds were authorized in 1934 in order to provide funds for the construction and improvement of state buildings,[50] the purpose of this construction program being to provide work for the unemployed. This authority was not used until 1936, when bonds amounting to $475,000 were sold.

The outstanding bonded debt of Maine on June 30, 1936, amounted to $29,654,500. Approximately ninety-four per cent of this debt was incurred for the purpose of highway and bridge construction. Interest and amortization charges for this debt will amount to $3,110,340 in 1937, which is eleven and one-half per cent of the expenditures in 1936. Whether or not Maine should continue to increase her debt for the purpose of highway construction is a debatable question, but with the necessity of providing several millions of additional revenue facing the state, it would seem that any further borrowing should be undertaken only after careful consideration.

At the beginning of this period the state government was in a strong financial position. Its debt had been extinguished, with the exception of $268,300 held by state trust funds and $700 due but uncalled for. Its revenue system yielded adequate funds to provide for expenditures on the level which then existed.

[49] Amendment li, *Revised Statutes of Maine 1930*, p. 51.
[50] Constitution of Maine, Article IX, Section 20.

This situation, however, did not long continue. Expenditures which amounted to $4,890,000 in 1913, began an increase which continued until they reached a peak of $29,460,000 in 1932. In 1933, the financial policy was reversed and the next year expenditures were only $20,053,000, but this economy program was short-lived, for in 1935 another increase began which continued into 1936, when expenditures amounted to $26,926,000. Every state service shared the increase which began in 1913, but there was a great change in the relative importance of the various services. The most notable change was in the expenditures for highways, which increased from eleven per cent of the total in 1913 to fifty-five per cent in 1930, and then decreased to thirty-five per cent in 1936.

The revenue system from the beginning of this period proved incapable of providing funds with which to pay for the rapidly increasing expenditures and borrowing was resorted to, with the result that the public debt, which in 1913 amounted to only $269,000, increased to $29,654,500 on June 30, 1936. The revenue system, with the exception of motor vehicle licenses and the gasoline tax, was changed very little during these years and, as stated by Professor Lutz, is in need of an extensive revision.

At present, the state faces a critical financial situation. To continue expenditures on the level of 1936, over $3,000,000 more revenue will be required. In addition, a majority of the present legislature has made campaign promises to enact legislation granting old age pensions and other social security aid, which will cost a number of additional millions. Moreover, the state debt is rapidly approaching a point where further borrowing would seem questionable financial policy.

PART TWO

STUDIES OF SELECTED ASPECTS OF THE FINANCES OF THE STATE

CHAPTER VI
THE PROPERTY TAX

MAINE, while under the political jurisdiction of Massachusetts, had been subject to property taxation for a great many years. An examination of the history of the tax laws of Massachusetts reveals citations of laws with reference to the taxation of property running back to the English statutes of Anne and the Georges. The earlier attempts at property taxation were crude, but gradually there developed a body of law which by 1820 was so complete that even today it constitutes the general framework of Maine's property tax laws. It was but natural that Maine should adopt the tax laws of Massachusetts, which was done by the acts of 1820 and 1821, with some variations due to local conditions.

To give a clear picture of the property tax as it operates in Maine, it is necessary to describe briefly the three units of government—the state, counties and municipalities. The state government performs the general functions which are common in all states, but the functions of county governments are unusually limited in Maine. This is because the township was the original unit of government and counties developed later to perform those functions which could not well be performed by the state or town government.[1] The first step in creating counties was taken in Massachusetts in 1636, when the state was divided into four districts for the purpose of equalizing taxes among the towns. By the time of separation in 1820, the counties were maintaining the registry of deeds, probate and county courts (which tried both civil and criminal cases), the jails and the roads. The legislature adopted the Massachusetts law in regard to county government almost *in toto*. In later years construction and maintenance of highways passed largely

[1] E. H. Bartlet, "Local Government in Penobscot County," *University of Maine Studies*, second series, no. 21.

to the state or to the towns. County officials, originally appointed, are now elected.[2]

Today the municipalities perform the greatest volume of governmental functions and expend the bulk of the money raised by property taxation. In Maine there are four different forms of municipal government: cities, towns, plantations and unincorporated places. The fundamental geographical unit for all four forms of municipalities is the township, which is approximately six miles square.[3] There is no general law for the chartering of cities and no requirements as to minimum population or form of government. The citizens of any town may petition the legislature to be chartered as a city and, if the legislature be favorably disposed, an act is passed making the town a city and prescribing the form of government it shall have. Despite the fact that each city has been chartered individually, there is a considerable uniformity in the provisions of charters. Towns and plantations are incorporated under general laws. Plantations are merely simplified towns, the chief difference being that, instead of having selectmen as administrative officers, the assessors serve as such. Unincorporated places are usually townships which have less than two hundred inhabitants and in which no local government exists, the schools being under the superintendence of the state department of education, the highways under the county commissioners, while law is enforced by the county sheriff. They are subject only to state and county taxes. In January 1931, there were 20 cities, 433 towns, 65 plantations and 361 unincorporated places. These unincorporated places or, as they are sometimes called, unor-

---

2 *Ibid.*, p. 22, *ad passim.*

3 Town and township should not be confused. A town is an incorporated unit of local government while the word township refers only to a geographical area. The surveys of these townships were not entirely uniform, varying to take account of the topography of the country and the boundaries of old land grants. Frequently the legislature changed the size of a township by changing the boundaries of towns.

ganized townships, cover an area of 8,057,000 acres, or 42 per cent of that of the whole state.[4]

The provisions regarding taxation, contained in Article X of sections 7 and 8 of the original constitution, were very limited. Section 7 reads as follows: "While the public expenses shall be assessed on the polls and estates, a general valuation shall be taken at least once in ten years." Section 8 provides that: "All taxes upon real estate, assessed by authority of this state, shall be apportioned and assessed equally, according to the just value thereof." This latter section differed from the Massachusetts provision, which had permitted a classification of real estate in order to make the tax burden conform to some extent to the rate of return on the property.[5]

The first legislature, meeting in 1820, passed only one law concerning taxation, which was "an act to ascertain the estates ratable within the state."[6] It provided that the assessors of each district, town and plantation should, on or before the first day of November, 1820, make a return to the secretary of state of the "Polls and Estates Ratable," and gave instructions as to how this valuation should be made. The remainder of the tax laws were passed in 1821. The laws of these two sessions will be treated together.

The valuation of taxable property will be treated first. The assessment district was the township. However, surveys establishing boundaries had been made only in the settled parts of the state. A large amount of wild land remained outside the political jurisdiction of any organized township and the valuation of this wild land was made the duty of the state treasurer. The law provided for the election of three to five assessors at the annual town meeting. In case no assessors were elected, the selectmen were to act as assessors, and in case no selectmen were elected, the county officers were empowered to appoint

---

[4] These figures obtained from the office of the State Board of Assessors.
[5] W. Williamson, *History of Maine*, vol. ii, p. 684.
[6] *Public Laws of Maine 1820*, ch. 19.

assessors and the town was chargeable for their pay and expenses and also subject to a fine of $300.00. This arrangement was necessary because in many towns the population was so small and scattered that frequently no regular town government was maintained. The law also specified that whenever any plantation should fail to elect assessors, the state treasurer should issue an order to a justice of the peace, living near the plantation, requiring him to issue a warrant to some "principal inhabitant" of the plantation, directing him to notify the voters of the plantation to meet on a certain date and to elect a moderator, clerk, assessors, and collector of taxes. If the "principal inhabitant," so notified, did not obey the order the whole of the state tax levied was to be charged to him personally. After the meeting, the "principal inhabitant" was to notify the justice of the peace of the names of the officers elected and the justice of the peace was in turn to notify the state treasurer and the county officers.[7]

The constitution, as noted before, required that a state valuation, which was needed for the purpose of apportioning the state tax among the towns, should be taken at least once in ten years. The act of 1821 provided that in the towns a valuation should be taken annually to serve as the base for local taxes.[8]

The tax law of 1820 ordered a state valuation to be made in that year[9] and gave detailed instructions as to how it should be done. The following is the form of the list required to be submitted to the assessors.

Be it further enacted that the following shall be the form of the list for the valuation, for the year one thousand eight hundred and twenty. A list of the polls and estates, real and personal, for the several proprietors and inhabitants of the town of ——————— in

[7] *Statutes of Maine 1820-1821*, ch. 116.
[8] *Statutes of Maine 1820-1821*, ch. 116.
[9] The law providing for the choosing of assessors was not passed until 1821. The assessors for 1820 were chosen under the laws of Massachusetts which did not differ greatly from the one enacted by Maine the next year.

the county of ——————— taken pursuant to an act of the Legislature of this State, passed in the year of our Lord eighteen hundred and twenty, entitled, "An Act to ascertain the estate ratable within this State, by the subscribers, Assessors of the said ——————— duly elected and sworn. Number of polls ratable, eighteen years old and upwards to twenty-one years; number of polls ratable, twenty-one years old and upwards; number of male polls not ratable, nor supported by the town, distinguishing State paupers from town paupers; number of dwelling houses, number of shops within or adjoining dwelling houses; number of other shops; number of distill houses; number of sugar houses; number of tan houses; number of slaughter houses; number of pot and pearlash works; number of warehouses; number of ropewalks; number of gristmills and the number of pair of stones in each; number of carding machines, with their buildings; number of fulling mills; number of spinning machines, going by water, with their buildings, number of saw mills and the number of saws; number of small arms manufactories, with their buildings; number of slitting mills; number of cotton and woolen mills with their buildings; number of other mills; number of iron works and furnaces; number of bakehouses; number of barns; number of all other buildings, and edifices of the value of twenty dollars and upwards; number of superficial feet of wharf, and the annual income thereof; number of tons of vessels, and small craft of five tons burthen and upwards, at home or abroad, computing the same according to the rule established by the United States; the annual amount of commissions arising from factorage; the amount of every person's whole stock in trade, good wares, and merchandise, at home or abroad, paid for or not paid for; the amount of securities of the United States, this State, or any other State, and at what rate of interest; the amount of money on hand, including such as may be deposited in any bank or with any agent, exclusive of such as may belong to any stockholders as such; the amount of stock held by any stockholders in any bank; number of ounces of plate; number of shares in any bridges or turnpikes, and the value of such shares and the income thereof; number of acres of tillage land, including orchards tilled; number of bushels of wheat; number of bushels of rye; number of bushels of oats; number of bushels of Indian corn; number of bushels of barley; number of bushels of peas and beans, raised on the said tillage land per year; number of pounds of hops, number of acres of English and upland mowing, including orcharding mowed; number of tons of hay the yearly produce of the same; number of acres of salt marsh; number of tons of hay the yearly produce of the same; number of acres of pasturage, including orcharding pastured; number of cows the same will keep; number of barrels of cider which can be made yearly upon the whole farm; number of acres of woodland, exclusive of pasturage enclosed; number of acres of unimproved land; number of acres of land unimprovable; number of acres of land owned by the town; number of acres owned by any other proprietors; number of acres of land used for roads; number of acres of land covered by water; number of horses three years old and upwards; number of oxen four years old and upwards; number of steers and cows three years old and upwards; number of swine six months old and upwards; number of carriages kept for transportation of persons and their baggage; amount of estates doomed.[10]

Nothing was said in the act of 1820 about the procedure of valuation for county and town purposes, but in the law of 1821 it was provided that the valuation for county and town purposes should be made according to the rules laid down in the act of 1820, for taking the valuation for state purposes.[11]

From a study of the preceding rules of valuation it is clear that the idea of a truly comprehensive *general property tax*[12] had not emerged. The constitution provided that all real estate should be taxed at a uniform rate but it did not specify that all property should be taxed. In following the practice of enumerating the property to be taxed, omissions were unavoidable. An examination of the list shows that stock in corporations, other than that of banks, toll bridges and turnpikes; bonds other than those of the United States and the state governments; household furniture and tools both of agriculturalists

10 *Public Laws of Maine 1820*, ch. 19.
11 *Statutes of Maine 1821*, ch. 116.
12 Taxation of all property at a uniform rate.

and mechanics were omitted. It is possible that stocks and bonds, other than those enumerated, were not of sufficient amount at that time to be important, but household furniture and tools must have been. Since these were exempted in later years, it may have been that the omission was intentional. Nothing was said in the law of 1820 about the deduction of debt, but in the law levying the state tax for 1821 the following appears: " including all monies at interest, more than they pay interest for, and all other debts due to them more than they are indebted for." [13] This passage was repeated in the laws of subsequent years until the comprehensive revision of the tax laws in 1845.

The procedure of levying the tax on polls and estates, commonly called the state tax, involved two steps by the legislature. First, a law was passed levying a certain amount on the polls and estates and appointing a committee of the legislature to apportion this amount among the cities and towns on the basis of assessed valuation. This apportionment would then be drafted into a bill and passed, levying a certain amount of money on each city and town. In this same act, there would be a provision that a certain part of this money should be raised by a tax on polls. The amount of the poll tax was specified at so many cents per poll, but with the provision that if in any city or town the total amount of poll taxes at the figure specified should exceed a certain fraction of the state tax levied on that city or town, the poll tax should be reduced until it equalled that fraction. Thus it is seen that the rate of the property tax in different cities and towns depended on the number of taxable polls.[14] This practice was followed until 1857, when the state tax became simply a property tax.

As procedure in collecting the state tax, it was provided that the state treasurer should deliver warrants to the sheriffs of each county, who, in turn, should distribute them to the

13 *Public Laws of Maine 1821*, ch. 134.

14 The amount of the poll tax in different years ranged from eighteen to twenty cents and the fraction of the total state tax which poll taxes could not exceed ranged from one-fifth to one-sixth.

assessors of the cities and towns. The towns were to choose tax collectors to whom the assessors were to deliver the tax bills.[15]

The provisions concerning delinquent taxes were severe as compared with present practices. If a person refused or neglected to pay his personal property taxes on demand, the collector was directed to distrain his goods and chattels, and if, on the expiration of four days, payment had not been made, they were to be sold at public auction. It was also provided that:

If any person assessed as aforesaid, shall refuse or neglect to pay the sum or sums assessed, by the space of twelve days after demand thereof, and shall neglect to show the constable or collector sufficient goods or chattels whereby the same may be levied, in every such case he may take the body of the person so refusing, and commit him to the common jail of the county, there to remain until the same is paid, or he therefrom be discharged by due order of law.[16]

In the case of real estate, it was provided that if taxes were not paid within two months after they became due, the collector should sell it at public auction, or enough of it to pay the taxes, providing that notice of the sale had been published in a paper of the county for three consecutive weeks before the sale. The owner was given two years in which to redeem the property by paying the taxes, together with interest at twenty per cent and all necessary charges.[17]

If any town should fail to pay the state tax, the law directed that the sheriff of the county in which the town was located should seize the property of the assessors and sell enough of it to pay the tax; if the property of the assessors was not sufficient, the sheriff was to seize enough of the property of any of the inhabitants to pay the deficiency. The inhabitants who had lost

15 *Statutes of Maine 1820-1821*, ch. 116.
16 *Ibid.*
17 *Ibid.*

THE PROPERTY TAX

their property could then sue the town and recover the value of the property lost, and damages.[18]

Local taxes for building and maintaining highways in the towns could be " worked out." The taxes were levied as other town taxes but the tax warrants were delivered to the highway surveyor and every person taxed was permitted to work on the highways with his oxen a sufficient amount to pay his tax, or in case he could not work himself, to send a substitute. If the amount of labor performed was not sufficient to pay the tax, the balance was payable in money to the surveyor.[19]

Special provision was made for the levy of taxes for religious purposes. Every parish and religious society could levy such taxes as it deemed necessary for the support of the ministry, for the building, repairing and maintenance of houses of religion, and all other necessary charges. These taxes were to be levied on the members of the religious society only, and were to be collected under the laws providing for the assessment and collection of other property taxes. There was no requirement that anyone join a religious society, but once having become a member he had to pay the taxes assessed while he was a member, and could not dissociate himself from the society until all his taxes had been paid.[20]

The methods of assessing taxes for town and county purposes were the same as those for state purposes, except that the estimates of county taxes were required to be submitted to the legislature for approval before they could be collected.[21]

In the acts of 1830 and 1840, which gave instructions as to how the state valuation should be taken, no changes were made except that the articles enumerated as subject to taxation became much more specific and much more numerous.[22] In 1836, the

---

[18] *Ibid.*
[19] *Statutes of Maine 1820-1821*, ch. 119.
[20] *Ibid.*, ch. 135.
[21] *Ibid.*, ch. 116.
[22] *Private and Special Laws 1830*, ch. 116; *Public Laws 1840*, ch. 71.

state treasurer was instructed to collect the county taxes on lands in unincorporated places at the same time he collected the state tax. He was also instructed to pay the counties the taxes due as soon as the warrants were presented to him, without waiting to collect them.[23] It was deemed necessary for the state treasurer to collect these taxes because a great portion of them were levied on wild lands with non-resident owners and the state, through the land agent, was the only agency which could satisfactorily do this. A considerable amount of these state and county taxes were never collected, and the uncollected county taxes became a drain on the state treasury.

In 1845, a revision of the tax laws was made, which definitely changed the property tax from a tax on a list of specified items of property to a true general property tax. Section two of this act provided that " All real property within this state, all personal property of the inhabitants of this state, and all personal property hereinafter specified of persons not inhabitants of this state, shall be subject to taxation as hereinafter provided." [24]

Real estate was defined as " All lands in this State and all other things affixed to the same." Real estate was made taxable where located and the land might be assessed either to the tenants or owners, each paying one-half the tax. The real estate of railroads other than roadbeds was made taxable in the towns where located: " The track of the road and the land on which it is constructed shall not for this purpose, be deemed real estate." [25]

Personal property was defined as follows, provision being made for the offsetting of debts against credits only:

All goods, chattels, moneys and effects, wheresoever they are; all ships and vessels, at home and abroad; all obligations for money or other property; money at interest and debts due the persons to

23 *Public Laws of Maine 1836*, ch. 201.
24 *Ibid.*, *1845*, ch. 159, sec. 2.
25 *Ibid.*, sec. 4.

be taxed more than they are owing; all public stocks and securities; all shares in moneyed, railroad and other corporations, within or without the state; all annuities payable to persons to be taxed when the capital of such annuity is not taxed within this state; and all other property included in the last preceding state valuation for purposes of taxation.[26]

Personal property was taxable at the residence of the owner, with the following exceptions: (1) all goods, wares, merchandise, logs, timber, lumber and all stock in trade were taxable where they were located, provided the owners occupied any store, shop, mill or wharf in that town; (2) all machinery and goods, either manufactured or unmanufactured, belonging to a corporation were taxable in the town where situated; (3) mules, horses, neat cattle, sheep and swine were taxable in the town where located.

Personal property which was mortgaged was deemed the property of the person who had possession of it. Partnerships were assessed in the partnership name for all property used in conducting the business. In assessing the shares of stock of manufacturing corporations, it was provided that the assessed value of their real estate, machinery and goods, either manufactured or unmanufactured, should be deducted from the value of the stock; no deduction for debt was allowed.

Since this law marked a change from a specific property tax to a general property tax, exemptions had to be enumerated. The following property was exempted: the property of schools and of benevolent, charitable and scientific institutions incorporated in the state; all property of the United States or of this state; household furniture not exceeding $200 to any one family; farming utensils and mechanics' tools; churches with their furnishings; mules, horses, neat cattle, swine and sheep not exceeding six months old; property of Indians and the property of all persons who, by reason of age, infirmity or poverty were in the judgment of the assessors unable to contribute

26 *Ibid.*

toward the public expenditures.[27] The rules concerning the assessment and collection of the taxes remained practically unchanged.[28] The changes made by this revision of 1845 with respect to jurisdiction, double taxation and liability of the tenant for the payment of the tax require special comment.

In Maine the question of the jurisdiction under which personal property should be taxed was an important one, because of the special conditions present in the lumbering and shipping enterprises. The general rule, that personal property should be taxable at the domicile of the owner, would work injustices in the case of such businesses named. Logs and sawed timber were seldom physically present in the town in which the owner resided, while the towns or townships in which it was located at the time of assessment had usually been put to expense on account of the presence of this timber. The new law recognized this by providing that it should be taxed where it was located April 1, on the condition that the owner occupied a store, shop, mill or wharf in that town. However, the manner in which courts interpreted the provision of occupancy not only practically nullified the intent of the law regarding the taxing jurisdiction, but virtually exempted vast quantities of timber nominally taxable. In the case of *Campbell v. Inhabitants of Machias,* the court held that " Occupancy should constitute a right to receive and not a liability to pay " [29] and that for timber to be taxable in a particular town, the owner of timber must own, rather than rent, a mill or wharf in that town. The result of this decision was to make a very large portion of the annual lumber cut taxable in the towns in which the owner had his domicile, and since the assessors of these towns had no means of learning of the existence of such property, hundreds of

27 *Ibid.,* sec. 5.

28 There were several other provisions in the act concerning the assessment of the property of minors, trust funds held by guardians, property of deceased people, etc., but these were not of sufficient importance to require description here.

29 33 Maine, 419.

thousands of dollars worth went untaxed. No particular difficulty seems to have been encountered in regard to the section which applied to shipping, as no cases were found bearing on the subject. The registry of ships evidently made possible the satisfactory assessment of this kind of property.

The possibility of double taxation was definitely recognized in the law and in two cases, railroads and manufacturing corporations, provision was made for its avoidance. In the case of railroads, the law read:

Provided, however, that the track of any railroad belonging to any railroad company incorporated in this state, and the land on which any railroad tracks is or may be constructed, shall not be deemed real estate;
The shares of the respective stockholders in any railroad company in the state shall be deemed personal estate and shall be taxable as such to the owners in the places where they reside.[30]

Although the intention of the legislature, as shown by comments of legislators and state officials, was to prevent the taxation of both the property and stock of railroad corporations, the practical effect was to exempt it from all taxation, because of the difficulty of assessing stock.

The prevention of the taxation of both the stock and property of manufacturing corporations was the objective of the following section:

All machinery in any branch of manufacturing and all goods manufactured or unmanufactured belonging to any corporation, shall be assessed to such corporation in the town or place where such real estate, machinery and goods are situated or employed; and in assessing the stockholders for their shares in any corporation, their proportional part of the value of such machinery, goods and real estate shall be deducted from the value of such shares.[31]

30 *Public Laws of Maine 1845*, ch. 165.
31 *Ibid.*, ch. 159.

In later years, there was considerable controversy as to the definition of a manufacturing corporation. In 1845, when this law was passed, practically all corporations were either manufacturing, railroads or banking corporations. Turnpike corporations had by this time gone out of existence and the general adoption of the corporate form of organization had not yet come about. Double taxation, consequently, as far as corporations were concerned, was eliminated, except in the case of banks.

In summarizing the evolution of the property tax laws up to this time, it may be said that they had now taken on a modern form and that future legislation was in the nature of refinement of the laws or meeting problems that at this time were either non-existent or of too slight importance to merit recognition.

Between 1845 and 1870, changes in the property tax laws were of minor importance. In 1858, interests in timber and improvements on the public lands were made taxable.[32] This was important because rights to cut timber on several hundred thousand acres of the public land had been sold.[33] Acts were passed which permitted cities and towns to exempt new manufacturing enterprises from local taxation for ten years.[34] The stock of manufacturing corporations was exempted outright, instead of being taxed to the extent that it exceeded in value tangible property on which taxes had been paid.[35] This marked the abandonment of the attempt to tax the good will of such corporations. Changes were also made in the method of taxing bank stock.[36]

From 1820 to the beginning of the Civil War, property taxes usually yielded approximately one-half the state revenue. Nearly

[32] *Public Laws of Maine 1858*, ch. 202.

[33] *Cf. infra*, pp. 207-209.

[34] *Public Laws of Maine 1859*, ch. 81; *1864*, ch. 234; *1867*, ch. 76; *1869*, ch. 65.

[35] Changed in revision of statutes 1871.

[36] *Cf. infra*, ch. vii, pp. 154-156.

all of the other revenue had been received from a tax on the stock of state banks and from sales of public land. By 1870, most of the public land had been sold and the state banks had gone out of existence, with the result that the property tax was the only large source of state revenue. In 1870, the state property tax yielded $1,175,741.67, while revenue derived from other sources amounted to only $48,322.25. The outstanding question at the end of this period was: Would Maine continue to secure all of the revenue required from the property tax or would she attempt to find other sources of revenue?

The depression of 1873 caused property taxes to bear very heavily on the people of the state and resulted in much agitation in favor of additional sources of revenue as well as for better administration of the property tax. Between 1870 and 1900, special taxes on bases other than property were imposed on savings banks, railroads, telegraph and telephone companies, insurance companies, and building and loan associations. As a result of these taxes, the property tax, which had produced ninety-eight per cent of the revenue in 1871, by 1890 was producing only fifty-five per cent of the revenue, and continued to produce about that percentage of the total revenue during the remainder of the century. The rate of the state tax was six mills in 1870. By 1890, it had declined to 2.75 mills and remained at approximately that figure until 1900.[37]

The chief burden of the property tax was not the state levy but the levies of the municipalities. In 1889, the average rate for the state and local taxes was 17.75 mills;[38] subtracting the state levy from this, there remained fifteen mills levied by the counties and municipalities. Moreover, one mill of the state levy was distributed to the common schools of the municipalities. Consequently, by 1889 the state tax which was used for state purposes had become almost negligible.

[37] *Annual Report of the State Board of Assessors 1918*, p. 300.
[38] *Report of the Special Tax Commission of Maine 1889*, p. 38.

From 1870, continuous complaints were made that intangibles were not bearing their share of the tax. Nearly every governor, in his message to the legislature, reiterated this complaint. It was also charged that tangible property in some counties was much undervalued.

In 1875, in an ill-advised attempt to remedy the intangible situation, the constitution was amended so as to provide that personal property, as well as real estate, should be taxed at a uniform rate.[39] Prior to this, the constitution had provided that real estate only should be taxed at a uniform rate. As a matter of fact, however, the legislature had all along been taxing personal property, except railroad shares and shares in manufacturing corporations, at the same rate as real property. It is difficult to understand what it was hoped would be accomplished by this amendment, and in fact nothing was accomplished.

The legislature of 1889 instructed the governor to appoint a special tax commission of three members to investigate the tax system of Maine and other states to make recommendations for changes in the tax system. This commission, as a result of its studies, recommended the creation of a state board of assessors and changes in the assessment of property, an inheritance tax, and several minor changes in the tax laws. The legislature of 1891 adopted only the recommendation for the state board of assessors and made certain changes in the methods of assessing property.

From statehood down to 1891, a valuation had been taken for state purposes every ten years. A Committee of the legislature equalized the assessments among counties and annually apportioned the state tax among the municipalities. This, of course, worked badly, because the work was done hurriedly by men who not only knew nothing about the subject, but each of whom considered himself a special representative for his own county, charged with the responsibility of securing for his own county as low a valuation as possible.

---

39 Constitution of Maine, art. ix.

In arguing for a state board of assessors, the commission pointed out many of the evils of the old system. In regard to valuation it said:

Property is assessed at much less than its just value in many towns. In the late returns of the assessors of all of the towns of the state for the use of the state valuation commissioners, it appears that the assessors of 132 towns based their taxes on less than a "just value" of the property assessed. Thirteen based them on four-fifths value, thirty-five on three-fourths value, fifty-three on two-thirds value and sixteen on one-half value, while in two towns assessors considered their duty done when they assessed at one-third of the cash value of the property assessed.[40]

The commission also pointed out that under the law no records were required to be kept and that none had been kept; that there was no way of determining the amounts of the different classes of assessed property of the state for past years and that without that information little could be done in equalizing the assessments, either as among classes of property or as among towns.

The law creating the state board of assessors provided that: (1) a board of three be elected by the legislature, only two of whom could belong to one political party, to hold office for six years, one member going out of office each biennium; (2) it should be the duty of the board to equalize the assessment of property both as among classes of property and as among towns and to make a state valuation every two years; (3) the board should have the power to summon town assessors and to require them to bring their records; (4) it should hold meetings in each county once every two years in order that the people of that county might have opportunity to present their evidence for valuation purposes; (5) the administration of the railroad tax, bank tax and other taxes which had previously been lodged with the governor and council should be placed on the board; (6) the salaries of the members of the board should

[40] *Report of the Special Tax Commission of Maine 1889*, p. 38.

be $1,500 annually and members should devote their full time to the work of the board.[41]

The reports of the state board of assessors for the first three years of its existence indicated that little was accomplished by way of equalization. It was claimed by the board that it was not possible to know the conditions of valuation in all parts of the state and that the local assessors had different ideas about methods of valuation. Some local assessors believed that property should be assessed on the basis of a forced sale, others at current sale price, and still others had the idea of a value based on prudent judgment. In 1893, the legislature passed a law compelling the local assessors to attend county meetings called by the state board of assessors for the purpose of instructing the local assessors in uniform policies of assessment and discussing the problems of assessment. After the meetings began to be held, the reports of the state board of assessors became more optimistic about the ability of the local assessors to perform their duties properly.

The escape of intangibles continued to be a troublesome problem. The state board, in its annual reports for 1899 and 1900, called attention to the small amount of intangibles which were on the tax rolls and stated that the local assessors either could not or would not search out this property and assess it.

The chief classes of property which escape taxation are promissory notes, bonds and stocks . . . while railroad bonds are taxed only $62,249. Yet the bonds issued by the steam railroads and the electric railway companies amount to over $40,000,000. . . . This unequal taxation causes discontent and complaint.[42]

It is not easy to appraise the accomplishments of the state board of assessors during the first decade of its existence. For the first time, information became available concerning the amounts of the different classes of property assessed. It became

---

41 *Public Laws of Maine 1891*, ch. 103.
42 *Annual Report of the State Board of Assessors 1900*, p. 6.

possible to know what the tax rate was for every township in the state. It developed that in general it ran between eighteen and twenty mills. This seems moderate compared with the rates at present, but the people at that time considered it heavy. The board was unsuccessful in placing intangibles on the tax rolls. The proportion of intangible property to the total property assessed was about the same at the end of the decade as it had been at the beginning. Undoubtedly greater equality of assessment among the towns was achieved. On the whole, the first decade of the existence of the board may be considered as a period of experimentation, the result of which was to build up a body of information and experience which enabled the board to function more efficiently in the period which followed.

There were several changes in the law regarding the state board of assessors between 1900 and 1932. In 1909, the method of selecting the members of this board was changed from that of election by the legislature to appointment by the governor and council. The designation of the chairman of the board was made a function of the governor, occupancy of the office of chairman to continue until the expiration of his term as member of the board. Qualifications for members of the board were established in the following language: " The members of such Board shall be such as are known to possess knowledge of and training in the subject of taxation and tax laws, and skilled in matters pertaining thereto." [43] So far as the author has been able to ascertain, these qualifications have seldom, if ever, been possessed by appointees to this board.

The same statute gave the state board of assessors authority to change local assessments. The board " at its own instance or complaint made to it," was to " diligently investigate all cases of concealment of property from taxation, of undervaluation, and of failure to assess property liable to taxation." If it found property in any town undervalued or not assessed, it could order the assessors of that town to reassess it, and if

[43] *Public Laws of Maine 1909*, ch. 220.

this was not satisfactorily done, the assessors were to be deemed guilty of wilful neglect of duty and subject to prosecution as provided by law in such cases.[44] In 1917, an addition was made to this law, which provided that in case the local assessors did not satisfactorily reassess property when ordered to do so by the state board of assessors, the board could employ men to do the work at the expense of the town.[45] This authority is adequate to enable the state board of assessors to exercise control over local assessment and to alleviate many of the evils which constantly come to the attention of the board. However, not a single case has been found in which it has chosen to exercise this authority.

The complaint, common in the Eighties and Nineties, concerning the escape from taxation of intangibles, continued and resulted in 1913 in an amendment to the constitution, giving the legislature authority to tax intangibles in any manner it saw fit and at a rate different from that applying to other property.[46] The legislature, however, has to date consistently refrained from extending any special treatment to intangibles and they continue to be taxable under the law, in the same manner and at the same rate as other property.

In the reorganization of the state government which took place in 1932, the state board of assessors was abolished and a bureau of taxation was created, with the authority to perform the duties formerly lodged with the state board of assessors, as well as to administer the gasoline tax which had formerly been a function of the state auditor. The office of state assessor was created, that officer to serve as head of the bureau of taxation and as chairman of a new board of equalization. This new board of equalization is composed of the state assessor and two other members, appointed by the governor and council for terms of four years. The two appointed members devote such time to

44 *Ibid.*
45 *Ibid., 1917*, ch. 24.
46 Constitution of Maine, art. xxxvi, *Revised Statutes*, 1930, p. 42.

their office "as the State Assessor shall require," and are paid on a per diem basis at such rate as determined by the governor and council. The duty of this board is "to equalize the state and county taxes among the several towns and unorganized townships in the manner provided by law." [47] This reorganization was in effect little more than a change in name, the only substantial modification being to place control of state property assessment in the hands of one man instead of three.

In 1909, the Maine forestry district was created, the purpose of which was to combat forest fires on the wild lands of the state. The law designated 9,500,000 acres to be included in this fire district and levied a special tax of one and one-half mills on the assessed value of the property so included. The revenue from this tax is used by the forest commissioner to prevent and fight forest fires.[48] In 1919, the rate was increased to one and three-quarters mills,[49] and in 1921, it was increased to two and one-half mills.[50] This tax is in addition to the regular state and local property taxes.[51]

In 1929 a special method of taxing growing forests was established, only to be almost immediately abandoned. The state auxiliary forest district was established and planted forests meeting certain requirements might be admitted to the district. Thereupon this land was assessed at the same value as stripped forest land, but in no case at a value greater than $2.00 an

47 *Public Laws of Maine 1931*, ch. 216, art. ii.
48 *Ibid.*, *1909*, ch. 193.
49 *Ibid.*, *1919*, ch. 104.
50 *Ibid.*, *1921*, ch. 4.

51 The question arises as to whether or not this law violates article ix, section 8 of the Constitution, which provides that "all taxes upon real and personal estate, assessed by authority of this state, shall be assessed and apportioned equally, according to the just value thereof." However, the supreme court held in *Hamilton v. Portland Pier District* (120 Maine 15) that the legislature has the constitutional authority to create special taxing districts for the purpose of providing revenue for the performance of some special act, or making some improvement. Consequently, this law is probably not unconstitutional.

acre. When the timber was cut, an additional tax was imposed at a rate which varied according to the number of years the land had received a preferential assessment.[52] The purpose of this law was to relieve owners of growing timber from the burden of paying taxes until such time as the timber should be cut and money obtained to pay the taxes. This law was not in effect long enough to test its worth. It was repealed in 1933 [53] at the request of certain towns, because so much land was withdrawn from the general property tax rolls that the burden placed on other property was deemed oppressive.

Having traced the evolution of property tax laws from the time Maine became a state, the task remains of summarizing the data relating to rates and yields in the various governmental jurisdictions and of appraising the tax as it has been administered in recent decades.

In the appendix,[54] the state property tax collections are shown for each year of the state's history. The more adequate data compiled in recent decades make it possible to present in Table 27 the annual property tax levies since 1900, segregated according to the jurisdictions levying them. In 1932, the state levied 20.08 per cent, the counties 5.54 per cent and the other local units 74.38 per cent of the total property taxes levied.[55] Table 28 indicates the rate of increase in property taxes levied by state, county, and local governments. It is seen that taxes levied by local governments increased at a much faster rate than those levied by state and county governments.

The combined rate for state, county and local governments for each year from 1902 is shown in Table 29. Since 1903, the low year for the period, the average rate of property taxes levied by state, county and local governments has increased from 20.25 mills to 46.56 mills in 1935. In 1900, the rate of

52 *Public Laws of Maine 1929*, ch. 306.
53 *Ibid., 1933*, ch. 139.
54 *Cf. infra*, pp. 232-233.
55 Computed from data in Table 27.

TABLE 27
Property Tax Levies Segregated According to Governmental Jurisdiction, 1900–1932 *
(Figures in thousands)

Year	State taxes	County Taxes Levied by town	County Taxes Levied by state	County Taxes Total levied	Municipal or local taxes	Total property taxes [a]
1900	$ 908	$ 429	$ 26	$ 455	$ 5,875	$ 7,148
1901	928	437	39	476	5,146	6,550
1902	928	437	39	476	5,452	6,856
1903	970	433	44	476	5,471	6,918
1904	970	430	44	474	5,728	7,172
1905	918	440	49	488	6,039	7,446
1906	918	439	49	488	6,218	7,623
1907	1,186	501	53	554	6,602	8,342
1908	1,186	497	53	550	6,378	8,114
1909	1,287	522	58	581	6,759	8,626
1910	2,143	522	58	581	6,387	9,111
1911	2,713	612	67	679	6,318	9,709
1912	1,809	612	67	679	7,037	9,525
1913	2,393	623	60	683	7,568	10,644
1914	2,154	622	60	682	7,680	10,515
1915	2,494	664	62	726	7,787	11,007
1916	2,494	664	62	726	8,276	11,496
1917	3,130	723	78	801	9,256	13,188
1918	3,130	723	78	801	10,047	13,978
1919	4,333	869	88	957	11,298	16,588
1920	4,188	869	88	957	15,122	20,268
1921	3,508	918	98	1,016	16,472	20,996
1922	3,827	918	98	1,016	17,158	22,001
1923	4,880	1,119	132	1,252	18,025	24,157
1924	4,543	1,117	132	1,250	19,117	24,910
1925	4,905	1,161	128	1,289	19,029	25,223
1926	4,905	1,161	128	1,289	20,667	26,861
1927	4,714	1,161	131	1,292	21,280	27,286
1928	4,714	1,161	131	1,292	21,903	27,909
1929	5,580	1,351	145	1,495	22,152	29,227
1930	5,580	1,351	145	1,495	22,166	29,241
1931	5,303	1,399	169	1,568	22,464	29,335
1932	5,682	1,399	169	1,568	21,051	28,301

* Taken from "Farm Taxation in Maine," Bulletin 363, Agricultural Experiment Station of Maine, p. 257.

[a] It should be noted that these are tax levies and that because of delinquencies the amounts shown here will vary from collections.

TABLE 28
TREND OF PROPERTY TAXES LEVIED, 1900–1932 *
1910–1914 = 100

Year	State	County	Municipal	Total
1900	40	70	84	72
1901	41	72	74	66
1902	41	72	78	69
1903	43	72	78	70
1904	43	72	82	72
1905	41	74	86	75
1906	41	74	89	77
1907	53	84	94	84
1908	53	83	91	82
1909	57	88	97	87
1910	96	88	91	92
1911	121	103	90	98
1912	81	103	101	96
1913	107	103	108	108
1914	96	103	110	106
1915	111	110	111	111
1916	111	110	118	116
1917	140	121	132	133
1918	140	121	144	141
1919	193	145	161	168
1920	187	145	216	205
1921	156	154	235	212
1922	171	154	245	222
1923	218	190	258	244
1924	203	189	273	252
1925	219	195	272	255
1926	219	195	295	271
1927	210	196	304	276
1928	210	196	313	282
1929	249	226	317	295
1930	249	226	317	295
1931	236	237	321	296
1932	253	237	301	286

* Computed from data in Table 27.

TABLE 29
TOTAL PROPERTY TAX RATES IN MAINE*
1902–1935

Year	Total tax rate in mills [a]
1902 [b]	21.70
1903	20.25
1904	20.57
1905	21.03
1906	20.87
1907	22.08
1908	20.83
1909	21.65
1910	21.77
1911	22.60
1912	21.55
1913	23.50
1914	22.72
1915	23.32
1916	23.95
1917	26.72
1918	26.67
1919	30.46
1920	34.63
1921	34.71
1922	35.77
1923	38.28
1924	38.49
1925	38.63
1926	40.36
1927	40.31
1928	41.03
1929	42.59
1930	44.28
1931	44.04
1932	43.47
1933	41.52
1934	45.06
1935	46.56

* Annual reports of state board of assessors.

[a] This rate is the sum of the state tax rate, the average of the rates levied by the counties, and the average of the rates levied by the cities and towns.

[b] These data not available prior to 1902.

the state tax was 2.75 mills; in 1935, it was 7.5 mills; the percentage of total revenues of the state government supplied by property taxes in 1900 was 55 per cent; in 1936 it had decreased to 19 per cent. Property taxes still supply almost all of the revenues for local government, having in 1932 accounted for 92 per cent of the receipts of cities and towns.

The foregoing tables reveal the preponderant importance of the property taxes collected by local governments. If a reduction in property taxes is made, it must come largely through reduction of local levies.

Quite aside from possible criticisms of the general scope and nature of the property tax in Maine, it is apparent that the administration of the existing statute leaves much to be desired. Assessment of property continues to be in the hands of elected local assessors or, in some cities, depending on the provisions of the city charter, of assessors appointed by the city government. The property owner is required to render a list of his property, but in case he does not, the assessors may value it and property owners may appeal to the county commissioners, or to the superior court, if the assessors change the value so rendered.

The State Board of Equalization has the duties of equalizing assessments among cities and towns and assessing the wild lands in unorganized townships, and the authority to order reassessment of individual properties improperly assessed by local officials.

The assessment of property achieved by this procedure is about as bad as it could possibly be and little or no improvement has been made for a hundred years.[56] The chief complaint is that property is assessed unequally. No truly adequate studies have ever been made of the inequalities of assessment or the percentage of true value represented by assessments. Two minor studies throw some light on the situation.

[56] See H. L. Lutz, *The System of Taxation in Maine*, ch. ii, for an excellent discussion of property tax administration.

In 1930, the state board of assessors sent instructions to the local assessors in each town and city to select a certain number of pieces of property of different types, to estimate the true value of this property and to state the percentage which assessed value was of true value. Table 30 presents the results of this study. The number of towns reporting was 507, a large share of the total. The range of variation of the percentage which assessed value was of true value was, for cities and towns from 19 to 100 per cent and for counties, from 48 to 79 per cent. For the whole state the average percentage assessed value was of true value was 67 per cent.

The secretary of the property division of the bureau of taxation points out that the results of this study can not be considered accurate, because the local assessors were not competent to estimate accurately the true value; but the figures certainly understate rather than overstate the degree of undervaluation that exists.

The second study, made by the agricultural experiment station of the University of Maine in 1933, attempted to show the variation in the assessment of farm property in the state. As a sample, 422 farms of different types, located in different parts of the state, were chosen. The value of those farms was estimated and the assessed valuation of them was ascertained from tax records. Table 31 presents the results of this study.

It can be seen that more farms were assessed between 20 and 30 per cent than were assessed in any other 10 per cent class. Considering the results of this study in connection with that of the preceding one, it would seem that farm property is assessed much lower than any other property in the state. Also, the rate of 43.47 mills does not seem high, in view of this degree of underassessment.

The responsibility for this unequal assessment rests both with the local assessors and the state officials. The evils of assessment by locally elected officials are too well known to call for extended treatment. The positions are part-time and the remun-

TABLE 30

PERCENTAGE OF ASSESSED VALUE TO ACTUAL CASH MARKET VALUE, AS DETERMINED FROM LISTS OF SPECIMEN PROPERTIES SHOWING ASSESSED AND ACTUAL CASH MARKET VALUE SUBMITTED BY THE LOCAL ASSESSORS IN 1930 *

Counties	Number of towns reporting	Percentage of assessed value to actual value (county-average)
Androscoggin	14	64%
Aroostook	66	48
Cumberland	26	67
Franklin	24	75
Hancock	37	71
Kennebec	30	69
Knox	18	70
Lincoln	18	74
Oxford	37	69
Penobscot	62	64
Piscataquis	24	70
Sagadahock	9	79
Somerset	37	73
Waldo	26	78
Washington	51	69
York	28	64
Total	507	
Average for state		67
The range was from 19% to 100%		

* Taken from records of property division of the Bureau of Taxation.

eration is so small that competent men as a rule can not be interested in taking the office. No scientific methods of valuation are used. In many towns and cities large property owners are able to influence assessors to place low valuations on their property, either by political pressure, or by threatening to appeal the assessment to the courts. By appealing to the courts, large property owners could impose such large expenses upon the towns that in many cases the towns would rather compromise for a lower valuation than try to enforce a fair valuation.

The history of the state board of assessors and its successor, the property division of the bureau of taxation, is a record of

TABLE 31
Variation in Assessment of Farm Property in Maine*

Percentage assessed is of estimated valuation	Number of farms
Less than 20	33
20–29	134
30–39	109
40–49	71
50–59	32
60–69	20
70–79	14
80 and over	9

* Bulletin 366, Agricultural Experiment Station, University of Maine 1933, p. 242.

failure in assessment of property. Over a period of forty years this board has not adopted any recognized scientific methods of property assessment. Its work has been confined to recording information sent in by local assessors and to visiting periodically the counties for the purpose of attending meetings of local assessors and granting hearings to towns which might be aggrieved at changes in valuation which the board proposed to make. The contribution of the board to these county meetings could have been of little value because the board itself had little, if any more knowledge or information than was possessed by local assessors. When the board changed the valuation of a city or town, the changed amount was likely to be as bad a guess as the valuation established by local assessors. During the whole period of its existence, no real study of property valuation has been instituted; no program providing for adequate assessment of property has ever been presented to the legislature for approval; and finally the authority to control original individual assessments, granted under the laws of 1909 and 1917,[57] has never been exercised.

The question may be raised as to why the state board of assessors has failed. The opinion of this writer is that it has

[57] Cf. supra, pp. 125-126.

failed primarily because the appointments were made for political reasons rather than on a merit basis. What training the members of this board may have possessed was obtained in having been local assessors and it was but natural that they carried the ideas which they had acquired as local assessors to the state board. None of the members, so far as the writer has been able to ascertain, ever had formal training in tax administration, law or theory.

In the opinion of the writer the defects in the administration of the property tax can be in a large degree corrected by the adoption of such steps as the following:

(1) Transform the general property tax system into a classified property tax, with rates designed to make the task of the assessor one capable of performance;

(2) Create a tax commission with such requirements as to qualifications for membership as will make it impossible for political appointments to be made;

(3) Give the tax commission authority to perform the following functions and insist that the commission perform these functions: (a) the study of property values in every township in the state; (b) the preparation of a tax map for every township in the state; (c) the preparation of rules of assessment for use of local assessors assuming sufficient control to insure that local assessors observe them; (d) the division of the state into assessment districts of convenient size and the provision of a full-time employee of the tax commission in each district to check on the work of local assessors and to instruct them, and (e) the removal of local assessors for incompetence or refusal to follow rules prescribed by the tax commission.

The writer is somewhat skeptical about the possibility of drafting a law which would compel the appointive authority to select properly qualified members. Failure to appoint qualified members to the state board of assessors in the past has probably not, in most cases, been due to wilful intent to evade requirements established by law, but to failure to understand what constituted adequate qualifications. If the governor and council could be made to understand what constitutes adequate qualifications, satisfactory appointments would in most instances be made.

A study of property values and the preparation of a tax map should, of course, be carried on jointly. Space will not permit a detailed explanation of what constitutes a tax map. Briefly, it is a map of a city or town on which each piece of property is designated and bounded. The map may have a primary division into blocks in a city or sections in a town, which in turn may be subdivided for individual pieces of property. From this, as a point of departure, descriptions of each piece of property can be worked up. Without some such device, adequate assessment is impossible.

Instead of retaining locally elected assessors, it would be desirable to have them appointed by a central authority, and to make assessment districts large enough so that the office of assessor could be one which would require full-time employment and thus permit the appointment of adequately trained men to do this work. However, at the present time, it would be impossible to secure a change in the law which would permit this. People in Maine are attached to the old and fearful of the new and even the modest changes suggested above are not certain to meet with approval.

The system of dividing the state into districts and placing in each one a representative of the tax commission who would have control over local assessors is one which has been successful in Wisconsin for a number of years. Conditions in Maine are sufficiently similar to those in Wisconsin to lead one to believe that this system of assessment would be successful there also.

CHAPTER VII
THE TAXATION OF FINANCIAL INSTITUTIONS

THERE have existed in Maine four different types of banking institutions: state chartered commercial banks, nationally chartered commercial banks, savings banks and trust companies. These banks have been subjected to different types of taxation and consequently must be treated separately. One other type of financial institution, the insurance company, deserves special mention.

State Chartered Commercial Banks. At the time of separation, the only banks in the state were commercial banks which had been chartered by Massachusetts. Table 32 shows the growth in number and capital stock of these banks. Following the passage of the national banking act in 1863, these institutions were rapidly converted into national banks or were liquidated. By the end of 1865, only nine were left and in 1879, the last one gave up its charter.[1] Such banks were subject to a special percentage tax on the par value of their capital stock, a property tax on their real estate and fixtures and in addition the stock of the banks was taxable to the owners.

The percentage tax on the par value of the capital stock of these banks was one of the three main sources of state revenue from 1820 until the Civil War. In 1812, Massachusetts had passed a law levying a semi-annual tax of one-half per cent on the par value of the capital stock of the banks.[2] This same law was placed in the statutes of Maine in 1821 and remained in effect until 1863[3] when, as a result of the passage by Congress of a law in 1862, levying a tax of one-fourth of one per cent per annum on demand deposits,[4] the legislature remitted one-

[1] Annual reports of the bank commissioners.
[2] *General Laws of Massachusetts 1812*, ch. 32.
[3] *Laws of Maine 1821*, ch. 147.
[4] *United States Statutes at Large*, vol. xii, p. 470.

TAXATION OF FINANCIAL INSTITUTIONS 139

half of the state tax.[5] Following 1865, when all but nine of the state chartered banks gave up their state charters, the revenue from this tax was negligible and finally ceased in 1879.

In addition to the percentage tax assessed against the banks, the act of 1820 establishing a state valuation, enumerated bank stock in the hands of individual owners as a part of the property tax base. As a result of the difficulty of finding bank stock and placing it on the tax rolls, an act was passed in 1837 which provided that the cashiers of banks should report to the assessors of towns in which the stockholders resided, the amount of stock owned by each resident of that town, where it was to be taxed as other personal property. This law worked better, but because there was no way to check back to see if the cashiers had complied with the law, a great deal of stock still escaped taxation. In order to reach the stock owned by persons residing outside the state, which escaped taxation in Maine and presumably elsewhere as well, the law was amended in 1863 so as to make stock owned by persons of unknown residence or by persons residing outside the state taxable in the town where the bank was located. No dividend could be paid on the stock, and no transfer could be effected while the tax remained unpaid. The cashier of a bank might pay the tax and deduct the amount from the dividends when paid, and if the tax remained unpaid for ninety days, the stock could be sold in the manner prescribed by law for selling property for delinquent taxes.[6]

National Banks. The creation of national banks raised a new problem, because they could be taxed only in the manner and to the extent permitted by Congress. The Federal Law of 1864 permitted the real estate of national banks to be taxed to the banks at the place where the banks were located, and included the following section concerning the taxation of bank stock:

5 *Public Laws of Maine 1863*, ch. 217.
6 *Ibid.*, *1863*, ch. 193.

TABLE 32*
NUMBER AND CAPITAL OF STATE COMMERCIAL BANKS, 1819–1880
(Figures in thousands)

Year	Number of banks	Capital	Year	Number of banks	Capital
1819	15	$1,537	1850	32	$3,248
1820	15	1,655	1851	39	3,854
1821 [a]			1852	44	4,261
1822			1853	58	5,457
1823			1854	71	7,301
1824			1855	77	7,569
1825			1856	77	8,107
1826			1857	66	7,521
1827			1858	68	7,309
1828			1859	69	7,577
1829			1860	70	7,833
1830	18	2,050	1861	69	7,969
1831			1862	69	7,983
1832			1863	69	8,008
1833			1864	50	8,786
1834	28	2,727	1865	9	
1835	29	2,931	1866	9	
1836	36	3,785	1867	9	
1837	55	5,227	1868	5	
1838	55	5,459	1869	5	
1839	50	4,959	1870 [b]	5	445
1840	48	4,672	1871	5	445
1841	42	3,514	1872	5	
1842	39	3,414	1873	5	225
1843	40	3,314	1874		
1844	35	3,009	1875	3	225
1845	35	3,009	1876	2	125
1846	35	3,059	1877		
1847	35	3,044	1878		
1848	31	2,920	1879 [c]		
1849	32	3,098			

*Sources: 1. U. S. 26th Congress 1st session, House Document 172: 1329, for years 1819, 1820, 1830 and 1834-1840 inclusive.
2. Annual reports of bank commissioners 1841-42; 1845-47; 1849-1870.
3. Annual reports of controller of currency for years 1843, 1844 and 1876.

[a] For years in which no figures appear the data are not available.
[b] Charters extended for five years in 1870 and for another five years in 1875.
[c] All banks liquidated in 1879: Bank Commissioner's Report 1879.

Provided that nothing in this act shall be construed to prevent all the shares of any such associations, held by any person or corporation, from being included in the value of the personal property of such corporation or person, in the assessment of taxes imposed under or by State authority at the place where such a bank is located, and not elsewhere, but not at a greater rate than is assessed on other moneyed capital in the hands of individual citizens of such state; . . . the tax so imposed shall not exceed the tax imposed on any of the banks organized under the authority of the State. . . . [7]

Until 1867, the real estate and stock of national banks were taxed as property without any additional legislation. The special percentage tax applying to the capital stock of state banks was, of course, not extended to national banks. In that year, cashiers of national banks were directed to report annually the names of stockholders and the amounts of stock owned to the assessors of the towns in which the bank was located. These assessors were required to value the stock and to report that value to the assessors in the towns where the stockholders resided, where it was to be taxed at the same rate as other personal property. Stock of nonresidents, as in the old law, was taxable in the town where the bank was located.[8] The real estate, as before, was taxable in the town where the bank was located.

Immediately there arose the question as to whether this state law, providing that the stock should be valued at the location of the bank but that the rate should be levied and the tax collected at the place where the stock was owned, conflicted with the provision of the Federal statute that specified that the stock should be included in the assessment at the place where the bank was located and not elsewhere. It is evident that the legislature had doubt concerning this point, because it asked the supreme court for an opinion and stated in the law that if the opinion of the court should be adverse, the shares should be taxable in the town where the bank was located.

[7] *Thirty-eighth Congress*, sec. i, ch. 104.
[8] *Public Laws of Maine 1867*, ch. 126.

The court decided that the new law was not in conformity with the Federal statute. However, Justice Dickerson, in a minority opinion, said that the Federal statute referred only to the assessment of taxes and was silent regarding where they were to be collected or what town was to receive them. He reasoned that the objective of the Federal government was to prevent national banks from being taxed unequally and that the matter as to where the tax was collected was immaterial so long as it was not in conflict with this objective.[9] Later in the year, the case of *Abbot v. the City of Bangor* came before the court. Abbot, who resided in Castine, owned stock in a Bangor bank. The city of Bangor levied taxes on this stock, which Abbot paid under protest and brought suit to recover. In this case, the court reversed its previous opinion and, adopting the line of reasoning given in Dickerson's minority opinion quoted above, declared the Maine law to be in conformity with the Federal statute.[10] Finally, later in the same year, the court reversed itself once more, going back to its original position, this time on the grounds that to declare the Maine law in conformity with the Federal provisions, would call for an interpretation of the clause regarding the assessment of taxes so unusual as to be unwarranted.[11] Congress, in 1868, settled this question definitely by passing an act declaring the word "place" in the act of 1863 meant the state in which the bank was located, and the legislature might determine the manner and place of taxing all shares provided that they did not tax them at a higher rate than other moneyed capital was taxed.[12] Thus, the arrangements outlined in the state law of 1867 were at last definitely validated.

This method of taxing national banks remained in effect until 1921, when the assessment and collection of the tax on

[9] 53 Maine 594.
[10] 54 Maine 540.
[11] *E. P. Packard v. City of Lewiston*, 55 Maine 456.
[12] *United States Statutes at Large*, vol. xv, ch. 34.

national bank stock and the stock of trust companies was transferred from the local to the state government. National banks and trust companies were now required to report annually to the state board of assessors the value of their real estate which was taxed locally, a list of the stockholders showing the residence and amount of stock owned by each. The state assessors were directed to place a value on these shares and deduct the value of the real estate which was taxed locally. Upon the value of the shares so determined a tax of fifteen mills was levied, to be paid to the state treasurer. The tax collected from the resident stockholders was to be remitted to the towns in which the stockholders resided while that collected from nonresident stockholders was to be paid to the towns in which the banks were located.[13]

Two factors were responsible for this change in the law. One was the widespread evasion under the old law. The other was the fear, engendered by the Richmond case [14] and subsequent court decisions, lest the old law might be imposing on some national banks a higher rate than that imposed on competing moneyed capital, as defined by the United States Supreme Court. Maine, by this law and by its refusal to reduce the rate on intangibles, has apparently succeeded in avoiding the difficulties experienced by many states. National banks are taxed more lightly than any other financial institutions in the state,[15] with the possible exception of building and loan associations; intangibles in the hands of individuals are taxed, so far as they are reached by the assessors, at the same rate as real property and consequently no claim can be made that competing moneyed capital in the hands of individuals is being taxed at a lower rate, except in the case of underassessment, or on the grounds that assessors did not succeed in reaching " other moneyed capital." It would be difficult for the banks to prove that bank

[13] *Public Laws of Maine 1921*, ch. 197.
[14] 256 U. S. 635 (1921).
[15] *Cf. infra*, p. 153.

stock was assessed at a higher rate than other intangibles because the bureau of taxation assesses bank stock at only sixty per cent of its true value. But even if there were underassessment of other "moneyed capital," the undervaluation would have to be very great before the banks could prove that they were being taxed more heavily than "other moneyed capital," because the rate of the bank stock tax is only fifteen mills, while the average rate of the property tax for the whole state in 1935 was 46.56 mills.

The only grounds upon which this law might successfully be attacked would seem to be on the grounds that assessors were, in practice, unsuccessful in reaching intangible property. The Moneyed Capital Tax Law of New York State was invalidated by the United States Supreme Court in 1931 on this ground.[16]

In 1931, the law was changed so that the tax on bank shares owned by corporations was retained by the state.[17] The reason for this change was that there had been a great growth in group banking in the state, which had resulted in the ownership of bank stock by corporations being concentrated to a large extent in two or three of the larger cities, and it was thought unjust that such a large share of the bank tax should go to these cities.

Trust and Banking Companies. Before 1880, all the state chartered commercial banks had ceased to function and no state chartered institutions which could do a commercial banking or a fiduciary business existed. The laws regulating national banks seemed too conservative to some, and it is not strange that a demand for state chartered banks should have developed. It is surprising, however, that in a state which had been so sound and conservative in its banking as Maine had been, financial institutions of the nature of these trust companies should have

[16] *Keating, Receiver v. Public National Bank of New York*, United States Supreme Court, Dec. 7, 1931, 284 U. S. 587 and 47 Fed. 561.
[17] *Public Laws of Maine 1931*, ch. 253.

been allowed to develop almost unregulated, to the exclusion of commercial banks.

The first charter for a trust company was granted in 1883 to the Portland Trust Company [18] but it did not open for business until 1885. Table 33 shows the growth of these trust companies. The charters of the first two banks provided that they should be taxed in the same manner as savings banks, but amendments in 1887 changed the method so that the shares of these banks were taxable precisely the same as national bank stock. This latter arrangement was inserted in all subsequent charters. The result was a discrimination against savings banks, they being obliged to pay a tax which at times absorbed as much as twenty per cent of their gross income. Consequently, in the Nineties trust companies were able to pay higher interest on deposits than many of the savings banks, with the result that savings banks began to lose deposits to trust companies. To offset this discrimination, a new tax was imposed on trust companies in 1901, in addition to the tax on their stock. Under this law, trust companies were directed to make semi-annual returns which should include the average amount of time deposits for the preceding six months, bearing interest at three per cent or more, and a record of their investments. From the deposits, the state assessors were to deduct the assessed value of taxable real estate, the amount of United States government bonds owned and other tax-exempt securities. On the remainder, a semi-annual tax of one-quarter of one per cent was levied.[19] This tax soon became one of the major sources of state revenue.

Subsequent legislation was concerned almost entirely with enlarging the list of investments that could be deducted in determining taxable deposits. Such additional deductions included bonds of counties, municipalities and municipal water districts, issued after February 1, 1909 (in 1909); [20] in 1915 mortgages

18 *Private and Special Laws of Maine 1883*, ch. 203.
19 *Public Laws of Maine 1901*, ch. 286.
20 *Ibid.*, *1909*, ch. 49.

TABLE 33
Trust Companies, Number and Assets, 1885–1936 *
(Figures in thousands)

Year	Number	Amount of assets	Year	Number	Amount of assets
1885	2		1911	42	$ 52,370
1886	2	$ 764	1912	44	58,672
1887	5	1,301	1913	45	62,980
1888	6	1,870	1914	46	66,371
1889	9	2,766	1915	46	69,707
1890	10	3,628	1916	46	89,462
1891	12	4,279	1917	49	104,900
1892	13	4,866	1918	52	111,854
1893	14	5,175	1919	53	124,539
1894	15	5,836	1920	55	141,723
1895	17	6,642	1921	55	145,429
1896	18	7,049	1922	55	142,440
1897	16	7,513	1923	not available	
1898	17	9,183	1924	54	156,779
1899	17	11,802	1925	53	167,547
1900	17	13,295	1926	53	173,146
1901	18	15,207	1927	52	182,817
1902	18	17,036	1928	50	195,300
1903	23	19,914	1929	48	211,395
1904	23	22,928	1930	47	214,225
1905	26	27,984	1931	43	220,662
1906	33	33,542	1932	40	195,489
1907	39	39,848	1933	24	92,108
1908	40	42,982	1934	30	97,030
1909	40	44,547	1935	31	105,805
1910	40	46,145	1936	31	109,162

* Annual reports of bank commissioners.

on real estate that were exempt from taxation in the hands of the holder,[21] bonds of municipal light and power districts (in 1919),[22] and in 1923 stock of national banks and trust companies.[23] In 1935, as a result of the general reduction in interest

21 *Ibid., 1915*, ch. 150.
22 *Ibid., 1919*, ch. 221.
23 *Ibid.,* 1923, ch. 144.

paid on deposits, trust companies were required to report deposits bearing interest at the rate of two per cent or over.[24] The imposition of this tax on the deposits of trust companies in addition to the tax on their stock placed a heavier burden on them than on national banks, because national banks were taxed only on the value of their shares.

Savings Banks. Savings banks in Maine did not reach any considerable importance until after the first half of the nineteenth century. The first report of condition of savings banks to the bank commissioners was made in 1855, which showed that in that year there were eleven banks with deposits of $867,027.89.[25] Table 34 shows the growth in number and deposits of these banks. After the disappearance of the state chartered commercial banks in the Sixties,[26] savings banks soon became the most important financial institutions in the state, their number increasing to forty-nine and deposits to $22,788,000 in 1870. It was but natural that people who had been accustomed to taxation of banks for over half a century should, when one type of bank disappeared with the consequent loss of revenue and another type seemed to have taken its place, turn to this new type as an object of taxation.

The first suggestion encountered for the taxation of savings banks was in the *Annual Report of the Bank Commissioners* in 1868. The movement rapidly gathered strength and resulted in a law being passed in 1872 which levied a semi-annual tax of one-quarter of one per cent on the total deposits as they stood on the dates when the savings banks rendered their semi-annual reports.[27]

A controversy over the burden of this tax arose at the time this law was passed and continued until the end of the century. Strangely enough, this controversy centered around the point

24 *Ibid.*, *1935*, ch. 50.
25 *Annual Report of the Bank Commissioners 1855.*
26 *Cf. supra*, p. 138-139.
27 *Public Laws of Maine 1872*, ch. 74.

TABLE 34
Number of Savings Banks and Deposits, 1855–1936*
(Figures for deposits in thousands)

Year	Number of banks	Deposits	Year	Number of banks	Deposits
1855	11	$ 867	1896	52	$ 54,477
1856 (a)	....		1897	51	59,598
1857 (a)	....		1898	51	60,853
1858	11	897	1899	51	64,009
1859	12	1,030	1900	51	71,076
1860	13	1,466	1901	51	74,623
1861	14	1,620	1902	51	77,853
1862	15	1,876	1903	51	80,538
1863	15	2,641	1904	51	82,741
1864	15	3,673	1905	51	85,590
1865	15	3,337	1906	51	89,681
1866	18	3,946	1907	52	92,853
1867	20	5,599	1908	52	93,783
1868	28	8,032	1909	52	96,254
1869	37	10,830	1910	52	98,402
1870	49	22,788	1911	49	97,705
1871	54	27,557	1912	48	102,211
1872	54	26,154	1913	48	104,515
1873	56	29,557	1914	48	105,995
1874	58	31,052	1915	48	106,523
1875	63	32,083	1916	48	107,784
1876	60	27,819	1917	45	105,872
1877	60	26,898	1918	45	104,097
1878	59	23,173	1919	44	107,463
1879	59	20,978	1920	43	114,138
1880	55	23,278	1921	43	116,264
1881	55	26,475	1922	43	117,788
1882	55	29,504	1923 (a)	....	
1883	54	31,372	1924	38	118,288
1884	54	32,914	1925	37	119,788
1885	54	35,118	1926	37	121,520
1886	54	37,215	1927	35	122,156
1887	55	38,820	1928	35	126,281
1888	55	40,970	1929	35	127,259
1889	55	43,977	1930	32	126,843
1890	54	47,781	1931	32	131,631
1891	53	50,278	1932	32	133,509
1892	53	53,398	1933	32	132,703
1893	52	53,261	1934	32	132,033
1894	51	54,531	1935	32	136,366
1895	52	56,376	1936	32	139,106

* Compiled from the annual reports of the state treasurer.
(a) Data not available.

that the assets of savings banks were taxed more heavily, as property, than were other types of property. In view of a supreme court decision [28] declaring this to be a franchise tax levied for the privilege of doing business, the persistence of the notion that its sole justification was to be found in its character as a property tax is remarkable. It also may be an occasion for wonder that in view of the quasi-benevolent character of these institutions a tax was imposed upon them.

The law was amended in 1875 so as to levy a semi-annual tax of one-half of one per cent on the average gross deposits for the preceding one-half year, minus the assessed value of the real estate of the banks, and one-half the yield of this tax was appropriated to the common schools.[29] In 1883, because of the decreased earnings of savings banks, the rate was lowered to three-quarters of one per cent per annum and the base was redefined as the average deposits after deducting real estate and United States government bonds.[30] The deduction of United States bonds was allowed in deference to the view that since these bonds could not legally be taxed as property, they might not properly be included in the tax base. In 1893, the law was revised so as to make explicit the legislative intent of making the tax a franchise tax. The method of determining the value of the franchise was involved and apparently so devised that banks having large investments within the state of Maine would be required to pay a smaller tax than those having large investments in other states.[31] The banks were required to make semi-annual reports to the bank examiner in such form that he could tell the average amount of the deposits for the preceding six months, the amount of the investments in the state and the amount outside the state, the amount acquired before January 1, 1892 and those subsequently acquired, and a

---

28 *Jones v. Winthrop Savings Bank*, 66 Maine 243.
29 *Public Laws of Maine 1875*, ch. 47.
30 *Ibid., 1883*, ch. 202.
31 *Annual Report of the Bank Examiner 1896*, p. xiii.

schedule of the investments. The bank examiner was required to "fix and determine" the market value of the investments and transmit all the information to the state board of assessors, which was to place a value on the franchise. The formula for the valuation of the franchise was as follows: add together the average deposits, undivided profits and reserve fund, and from the result, deduct (1) the amount of United States government bonds owned, (2) the shares of corporation stock owned which were by law exempt from taxation,[32] (3) an amount equal to one-seventh of the market value of investments owned prior to January 1, 1893, (4) an amount equal to two-sevenths of investments in Maine acquired subsequent to January 1, 1893, (5) real estate owned and (6) two-sevenths of cash on hand or deposited in Maine. On the value of the franchise thus determined, an annual tax of seven-eighths of one per cent was levied, one-half of which was appropriated to the use of the common schools.[33]

This law introduced a new variable into the factors which caused the amount of the bank tax to fluctuate. The bank examiners continually pointed out that changes in the market value of securities which were deductible had the opposite effect on the amount of the bank tax than that which was desirable. When the market value of the securities was high, it was desirable that the tax should be high, but the deductions rendered it less. Moreover, under this 1893 law, the burden of the tax was so heavy that the savings banks found the competition of the trust companies embarrassing. In addition to the increased taxation imposed on trust companies in 1901, already noted,[34] it was found desirable in 1903 to lower the tax on savings banks. This was accomplished by increasing the two-sevenths deduction allowed for investments in Maine to two-fifths, the distinction between securities owned before and after January 1,

---

[32] Railroad, telephone and telegraph stock.
[33] *Public Laws of Maine 1893*, ch. 258.
[34] *Cf. supra*, p. 145.

1893 being dropped, and by decreasing the tax from seven-eighths to five-eighths per cent.[35]

During the next twenty years the same changes as were made in the case of trust companies in the list of securities deductible were made in the savings bank tax law.[36] In 1919, the rate of the tax was further reduced to one-half of one per cent and deductions for investments in Maine and cash were increased from two-fifths to three-fifths.

General Comments on the Taxation of Banks. There seems to be little reason in the existing method of taxing savings banks and trust companies. It is the remains of the old method of taxing banks on their deposits. As the years have passed, special interests have succeeded in securing exemptions for the securities in which they were interested, resulting in a form of taxation which is grotesque and which should be abolished. The writer would recommend that the present savings bank tax be repealed and a tax on deposits be substituted for it. There are certain tax-exempt securities which must be deducted from deposits. The rate of the tax should be adjusted so that the burden of taxation would be approximately the same as that imposed on trust companies and national banks.

Moreover, to the writer it seems unjustifiable to subject trust companies to the same share value tax as national banks and, in addition, to impose a franchise tax upon them. Trust companies and national banks are competing institutions, and to tax trust companies heavier than national banks gives an unfair advantage to the latter. The only way, unless income taxation is resorted to, in which this inequality can be eliminated is to relieve trust companies from the franchise tax.

The taxation of banks is complicated by the fact that national banks must be taxed as provided by the United States statutes.[37]

35 *Public Laws of Maine 1903*, ch. 9.

36 *Cf. supra*, pp. 145-146.

37 Section 5219, *Revised Statutes of the United States*, as amended by sec. 548, laws of the 69th, 70th, 72nd and 73rd Congresses (1933).

Because of the competitive conditions, state banks can not be taxed substantially more than national banks. The present Federal statute permits national banks to be taxed only in the following ways: (1) on the value of the shares providing they are not taxed more heavily than competing moneyed capital in the state; (2) by states which have personal income tax laws, on the dividends on the stock when received by the shareholders; (3) on the net income of the banks and (4) by an excise tax measured by the net income of the bank from all sources. If national banks are taxed by methods 3 or 4, the rates may not be higher than those on other financial institutions or manufacturing, mercantile or business corporations doing business within the state. Only one of these four methods may be used, except that method 2 may be used in connection with methods 3 or 4.

Prior to 1923, the only method provided by law for the taxing of national banks was the share value method. In 1921, a decision of the United States Supreme Court caused great confusion in the bank tax laws in many states by declaring the term " moneyed capital " should mean investment funds in the hands of individuals.[38] Many states had adopted laws levying low rates of taxation on intangibles, which caused the laws of those states taxing national banks to be contrary to the United States' law. In 1923, the United States' law was amended. The United States Supreme Court soon interpreted this amendment to be merely an affirmation of its decision in the Richmond case.[39]

The effects of these decisions were to make it necessary for states which taxed national banks by the share value method, and which exempted intangibles or subjected them to low rate taxes, to reduce tax rates on national bank shares so low that little income would be derived from them or to adopt one of

38 *Merchants National Bank v. City of Richmond*, 256 U. S. 635.
39 *First National Bank of Hartford v. City of Hartford*, 273 U. S. 548 (1927).

the other methods of taxing them. For states such as Maine, which had no income taxes, the only method available was the share value method. They must either tax intangibles at high rates or be content to obtain small amounts of revenue from the taxation of national banks.

In Maine, intangibles are taxed under the general property tax law which, in 1935, averaged 46.56 mills for state, county and local governments, as has been previously pointed out.[40] Maine has thus far experienced no legal difficulties in taxing national banks under the present law. There is, however, the possibility that this law might be successfully attacked on the grounds that assessors failed to reach " other moneyed capital " in the hands of individuals.[41] It might also be attacked because of the very low taxes which are imposed on building and loan associations.

If Maine should adopt personal and business income tax laws, it would be wise to subject national banks and trust companies to these two taxes instead of the present laws. However, one possible legal obstacle would still remain, namely, the light tax on building and loan associations. In 1932, the total assets of building and loan associations amounted to $25,221,882.13,[42] while the amount the state received from the tax on these associations was $4,623.21. It is surprising that this low rate of taxation on building and loan associations has not been used as a basis for contesting the share value tax on national banks.

Under the present Federal law, there is a lack of freedom for the states to develop their tax systems as they see fit. The original purpose which Congress had in mind when it regulated the taxation of national banks was to prevent states from discriminating between them and state banks. The Federal law should be changed so that this object can be achieved without prescribing definite forms of taxation.

40 *Cf. supra*, p. 131.
41 *Keating, Receiver v. Public National Bank of New York*, United States Supreme Court, December 7, 1931, 284 U. S. 587 and 47 Fed. 561.
42 *Report of the State Bank Commissioner 1932*, p. 26.

Taxation of Insurance Companies. Judging from a statute passed in 1821, the insurance business must have been developed in Maine prior to separation from Massachusetts.[43] However, the first data concerning the amount of insurance in force and the amount of premiums collected were found in the annual report of the bank and insurance commissioner in 1869. The commissioner said that in 1868 there was in force $116,-000,000 of life, fire and marine insurance and that the premiums collected for that year were $2,500,000. About this time a movement arose for the taxation of the insurance business, which culminated in legislation in the Seventies.

In 1874, the legislature passed an act taxing foreign insurance companies doing business in the state, at the rate of two per cent on their net premiums. The premiums were computed by subtracting from the gross premiums, losses during the year, returned premiums and legal reserve requirements.[44] Governor Dingley, in his message to the legislature in 1875, complained that the tax was too light. He said:

Of the twenty-seven states which tax the business of life insurance and of the thirty-two which tax the business of fire and marine insurance companies . . . on the just principle that whoever is protected by the state should contribute to the public burdens . . . scarcely any one of them imposes so light a tax.[45]

In 1875 and 1876 [46] laws were passed clarifying the meaning of the act of 1874. The law of 1876 also introduced the so-called retaliatory feature, providing that a foreign insurance company incorporated in a state which levied a higher tax than the one levied in Maine should be subject to the tax imposed in the state where it was incorporated.

43 *Public Laws of Maine 1821*, ch. 139.
44 *Ibid., 1874*, ch. 251.
45 *Message of Governor Dingley 1875.*
46 *Public Laws of Maine 1875*, ch. 46; *1876*, ch. 129.

TAXATION OF FINANCIAL INSTITUTIONS   155

The laws of 1874 and 1875 resulted in the practical exemption of life insurance companies because of the amount of deductions from the gross premiums which they were permitted to make. Fire and marine insurance companies received gross premiums to the amount of $960,403.93. Allowable deductions amounted to $418,201.83, leaving a taxable amount of $542,-202.10. The life insurance companies received gross premiums of $813,101.37 from which were deducted $347,716.89 for losses paid and $390,086.27 for other items, thus reducing the taxable amount to $75,298.21. The amount of the tax assessed on fire and marine companies was $10,928.83, while that assessed on life companies amounted to $1,505.94.[47] The amount of the gross premiums being nearly the same, it would seem that the tax should have been more nearly equal. The cause of this discrepancy is explained by the treasurer:

> In the case of fire and marine companies, no sum is deducted for that portion of the premiums which the companies are obliged to retain on hand to meet emergencies of loss, and known as the reinsurance fund, while in the case of life companies a deduction is made for the corresponding portion known as the reserve, thus leaving but a very small sum liable to taxation.[48]

The law of 1876 changed the deductions allowed and that year the assessment of life insurance companies increased to $6,084.87, while the fire and marine insurance companies were assessed only $12,255.02.[49] It is seen that the fire insurance companies were still assessed more but the discrepancy was not so great.

In 1885, it was provided that domestic life insurance companies should be taxed on their real estate by the towns in which they were located; that they should be taxed two per cent on their premiums, first deducting the dividends paid to policy-

[47] *Message of the Governor 1876.*
[48] *Annual Report of the Treasurer 1875*, p. 22.
[49] *Ibid.*, *1877*, p. 18.

holders; and that they should pay a tax of one-half of one per cent on their surplus, as determined by the laws of the state, after deducting real estate owned.[50] This resulted in taxing domestic life insurance companies at a higher rate than foreign life insurance companies. No tax at all was paid by domestic fire and marine insurance companies. No reason is obvious for the unfavorable treatment of domestic life insurance companies. It is possible that domestic fire insurance companies were not taxed because they were nearly all mutual companies and did a comparatively small portion of the fire insurance business of the state.

In 1897, a law was passed changing considerably the law taxing foreign insurance companies. The rate was changed to one and one-half per cent on premiums and taxable premiums were computed by a new method which resulted in an increase in that figure. It will be remembered that under the old law, taxable premiums were computed by deducting from gross premiums received, losses paid, premiums returned, legal reserves and reinsurance costs. Under the new law only premiums returned on policies cancelled and reinsurance costs were allowed as deductions.[51] Collections remained about the same after allowance for increased amounts of insurance. Evidently the lowering of the tax rate roughly offset the increase in taxable premiums.

After 1897, only minor changes were made in the insurance tax law. These changes were concerned with subjecting unusual types of insurance to special types of taxes. In 1909, premiums paid for insurance of farm property were exempted from taxation.[52] In 1911, an attempt was made to tax unauthorized insurance. This was insurance sold by mail or the contract for the sale of which was completed outside the state. Such insurance was not taxable under the regular insurance tax laws

---

50 *Public Laws of Maine 1885*, ch. 329.
51 *Ibid.*, *1897*, ch. 274.
52 *Ibid.*, *1909*, ch. 114.

TAXATION OF FINANCIAL INSTITUTIONS

because the companies had no agents in the state. This law levied a tax of five per cent on the gross premiums paid for unauthorized insurance. The tax was levied on the assured.[53] In 1913, the base of the tax was changed to net premiums and the rate reduced to two and one-half per cent.[54] In 1915, the base was changed back to gross receipts and in 1931 the tax was repealed.[55] This law was never successful because its constitutionality was so doubtful that the state hesitated to take steps to compel its payment. The effect of the law was to cause purchasers of small policies to pay the tax, while purchasers of large policies, acting under legal advice not available to small purchasers, refused with impunity to pay it.[56]

In 1913, mutual fire insurance companies, incorporated under the laws of other states, that insured only factories and mills or property connected with factories and mills, were subjected to a two per cent tax on gross premiums less the amount of premiums returned. The purpose in singling out this type of insurance for a special tax was to discriminate against these companies and to give an advantage to companies incorporated in Maine.[57]

Finally, in 1933, the law was amended so that all insurance companies, except domestic life and foreign mill mutuals, were subject to the one and one-half per cent tax on net premiums. This change in the law provided a means of taxing domestic fire and casualty insurance companies which had not before existed.

A few words of comment and suggestion may be added. In the first place, there is no justification for taxing domestic life insurance companies heavier than foreign companies. This tax has been imposed a great many years and since the single do-

---

53 *Ibid.*, *1911*, ch. 131.
54 *Ibid.*, *1913*, ch. 114.
55 *Ibid.*, *1915*, ch. 340; *1931*, ch. 175.
56 This information secured from the insurance commissioner.
57 *Ibid.*

mestic life company the state possesses has not complained about the tax, there has never been any incentive to change it.

The premium method of taxing insurance companies is the one generally used throughout the country. In 1931, 92 per cent of the revenues collected from insurance taxes in the United States was collected by this method.[58] This method of taxing insurance companies has become so general because it is difficult to determine the net income of insurance companies and impossible to tax them on a property basis. The most common rate applied to premiums is two per cent. Under the Maine law, the rate is one and one-half per cent. The commission for the revision of the tax laws in New York State, in 1932, recommended that a rate of two per cent be applied to fire insurance premiums and 1.75 per cent to life insurance premiums.[59] The writer is of the opinion that Maine might well consider raising the rates now applied.

[58] *Report of the New York State Tax Commission for the Revision of the Tax Laws* (1932), Memorandum 13.

[59] *Ibid.*, p. 32. This recommendation was enacted into a law in 1935.

CHAPTER VIII
THE TAXATION OF PUBLIC SERVICE CORPORATIONS

Taxation of Railroads. The state of Maine was a pioneer in the building of railroads. The first charters were granted in 1832, one to the Calais Railway Company for the purpose of building a railroad from Milltown to the place of shipping lumber on the St. Croix River,[1] the other to the Bangor and Oldtown Railway Company for the purpose of building a railroad from Bangor to Oldtown.[2] It is interesting to note that the charters of these two roads stipulated the rates that should be charged on both freight and passengers, and that, after ten years, the legislature should have the right to revise these charges. They also stipulated that the railroads must run speedy and safe trains and that the number of votes of a single stockholder should be limited.[3] While regulation of railroads is usually thought of as beginning in the Seventies and Eighties, it is apparent that in the case of Maine, the need for regulation was realized from the beginning.

The charter of the Bangor and Oldtown Railway Company passed into the hands of the Bangor and Piscataquis Canal and Railway Company, which had been chartered in 1833. The road between Bangor and Oldtown was completed and put into operation in 1836, being the first railroad to operate in Maine and the second in New England.[4] The subsequent history of railroad building in Maine did not differ greatly from that in other states. At first there were short lines built between two cities. Later the lines were consolidated longitudinally. Those consolidations were followed by combining these longitudinal consolidations into systems.

1 *Private and Special Laws of Maine 1832*, ch. 238.
2 *Ibid.*, ch. 236.
3 Ten in the case of the first company and forty in the case of the second.
4 *Industrial and Labor Statistics of Maine 1883-86*, pp. 46-66.

Public aid in building railroads was not extensive in Maine. The first aid by the state was in making surveys for the routes of several railroads. While exact figures showing the extent of this aid are not available, it is probable that not more than $100,000 was spent for this purpose. The legislature granted permission to several cities and towns to purchase the stocks and bonds of certain railroads, but aid of this nature was not great in the aggregate. The state government itself aided only one railroad, the European and North American, which was to run from Bangor to the northeastern boundary to connect with a Canadian railroad to Halifax. About 700,000 acres of land and $824,956.16 was granted to this company.[5]

The first specific law taxing the railroads, passed in 1845, provided that the track and roadbed of railroads should not be taxable as real estate and that shares of the railroad corporations should be taxable as personal property to the owners where they resided.[6] The real estate, other than track and roadbed, was made taxable as other real estate in the town in which it was located. The exemption of the track and roadbed was an attempt to offset the double taxation which would occur if both the shares and property were taxed. This law remained in effect until 1874. In many of the charters granted to railroads after 1845 were clauses providing for specific methods of taxation. In 1845, charters were granted to the Atlantic and St. Lawrence Railroad, the Androscoggin and Kennebec Railroad, and the Penobscot and Kennebec Railroad, with the following provisions concerning taxation:

And whenever the net income of such corporation shall have amounted to ten per cent per annum upon the cost of the road and its appendages and incidental expenses, the directors shall make a special report of the fact to the legislature; from and after which time one moity, or such other portion as the legislature may from time to time determine, of the net income from said railroad,

---

5 *Cf. infra*, p. 45; p. 188.
6 *Public Laws 1845*, ch. 165.

accruing thereafter over and above ten per cent, first to be paid to stockholders, shall annually be paid over by the treasurer of said corporation, as tax, into the treasury of the state for the use of the state. . . . But no other tax than herein is provided shall ever be levied or assessed on said corporation, or any of their privileges or franchises.[7]

The same charters also provided that the real estate of the roads should be taxed as other real estate, and that the shares should be taxed as personal property to the owners at their residences. However, it should be noted that the general statutes concerning taxation provided that the track and roadbed of railroads should not be considered as real estate, and therefore railroads were exempt from property taxes on their tracks and roadbeds.[8] In granting or renewing charters in subsequent years, the above provisions concerning taxation were included. Apparently the legislatures thought that the railroad business would be very profitable and that the state should receive part of this profit as a franchise tax.

Following 1870, a considerable movement took place to relieve property from bearing such a large part of the burden of the state government. In that year, the state tax on property comprised 96 per cent of the revenue from state sources. Governor Dingley, in his message to the legislatures of 1873 and 1874, urged that sources of revenue other than the property tax be found. The first step in this direction was the passage of an act in 1874 providing for the special taxation of railroads. This act provided that railroads should report annually to the gov-

[7] *Private and Special Laws of Maine, 1845*, chs. 195, 270 and 285.

[8] Since the charters of these railroads provided means by which they should be taxed, the question might be raised as to whether the general laws exempting track and roadbed from property taxes would apply to them. No records of property assessment were found which would answer this question, but in the case *Maine v. Maine Central* (66 Maine 488) evidence which seemed conclusive to the writer was presented, indicating that the general statutes, exempting track and roadbed from property taxes, applied to all railroads in the state.

ernor and council the amount of their capital stock, number and par value of their shares, the length of line located within the state and outside the state and the value of their property assessed for taxation; that the governor and council should then determine the cash value of the roads, deduct the value of the property assessed for taxation and levy a one and one-half per cent tax on the remainder; and that the treasurer should distribute to the towns that portion of the tax which the number of shares owned in the towns bore to the total number of shares outstanding. This tax was to be in lieu of all taxes on railroad stock.[9]

The governor and council levied the first tax under this act in 1874. The amount of the tax levied was $105,059.33, but only $13,820.40 was collected. All but three railroads, the St. Croix, Boston and Maine, and the Portland refused to pay it. The grounds for refusal were that their charters provided for another means of taxation.

In 1875, a suit was brought against the Maine Central Railroad to force payment of this tax. Only one suit was brought because it was thought that the cases against the other railroads were so similar that this decision would cause the others to pay. The Maine Central was a consolidation of seven railroads. Its charter, granted in 1862, specified that it should have all the rights and immunities enjoyed by the corporations out of which it was created. Two of the merged railroads, the Androscoggin and Kennebec Railroad and the Penobscot and Kennebec Railroad, had provisions in their charters providing that real estate should be taxable where it was located, that the shares of the corporations should be taxable as personal property at the residences of the owners, and that earnings in excess of ten per cent should be paid to the state as a franchise tax, if the legislature so directed.[10] The charters also provided that no other taxes should ever be levied on the corporations without their

[9] *Public Laws 1874*, ch. 258.
[10] *Cf. supra*, pp. 160-161.

consent. The Maine Central claimed that since its charter granted to it all the rights and immunities enjoyed by the corporations out of which it was created, the state's right to tax it was limited to the provisions of the charters of the Androscoggin and Kennebec and the Penobscot and Kennebec Railroads. It was claimed that the charter of the railroad was a contract between the state and the railroad and that for the state to pass legislation which was contrary to the provisions of the charter was a violation of contract and thereby contrary to the United States Constitution.

The Maine Supreme Court rendered its decision on January 5, 1877. It based its opinion on four points:

1. Since alienating the right to tax was giving up one of the most important attributes of sovereignty, and one which was necessary for its existence, such grant must be stated in such clear terms that there could be no doubt of the intent to grant this privilege. In the charter of the Maine Central the grant of the right was not absolutely clear.

2. In granting these privileges to the Androscoggin and the Penobscot and Kennebec Railroads, the duties were imposed of making annual reports to the governor and council. Since the railroads had been merged, they could no longer do this and consequently the grant was void because in every contract there must be a consideration for a right or privilege granted. In this charter, the consideration was making the annual reports and since the railroads could no longer perform their part of the contract, it became void.

3. As stated above, two of the merged railroads had clauses providing a specified method of taxation, but the other railroads which were a part of the merger did not have such provisions. The court stated that it was a recognized principle of law that the rights of a corporation created by a merger of other corporations was not the sum of the rights of all the corporations but only those which were common to all of the corporations being merged. On this ground, the state had a right to tax the Maine Central.

4. In 1831, the legislature had passed a law stating that after that date the legislature should have the right to amend any corporation charters granted subsequently. The court said that since this law had been continued in the statutes, the charter of the Maine Central was subject to its limitations. The decision of the court was in favor of the state.[11]

The railroad appealed the case to the United States Supreme Court, which upheld the decision of the Maine court.[12]

The other railroads that had refused to pay the tax had the same provisions in their charters as the Maine Central had, and it was thought that they would follow the decision of the Maine Central and pay the tax. All but the Dexter and Newport, and the Knox and Lincoln did so. The state brought suits against these two railroads and the Supreme Court of Maine decided in favor of the railroads on the grounds that their charters stated clearly that they were to be taxable only in the way provided in their charters, and also that their charters stated clearly that the law of 1831 did not apply to them.[13] These railroads merged later with the Maine Central and then became subject to taxation.

The law of 1874 had a serious defect growing out of the effort to avoid double taxation. It will be recalled that as early as 1845 the roadbeds of railroads were exempted from property taxation and that only the stock and property other than roadbeds were taxable. The law of 1874 did little but transfer the assessment and collection of the taxes on stock from the jurisdiction of local officials to that of state officials. In 1845, there was probably little wrong with this method of taxing railroads, because the capitalization of the railroads was made up almost entirely of stock, but by 1874 a large portion of the capitalization of the railroads was composed of

11 *Maine v. Maine Central*, 66 Maine 488.
12 *Railroad Company v. Maine*, 96 U. S. 499.
13 *State v. Dexter and Newport Railroad*, 69 Maine 44; *State v. Knox and Lincoln Railroad*, 78 Maine 93.

TAXATION OF PUBLIC SERVICE CORPORATIONS 165

bonds. While these bonds were in theory subject to local property taxes, in practice most of them were concealed from the assessors and escaped taxation. As a result of this, little railroad property except that represented by stock was taxable. Governor Plaisted, in his message to the legislature in 1881, stated the defect in the following words:

Prior to the law of 1880, providing for the taxation of railroad corporations, the capital stock only, of these corporations, in other words the right of redemption only, was taxable. Property of more than $20,000,000 in value, therefore, escaped with trifling taxes compared with other kinds of property in the State.[14]

In 1880, the legislature tried to remedy this defect by changing the base upon which the tax was levied from stock to property. The governor and council were ordered

to appraise the roadways, rolling stock and franchises at their cash value, and upon this valuation to levy a tax of one per centum so as to make said tax as near as may be equal to the taxes of all kinds upon other property through which said roads may extend.[15]

The stocks of the corporations were exempted from taxation and their property other than the roadbed was taxable locally where situated. There seems to have been some confusion as to whether this was a franchise tax levied for the privilege of doing business in the state, or a property tax. The quotation from Governor Plaisted's message indicates that he thought it was a property tax. The law uses the word franchise but from the construction of the text of the act it appears that the franchise should be considered as property and taxed as such. The attorney general, in a discussion of the act, seemed to entertain the view that it was an excise tax levied for the privilege of doing business in the state.[16] No attempt had ever

14 *Annual Message of the Governor 1881*, p. 7.
15 *Public Laws of Maine 1880*, ch. 249.
16 *Annual Report of the Attorney General 1880*, p. 3.

before been made in the state, except in the case of the old state commercial banks and insurance companies, to levy any taxes on business except property taxes. The litigation growing out of the attempts to collect taxes levied under this law showed that the idea of a tax levied for the privilege of doing business in the state had definitely emerged and that the courts would uphold such a tax.

The tax was levied by the governor and council and paid by all of the railroads except the Maine Central, Boston and Maine, and the Portland, Saco and Portsmouth. Suit was brought against the Maine Central, but the case was not decided by the Supreme Court of Maine until 1883, two years after the law had been repealed. The case is important, however, because it settled the question of whether the state had the right to levy a franchise tax.

The Maine Central claimed that this was a property tax, and as such violated the provision of the constitution of Maine that property taxes should be assessed and apportioned equally.[17] If this were a property tax there could be no question but that it was not assessed equally, because it imposed a uniform rate on all railroad property in the state, while the property tax on other property was assessed at varying rates in different towns. In answering this claim, the Court said: " If it is a franchise tax . . . that is a tax imposed upon railroad corporations on account of their powers and privileges . . . then it is one which it was competent for the legislature to impose; for the power of the legislature to levy such a tax is well settled. . . ."[18] The court then went on to say that it considered this tax a franchise tax, measured by the value of the roadway, rolling stock and franchises, and as such it was constitutional. In regard to measuring the tax by valuation of property it had the following to say: " Possessing the power to impose a franchise tax to any amount it deems proper, the

---

17 *The Constitution of Maine*, art. ix, sec. viii.
18 *State v. Maine Central Railroad*, 74 Maine 376.

legislature may measure the amount of the tax by any means it deems proper." [19] This case settled the question concerning the power of the legislature to levy franchise taxes on corporations, but it did not clearly define a franchise tax as a tax levied for the privilege of doing business in the state. It was ten years before that point was definitely determined.

Evidently motivated by the fear that the law of 1880 would be declared a property tax and consequently unconstitutional, the legislature, in 1881, changed the method of levying the tax and specifically stated that it was an "excise tax for the privilege of exercising its franchise in this state." [20] This law provided that the tax should be measured by the gross receipts. Each railroad was required to report annually its gross receipts and its total mileage. The gross receipts were to be divided by the number of miles to get the average gross receipts per mile. The rate of the tax was applied to the average gross receipts per mile. The rates, were, when not exceeding $2,200 per mile, one-quarter of one per cent; when betwen $2,200 and $3,000, the rate was one-half of one per cent; from that amount the rate increased one-quarter of one per cent for every increase in receipts of $750 per mile, but in no case was it to be more than three and one-quarter per cent. This tax was in lieu of all other taxes on roadbed, rolling stock, franchise, and stock. The towns in which railroad stock was owned were to receive from the state one per cent of the par value of all stock owned, except that in no case should the amount distributed to the towns exceed the amount collected by the state.

The only change made before 1900 was a change in rates in 1893. Under this law, earnings of $1,500 per mile or under were taxed one-quarter of one per cent; from that point, the rate increased one-quarter of one per cent for every increase of $750 earnings per mile, but in no case was the tax rate to be more than three and one-quarter per cent.[21]

19 *Ibid.*
20 *Public Laws of Maine 1881*, ch. 91.
21 *Ibid.*, ch. 166.

A case arising from the law of 1881 more closely defined a franchise tax than had the Maine Central case. The Grand Trunk Railroad refused to pay the tax assessed under the law of 1881 on the grounds that it was in interference with interstate commerce and therefore contrary to the United States Constitution. The state brought suit in 1882 in the state courts. By agreement, the suit was transferred to the United States Court of Appeals, which rendered a decision in favor of the railroad. The state then appealed the case to the United States Supreme Court, which reversed the decision.[22] In its opinion, the court said:

The tax for the collection of which this action is brought, is an excise tax upon the defendant corporation for the privilege of exercising its franchises within the State of Maine. . . . The designation does not always indicate merely an inland imposition or duty on consumption of commodities, or to exercise particular franchises. It is used more frequently in this country in the latter senses than in any other. The privilege of exercising the franchise of a corporation within a State is generally one of value, and often one of great value and the subject of earnest contention. It is natural, therefore, that the corporation should be made to bear some proportion of the public burdens of government. As the granting of the privilege rests entirely in the discretion of the State, whether the corporation be of domestic or foreign origin, it may be conferred upon such conditions, pecuniary or otherwise, as the State in its judgment may deem most conducive to its interests or policy. It may require the payment into its treasury, each year, of a specific sum, or may apportion the amount exacted according to the value of the business permitted, as disclosed by its gains or receipts of the present or past years. The character of the tax or its validity is not determined by the mode adopted in fixing its amount for any specific period or the times of its payment.[23]

22 142 U. S. 217.
23 *Ibid.*

TAXATION OF PUBLIC SERVICE CORPORATIONS 169

This case established clearly that the state had the right to levy a tax for the privilege of doing business in the state and that the mode of determining the amount of the tax was not material.

Between 1893 and 1927 there were frequent changes in the law, but they were concerned with rates, times of making reports and times of making payments; the gross receipts method of taxing the railroads was not changed. In 1901, the maximum rate was increased to four per cent;[24] in 1907, it was increased to four and one-half per cent.[25] In 1909, the whole rate schedule was changed, the provisions being that when the gross receipts were under $1,500 per mile, the rate should be one-half of one per cent; from $1,500 to $1,900 per mile, the rate should be three-quarters of one per cent; and for every additional $400 per mile, the rate should increase one-quarter of one per cent, but in no case should it exceed five per cent. For railroads engaged exclusively in carrying freight, the maximum rate was fixed at three per cent.[26] In 1911, the maximum rate was increased to five and one-half per cent.[27]

Following the World War, the financial condition of the railroads in Maine was very bad. Strenuous efforts were made, both by the railroads and their stockholders, to secure reduction in taxes. As a means of achieving this end, they proposed a change from the gross receipts to the so-called "gross-net" method, which had been recommended by the National Tax Association.[28] Mr. Curtis, chairman of the House committee on taxation, presenting arguments in favor of this plan, said:

For a long time, there has been a growing feeling that the method of taxing railroads on their gross earnings was funda-

24 *Public Laws of Maine 1901*, ch. 145.
25 *Ibid., 1907*, ch. 168.
26 *Ibid., 1909*, ch. 81.
27 *Ibid., 1911*, ch. 168.
28 *Proceedings of the Fifteenth National Tax Conference* (1922), pp. 173-178.

mentally wrong, and that the gross-net plan, as advocated in this bill under discussion, was the more equitable method. . . . The National Tax Association, consisting of assessors from all states, the United States Chamber of Commerce and the Special Tax Commission of New York recommend the gross-net method of taxing the railroads of the country, and their recommendations ought to have weight.[29]

After a bitter struggle lasting several years, the change was made to the "gross-net" method. Under this plan, the net railway operating income for the preceding year ended December 31, is compared with the gross transportation receipts and a tax imposed, the rates of which are graduated according to the percentage which the said income is of the gross transportation receipts. The rates are as follows: when the net railway operating income does not exceed ten per cent of the gross transportation receipts, the rate is three and one-half per cent of the said receipts; if exceeding ten per cent and not exceeding fifteen per cent, the rate is four per cent; fifteen to twenty per cent, four and one-half per cent; twenty to twenty-five per cent, five per cent; and five and one-half per cent when the said income exceeds twenty-five per cent of the gross receipts.

It is provided, however, that in the case of railroads operating not over fifty miles of road, the tax is not to exceed two per cent of the gross transportation receipts. It is further provided that when the net railway operating income of any narrow gauge railroad located wholly in this state exceeds five per cent of its gross transportation receipts, but does not exceed ten per cent of the said receipts, the tax shall be one-half of one per cent of the gross transportation receipts; if in excess of ten per cent, the tax shall be one per cent; and when the said income does not exceed five per cent of the gross receipts, no tax is assessed.[30] This law was vetoed by the governor, but it was

[29] *Legislative Record of the Eighty-second Legislature of the State of Maine 1925*, p. 811.
[30] *Public Laws of Maine 1927*, ch. 27.

passed over his veto. The opponents secured a referendum vote on it, with the result that it was passed and it became a law October 6, 1928.[31]

The history of railroad legislation in Maine is notable for several things: first, it was recognized from the beginning that railroads were not similar to ordinary businesses, and consequently should be regulated; second, many of the early charters provided that the state should share in the profits of the railroads above certain amounts in lieu of taxation; third, it was early (1845) recognized that to tax both tangible property and stocks of railroads was double taxation; and lastly, Maine pioneered in applying the "gross-net" method of railroad taxation.

TABLE 35

Excise Taxes and Gross Transportation Receipts for Steam Railroads in Maine 1923–1934 *

(Figures in thousands)

Year	Gross receipts	Amount of tax
1923	$35,337	$1,915
1924	34,995	1,897
1925	33,212	1,799
1926	33,231	1,804
1927	34,740	1,879
1928	35,019	1,897
1929	34,382	1,527
1930	35,731	1,658
1931	33,298	1,565
1932	26,606	1,146
1933	21,047	942
1934	19,812	936

* Annual reports of State Board of Assessors and records of Bureau of Taxation.

In view of the general interest in the "gross-net" plan among American students of taxation, the operation of the law will be examined in considerable detail. Table 35 presents the gross transportation receipts and the amount of the excise taxes

31 *Ibid.,* *1929,* p. 919.

levied. As was to be expected, taxes decreased as gross receipts decreased. The provisions of the law which gave lower rates to narrow gauge and short railroads render the total figures of little value for comparative purposes.

In order to obtain information that would permit conclusions to be drawn, a special study was made of two railroads which operate almost wholly in Maine: the Bangor and Aroostook, and the Maine Central. These two railroads operate seventy-two per cent of the total railroad mileage in the state. The Bangor and Aroostook was increasingly prosperous during most of the years from 1923 to 1934, while the Maine Central was not prosperous and in some years operated at a loss. Tables 36 and 37 present the data.

The law in effect prior to 1929 was a gross receipts tax. The rate of the tax was determined by the amount of gross receipts per mile of track operated, increasing as the gross receipts per mile increased.[32] The gross receipts per mile of both the Maine Central and the Bangor and Aroostook were sufficient to cause the maximum rate, five and one-half per cent, to be applied to them each year. Thus in effect, the old law was a gross receipts tax for these two railroads and affords an opportunity to make a comparative study between the operation of the " gross net " and the gross receipts methods.

Before analyzing the data presented in tables 36 and 37, it will be well to explain the difference between the two items in the tables, " net railway operating income " and " net income." The data in the tables under the heading " net railway operating income " are computed according to the Maine law, which reads as follows:

The term " net railway operating income " means the railway operating revenue less the railway operating expenses, tax accruals and the uncollectible railway revenues, including in the computation thereof debits and credits arising from equipment rents and joint facility rents.[33]

32 *Cf. supra*, p. 169.
33 *Public Laws of Maine 1927*, ch. 27.

TAXATION OF PUBLIC SERVICE CORPORATIONS

TABLE 36
BANGOR AND AROOSTOOK RAILROAD DATA CONCERNING EXCISE TAXES AND INCOME, 1923-1934 *

(Figures in thousands)

Year	Gross receipts (b)	Rate of tax	Amount of tax	Amount of tax under old law that would have been levied	Net railway operating income (b)	Net income (a)
1923	$7,366	5.5%	$405			$ 676
1924	6,692	5.5	368			594
1925	6,865	5.5	377			722
1926	6,789	5.5	373			723
1927	6,874	5.5	378			914
1928	7,340	5.5	403			1,139
1929	7,132	5.5	392	$392	$1,899	983
1930	8,066	5.5	443	443	2,277	1,398
1931	8,285	5.5	455	455	2,335	1,557
1932	6,823	5.0	341	375	1,388	623
1933	5,850	5.5	321	321	1,465	701
1934	5,753	5.5	316	316	1,741	993

* Annual reports of State Board of Assessors and records of Bureau of Taxation.
(a) Interstate Commerce Commission, *Statistics of Railways in the United States*.
(b) Because the tax is figured on returns of the previous year, gross receipts, net railway operating income, and net income are for years one year prior to what they appear on the table.

"Net income," as used in Tables 36 and 37, is computed according to the Interstate Commerce Commission Rules, and provides for deductions from "net railway operating income," as determined under the Maine law, of interest, losses incurred in the operation of leased roads, and several items of minor importance; or in other words, net income as prescribed by the Interstate Commerce Commission means that amount which is left after all expenses, charges and losses are deducted from the total gross income. This amount the directors of a railroad corporation may, as they see fit, distribute as dividends or transfer to surplus. Under the Maine law, "net railway operating income" is used in determining the rate of the tax.

TABLE 37

MAINE CENTRAL RAILROAD DATA CONCERNING EXCISE TAXES AND INCOME *
(Figures in thousands)

Year	Gross receipts (b)	Rate of tax	Amount of tax	Amount of tax under old law that would have been levied	Net railway operating income (b)	Net income (a)
1923.....	$16,880	5.5%	$928			$ 376
1924.....	17,510	5.5	963			10
1925.....	16,644	5.5	915			51
1926.....	16,613	5.5	913			1,177
1927.....	17,397	5.5	956			1,270
1928.....	17,206	5.5	946			551
1929.....	16,466	4.0	658	$905	$2,704	788
1930.....	17,364	4.5	781	955	3,680	1,746
1931.....	16,275	4.5	732	895	3,000	1,112
1932.....	12,767	4.0	510	702	1,836	63 (c)
1933.....	11,038	4.0	441	607	1,550	416 (c)
1934.....	10,324	4.5	464	567	1,993	19

* Annual reports of State Board of Assessors and records of Bureau of Taxation.
(a) Interstate Commerce Commission, *Statistics of Railways in the United States.*
(b) Because the tax is figured on returns of the previous year, gross receipts, net railway operating income, and net income are for years one year prior to what they appear on the table.
(c) Deficit.

Study of the data for the Maine Central Railroad shows that in 1929, the year when the "gross-net" method went into operation, the tax levied decreased $288,000 or 31.5 per cent, and the rate of the tax decreased to four per cent from five and one-half per cent; from 1929 to 1934, there was a rather constant relationship between the net railway operating income and the gross receipts, as evidenced by the fact that during these years the rate of the tax varied only one-half of one per cent; in 1932 and 1933, the railroad operated at a loss yet the rate of the tax did not decline to the minimum allowed by the law because of the constant relationship between gross receipts and operating income; from 1929 to 1934 the yield of the tax under the new "gross-net" law was from seventy-two to eighty-two per cent of what it would have been under the old gross receipts law.

The decline in the rate for the Maine Central in 1929, when compared with the rate for the Bangor and Aroostook, which did not decline because that railroad was in a prosperous condition, indicates that this law accomplished the purpose of imposing less taxes on a railroad that was not prosperous than on the one which was making satisfactory profits.

The constant relationship between the gross transportation receipts and the net operating income is contrary to the theory upon which the successful operation of the "gross-net" plan depends. According to this theory, net income, because of fixed charges, should vary to a greater extent than gross receipts. Thus, if gross receipts decreased 20 per cent, net income should decrease more than 20 per cent because there are certain items of expense which will not decrease regardless of the amount of business done. In this case a greater decrease than 20 per cent would bring about a lower ratio between gross and net receipts and cause a lower tax rate to be levied. If gross receipts and net income increase or decrease to the same extent there will be no change in the tax rate and the effect of the tax will be the same as that of a gross receipts tax. From the fact that the tax rate of the Maine Central varied only one-half of one per cent from 1929 to 1934, while during the same period the gross receipts declined twenty-seven per cent and in some years the railroad was operating at a loss, it is evident that the net operating revenue declined at about the same rate as the gross receipts. This may be accounted for by undermaintenance, as well as operating economies. The result of this constant relationship between the gross receipts and the net operating income was that even when the net income was negative the minimum rate did not apply to the Maine Central.

The data for the Bangor and Aroostook do not call for extended comment. During this whole period the Bangor and

Aroostook was prosperous and the maximum rate applied in all but one year, 1932.

In general, the Maine "gross-net" law conforms to the recommendations of the committee of the National Tax Association. There is, however, one point of dissimilarity. The committee recommends "net earnings" as one of the criteria by which the rate of the tax should be computed, while the Maine law uses net operating income. The committee, in its report, uses the term "net earnings" but gives no explanation as to how "net earnings" should be computed. Did it mean net operating income, as incorporated in the Maine law? Did it mean net earnings after the deduction of interest and other charges which would make it similar to "net income" as defined by the Interstate Commerce Commission? What did it mean? Accounting practices are not sufficiently standardized for a bare statement of that nature to have much of any meaning. "Net earnings" computed in one way will give results in the operation of the "gross-net" plan which are very different from those given if "net earnings" are computed in another way. Before any "gross-net" law is drawn up, careful studies should be made of the ratios between "net earnings" computed in various ways, and gross receipts. It will be found that these ratios differ for different businesses and that to apply the same ratios to different businesses will result in levying unequal tax burdens on these different businesses.

Certain conclusions may be drawn from this study: (1) the tax rate was less for a railroad that was not prosperous than for a prosperous one; (2) taxes conformed more to ability to pay, as measured by net income under the "gross-net" plan than under the gross receipts plan; (3) even when operating at a loss substantial taxes were imposed on the Maine Central; and (4) the method of computing "net earnings" needs careful study.

The question may now be considered as to whether or not the "gross-net" law should be continued in Maine. The writer is of the opinion that under the present conditions, it should be.

TAXATION OF PUBLIC SERVICE CORPORATIONS 177

With property assessments what they are, there would be no possibility of assessing equitable property taxes on railroads. There is a valid objection that the burden of taxes on railroads corresponds more nearly to the ability of railroads to pay than do taxes levied on other businesses. This objection is perhaps outweighed by the fact that because of present economic conditions, railroads are less able to pay arbitrary taxes than many other types of businesses.

If conditions should change in Maine so that all property is adequately assessed and if a net income tax is levied on all business done within the state, the writer would prefer that railroad property be taxed as other property, and that the railroads be subject to the same business net income tax as would be applied to other businesses.

Telephone and Telegraph Companies. The first mention of taxation of telegraph companies was found in the message of Governor Dingley to the legislature in 1875. In connection with a general recommendation for the taxation of public service corporations, he said:

In my judgment it is possible . . . certainly so with amendments to the State Constitution to provide for all expenditures for State purposes by a just tax on National and savings banks, railroad, insurance, telegraph and express companies, wild lands and other interests without assessing a single dollar on the several towns of the State.[34]

This recommendation was but a continuance of the movement which had resulted in the passage of the act in 1874, taxing railroads. The temporary lack of success with the railroad tax prevented the immediate extension of the policy of taxing businesses affected with a public interest. After the railroad tax had been declared constitutional by the Supreme Court the movement gained strength, resulting in the passage of an act in 1880 taxing telegraph companies in a special manner.

[34] *Message of Governor Dingley to the Legislature 1875*, p. 16.

178   A FINANCIAL HISTORY OF MAINE

This law provided that:

Every telegraph company, corporation or person doing business in this State shall pay an annual tax of two and one-half per cent of the value of any telegraph lines owned by said corporation, company or person within the limits of this State, all poles, wires, insulators, office furniture, batteries and instruments, and any circumstance or condition which affect the value of its property.[35]

This law also provided that this tax should be in lieu of all other taxes, including taxes on the stock of these companies; that it should be assessed by the governor and council; and that part of it should be distributed to the cities and towns in proportion as the amount of the stock owned in each city or town was to the total stock owned in the state.

The Western Union and International Telegraph companies refused to pay the tax and a suit was brought against the Western Union. The taxes were paid by the three smaller companies.[36] The Western Union claimed that this was a property tax and as such violated the uniformity clause of the constitution of Maine, which provided that: " All taxes on real estate and personal estate, assessed by authority of this State, shall be apportioned and assessed equally according to the just value thereof." [37] The company pointed out that this was a tax of twenty-five mills on all of its property in the state, while the rate of the property tax on other property varied in different towns. The company also called attention to the fact that the rate of the state property tax was only five mills, while the remainder of the property tax, levied on property in general, was assessed by counties and municipalities. It contended that if this tax was intended to be in lieu of county and municipal property taxes, it was one which the state government had no power to levy. Thus the issue to be decided by the court was

35 *Public Laws of Maine 1880*, ch. 246.
36 *Annual Report of the Treasurer 1880*, p. 17.
37 *Constitution of Maine*, art. ix, sec. 8.

the question of whether or not this was a property tax. Since this is the first case which involved the power of the state to levy an "excise tax for the privilege of exercising ... corporation franchise within the state," and since it implied that the state had the power to levy a tax for the privilege of doing business in the state, it will be treated in some detail. It should be recalled that in the Maine Central case,[38] the court did not pass on these points but only on the point of whether the law of 1874 taxing railroads was a violation of contract.

The supreme court of Maine declared that the tax on telegraph companies was not a property tax but "an excise tax levied for the privilege of exercising its franchise in the state." After classifying this tax as an excise tax, the court declared that the state had the right to levy an excise tax. The reasoning supporting this opinion can best be presented in the words of the court:

That the State has the power to tax a foreign corporation to any extent it pleases as a condition upon which it may exercise its franchise in the State may be considered well settled law. Dryden v. G. T. Railroad of Canada, 60 Maine 512; Paul v. Virginia, 8 Wallace 168; Liverpool Insurance Co. v. Massachusetts, 10 Wallace 566.

In this discussion we must start with the fundamental principle, now well settled, that all acts passed by proper authority in conformity with established forms, are presumed to be in accordance with the constitution and none will be declared otherwise so long as any reasonable doubt of its violation of the fundamental law remains.

Thus the real question at issue is the proper interpretation of the act, or more properly, will it fairly bear the construction necessary to make the tax one upon business.

The business is a necessary incident to the tax; without it the tax falls and ceases to be. The corporation is assessed not because it is a corporation but because it carries on that particular business,

[38] *Maine v. Maine Central*, 66 Maine 488 and *Railroad v. Maine*, 96 U. S. 499.

and the amount of that assessment is not a given sum but ascertained by a valuation put upon that which is used in the business. In a word the corporation is assessed because it is engaged in that particular business.[39]

The interesting feature of this case is that the court justified levying the tax not on the grounds of its being a tax on the corporate franchise, but a tax levied for the privilege of doing business in the state, regardless of whether or not it was a corporation.

No further changes in the law taxing telegraph companies was made until 1901, when the gross receipts of both telegraph and telephone companies were taxed. Since after 1901, telegraph and telephone companies have been taxable in the same manner, the history of the taxation of telephone companies before 1901 will be taken up next.

The first law taxing telephone companies was passed in 1883. This law provided that:

Every telephone corporation, company or person doing business within the limits of this State, shall annually pay into the Treasury of the State, a tax of two and one-half per cent of the value of any line owned by said corporation, company or person, within the limits of this State, including all poles, wires, insulators, transmitters, telephones, batteries, instruments, telephone apparatus, office furniture, and any circumstances or conditions which may affect the value of the property.[40]

The law also provided that this tax should be in lieu of all taxes on the property or on the stock of telephone companies. It should be noted that this law did not provide for the distribution of any of the proceeds of the tax to the cities and towns.

In 1893, the law was amended by specifying that the tax should be levied on property used by a company as well as on that owned. The reason for this change was that the larger

39 *State v. Western Union Telegraph Company*, 73 Maine, pp. 525-528.
40 *Public Laws of Maine 1883*, ch. 213.

companies were leasing the lines of smaller companies and it was difficult to collect the tax from these small companies. The law taxing telephone companies was never contested because it was similar to that taxing telegraph companies, which had been held constitutional.

In 1901, taxation of telegraph and telephone companies was consolidated under one law and the method was changed to that of a gross receipts tax. The method of ascertaining the amount of the tax was as follows: when the gross receipts were less than $5,000, the rate was one and one-quarter per cent; from $5,000 to $10,000, one and one-half per cent; from $10,000 to $25,000, one and three-quarters per cent; from $25,000 to $50,000, two per cent; and for every additional $25,000, the rate was to increase one-quarter of one per cent, but in no case should it exceed four per cent. The amount collected was to be distributed to the cities and towns in proportion as the number of shares owned in each city or town was to the total amount owned in the state. In no case was more to be paid to the cities and towns than was collected nor a greater portion of the tax collected than the proportion which the amount of stock owned in the state was to the total stock of the companies.[41]

In 1911, the law was changed so that the rates were as follows: when the gross receipts were less than $5,000, the rate was one and one-quarter of one per cent; from $5,000 to $10,000, one and one-half per cent; from $10,000 to $20,000, one and three-quarters per cent; from $20,000 to $40,000, two per cent; and for every additional $20,000 the rate increased one-quarter of one per cent but in no case was the rate to exceed six per cent.[42] No other change of importance was made until 1933, when it was provided that in case the amount of the stock owned in the state did not amount to two per cent of the total stock of any company, or unless the amount to be

41 *Ibid., 1901*, ch. 201.
42 *Ibid., 1911*, ch. 142.

apportioned exceeded $250,[43] no distribution should be made and the company should be relieved of the duty of reporting names and residences of stockholders.

The effect of the graduation of the rates of the tax on telegraph and telephone companes is to apply low rates to a few rural telephone lines. The other companies always pay the maximum rate. This tax is simple and inexpensive in its administration.

The Taxation of Express Companies. The express business was one of the first businesses to be singled out for taxation in some way other than by the property tax. The reasons for this were that express companies used very little property in comparison with the volume of business done and the property, being mostly railroad cars, was difficult to assess. The first law taxing express companies, passed in 1880, provided that:

> Every express corporation, company, or person doing express business on any railroad, steamboat or vessel in this State, shall annually before the first day of May, apply to the State Treasurer for a license authorizing the carrying on of such business; and every such corporation, company or person shall annually pay to the State Treasurer on or before the first day of May, three-fourths of one per cent of the gross receipts of said business for the year ending on the first day of April preceding. Said three-fourths of one per cent shall be on all of said express business done in this State, including a prorata on all express business coming from other States or countries; provided that nothing in this act shall be construed to apply to goods or merchandise in transit through the State.[44]

This law provided, also, that this tax should be in lieu of local property taxes and taxes on the stock of these corporations.

43 *Ibid., 1933*, ch. 224.
44 *Public Laws of Maine 1880*, ch. 244.

In 1883, real estate was made taxable locally and the amount deductible from the state gross receipts tax.[45] In 1885, the administration of the tax was placed in the hands of the state board of assessors.[46] In 1889, the rate of the tax was increased to one and one-half per cent;[47] the rate was increased to two per cent in 1901;[48] in 1907 to two and one-half per cent;[49] and in 1911 to four per cent.[50]

It is customary to employ the gross receipts method in taxing express companies. The writer believes the present method is satisfactory and recommends no change.

45 *Ibid., 1883*, ch. 135.
46 *Ibid., 1885*, ch. 49.
47 *Ibid., 1889*, ch. 109.
48 *Ibid., 1901*, ch. 147.
49 *Ibid., 1907*, ch. 167.
50 *Ibid., 1911*, ch. 115.

CHAPTER IX
THE PUBLIC LANDS

THE public lands were of great importance during the first half century of the existence of Maine as a separate state. The policy followed in disposing of the public land had a great influence on the finances of the state government and on the economic and social development of the state.

A glance at the accompanying map will show that in 1820, a large portion of the state was still an unsettled wilderness. The area of the state under the boundaries, as finally determined, is 19,132,800 acres.[1] According to Greenleaf's computations, the settled and incorporated towns in 1820 embraced an area of 8,555,596 acres, or approximately one-third of the state.[2] Part of the unsettled land was owned by the state and part by individual proprietors. Greenleaf computed, from the Massachusetts records, that by 1820 there had been 9,856,126 acres disposed of.[3] If this figure is subtracted from the present area, there remains 9,276,674 as the amount of the public land, or approximately one-half the area of the state. The joint committee of Maine and Massachusetts estimated in 1821 that the amount of public land was 8,218,320 acres.[4]

The boundaries of the state had not been determined at that time and a large portion of the state had not been surveyed; consequently, the estimate made by the committee could have been little more than an intelligent guess.

From 1783, the year Massachusetts became a sovereign state, to 1820, public land in Maine was disposed of rapidly; 1,103,415 acres were granted to " literary and other public institutions; "

---

1 *Maine Forestry Bulletin*, no. 8, p. 22.

2 Moses Greenleaf, *Survey of Maine*, 1829, p. 416. Greenleaf said that to consider the incorporated towns as the settled portion of the state was not entirely accurate but for all practical purposes it was adequate.

3 *Ibid.*, p. 418.

4 *Cf. supra*, p. 17.

THE PUBLIC LANDS 185

4,320,617 acres were sold at an average price of twenty-two and three-fourths cents an acre, bringing into the treasury $923,871.14. Most of this land was sold in large tracts, only 79,010 acres having been sold to settlers.[5]

At the time of separation, the most important question to be settled was the ownership of the public land. An agreement was reached whereby the public land was to be divided equally between the two states and a commission was established to make the division. It was also provided that all grants of land which had been made by Massachusetts should continue in full force after separation.

In order to get a complete picture of the amount of land which was eventually at the disposal of Maine, it will be necessary to consider two problems: the Northeastern Boundary controversy and the purchase by Maine of the Massachusetts lands.

At the time Maine became a state, the northern and eastern boundaries had not been definitely located. The treaty between Great Britain and the Colonies in 1784,[6] which established these boundaries, was worded in such general terms that a controversy immediately arose as to the exact location of the dividing lines. The eastern boundary was determined in 1795, but the northern boundary remained a subject of controversy for many years and it was not until after a clash of arms had taken place between Maine and the province of New Brunswick in 1839 that the governments of Great Britain and the United States energetically attempted to settle the matter. In 1842, Lord Ashburton came to this country and made an agreement with the American Secretary of State, Mr. Daniel Webster, by which 4,489,600 acres of the disputed territory was awarded to Maine and 3,207,680 acres to Great Britain. The state of Maine accepted this settlement on the condition that the United States government pay her an indemnity of $125,000 and reimburse her for the expenses she had undergone as a result of the con-

5 Moses Greenleaf, *op. cit.*, p. 427, ad. *passim.*
6 Treaty between Great Britain and the United States, 1784, art. ii.

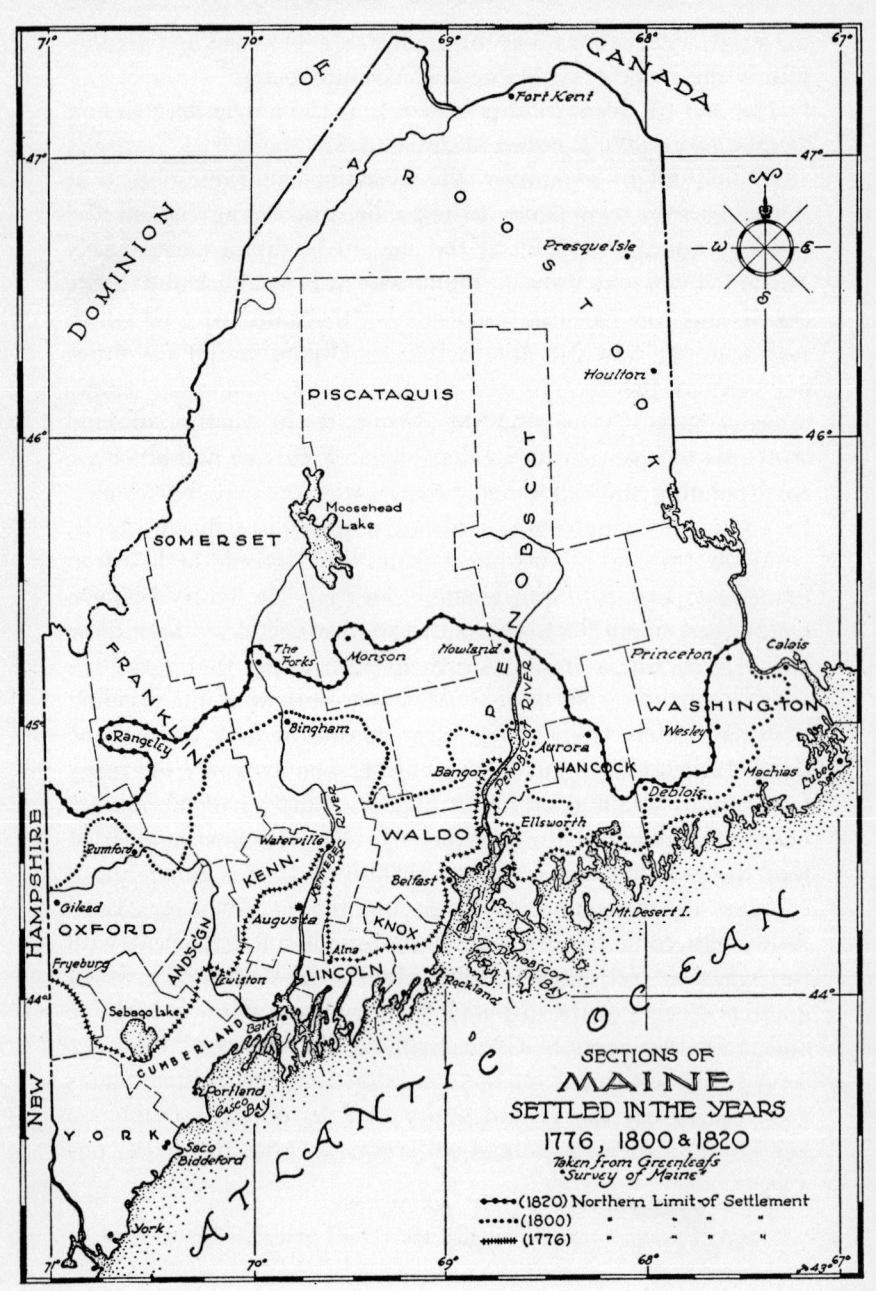

SECTIONS OF MAINE SETTLED IN THE YEARS 1776, 1800 & 1820
Taken from Greenleaf's "Survey of Maine"

●●●● (1820) Northern Limit of Settlement
●●●● (1800)
━━━━ (1776)

troversy.[7] Practically all of this land was public land and became jointly the property of Maine and Massachusetts.

The Act of Separation provided that the public land should be divided equally between Maine and Massachusetts. Between 1820 and 1830, a number of divisions of several hundred thousand acres were made. In 1832, because of the difficulty of making equitable division of the public land, an agreement was concluded whereby the public land was to be sold without dividing it and one-half the proceeds of the sales was to go to each state. It was also agreed that each state would spend ten per cent of the receipts for roads, surveys and other public improvements.[8] After 1848, Massachusetts refused to continue with this ten per cent agreement, leaving the whole burden of road building and other improvements on the state of Maine.[9] In 1850, Massachusetts passed a law providing that no more public land should be sold but that the policy should be followed of selling permits to cut timber and that the land should be held in perpetuity.[10] This policy was objectionable to Maine for two reasons: first, it would greatly hinder the opening of the settling lands, because those of Massachusetts were intermingled with the settling lands belonging to Maine; second, because the public land belonging to Massachusetts was exempt from taxation while the title rested with the state, and an undue burden of taxation would be placed on other land for the support of local functions of government.

After considerable negotiation, Maine in 1853 purchased Massachusetts' interest in the public land for $362,000, paying $112,000 in cash and the balance in serial bonds. The total amount of land purchased was 1,198,000 acres.[11]

[7] Henry S. Burrage, *Maine in the Northeastern Boundary Dispute*, p. 336, ad. passim.

[8] *Resolves of Maine 1832*, ch. xi.

[9] "Message of Governor Hubbard to the Legislature 1853," found in Public Documents 1853, pt. ii.

[10] *Annual Report of the Land Agent 1851*, p. 7.

[11] *Annual Report of the Treasurer 1853*.

In considering the alienation of the public land, there are three main phases to follow: grants, sales of timber land and sales of settling land. In general, the policies were: (1) to be generous in making grants to educational institutions and for other public purposes; (2) to sell the timber land as rapidly as possible and (3) to sell the settling lands to actual settlers for a nominal price on very easy terms.

In the grants of land made, Maine was very liberal in supporting education. Over 700,000 acres were set aside for the establishment of a permanent school fund, the principal of which was to be kept inviolate and the interest to be used for the support of the common schools of the state.[12] In each township, 1,000 acres were reserved for the use of the common schools of that township when it should be incorporated.[13] All of the colleges in the state received grants of land. Nearly all of the academies received grants.

Grants were also made for purposes other than education. Revolutionary soldiers were given 200 acres each. In a number of cases, grants were made to towns for the purpose of aiding them in constructing roads. Only one case was found where a grant was made to a private company. This was a grant in 1868 of 700,000 acres to the European and North American Railroad for the purpose of encouraging the construction of a railroad from Bangor to the eastern boundary of the state. This grant later became known as the "state steal."

Because the policies followed in disposing of timber lands were different from those followed in disposing of settling lands, the alienation of these two types of lands will be treated separately. The first law concerning the disposal of the public land was passed in 1824. This law created the office of land agent, charged with the duty of administering the public land. It provided that the land agent should select townships,[14] the

12 Cf. infra, pp. 209-210.
13 Cf. infra, pp. 205-209.
14 The system of surveying land into townships of six miles square containing 23,040 acres had been adopted by Massachusetts before 1820.

THE PUBLIC LANDS 189

land of which was suitable for settling, and designate them as settling lands. Other townships were to be designated as timber lands.[15] The first policy adopted for disposing of the timber lands was that of restricting narrowly the amount to be sold to any one person, so that the land might not fall into the hands of large land holders and become a subject of speculation. The restrictions originally imposed were set forth in the following section of the law:

Be it further enacted, that such land as may be unfit for settlement and cultivation, and properly falling under the denomination of timberland shall be laid out in lots and sold for its just value, not exceeding five hundred acres to any one person; one-half of the purchase money to be paid at the time of contracting, and the other half to be paid in three annual payments, with interest annually, with good and sufficient surety for the payment thereof.[16]

Little timber land was sold under this law. Evidently the policy was not satisfactory, because in 1826 the law was changed, providing that the land agent, acting under the advice of the commission created by the act of separation, should designate the townships which were "considered valuable chiefly for the timber thereon" as timber land and should set a minimum price on them. The land agent was then to sell them at public auction after ninety days' notice, whenever he could obtain a price greater than the minimum set. The terms of payment were similar to those in the preceding act.[17] Reference to Table 38 will show that under this act, sales greatly increased. In 1826, sales amounted to only 12,092 acres, while in 1827, 101,909 acres were sold. From this time until the depression, which began in Maine in 1836, annual sales continued to be large.

15 *Public Laws of Maine 1824*, ch. 993.
16 *Ibid.*, ch. 280.
17 *Ibid.*, *1826*, ch. 366.

TABLE 38
SALES OF PUBLIC LAND IN MAINE, 1824-1878 *

Year	Number of acres	Average price per acre	Amount received
1824	1,448	$ .84	$ 1,219.84
1825	36,711	.50	18,369.92
1826	12,092	.40	4,822.63
1927	101,909	.22	22,920.90
1828	263,676	.31	82,206.51
1829	129,483	.21	26,627.79
1830	162,282	.28	45,234.45
1831	21,661	.68	14,779.64
1832	92,393	.66	61,091.73
1833	70,989	.42	30,469.27
1834			
1835	230,146	1.45	335,478.62
1836	2,630	.99	2,612.80
1837	3,274	1.66	5,447.00
1838	12,837	.74	9,504.77
1839	33,558	1.48	49,718.79
1840			
1841	18,050	.88	15,915.92
1842	17,868	.43	7,862.27
1843	1,661	.28	465.77
1844	147,637	1.08	159,924.64
1845	48,459	.45	22,230.26
1846	47,310	.60	28,514.90
1847	105,625	.86	91,678.04
1848	101,220	.77	78,451.95
1849	145,708	.46	67,074.28
1850	324,913	.49½	169,538.99
1851	39,823	.31	12,446.42
1852	310,802	.47	145,714.01
1853	316,926	.49	155,520.21
1854 [a]	5,050		1,431.00
1855	10,456		4,150.45
1856	34,351		
1857	4,968		
1858			

TABLE 38—*Continued*

Year	Number of acres	Average price per acre	Amount received
1859	76,605		
1860	87,479		
1861	54,396		
1862	55,566		
1863	193,509		
1864	68,376		
1865	75,450		
1866	132,901		
1867	158,695		
1868	39,314		
1869	30,390		
1870	19,707		
1871	69,161		
1872	26,203		
1873	57,481		
1874	150,328		
1875	113,826		
1876	22,764		
1877	12,709		
1878	30,083		

* Annual reports of the treasurer for years 1824-55. Annual reports of the land agent for years 1856-78.

(a) No data available after 1853 concerning price of land per acre or amount received.

Two changes were made between 1826 and 1836 in the laws regulating the sale of timber lands. The law of 1828 limited the amount of land which could be sold in any one year to eight townships, or an amount equal to eight townships. The cash payment received was reduced from one-third of the purchase price to one-fourth.[18] In 1832, a plan was adopted, in conjunction with Massachusetts, which made the sales of timber land much easier. It was provided that no further divisions of the public lands should be made, but that the land agents of

18 *Ibid.*, *1828*, ch. 313.

the two states, acting jointly, should sell the land and the proceeds should be divided equally between the two states, after deducting the expenses of surveying, road building, and exploration. The expenses were not to exceed ten per cent of the sales price. The land was to be classified into six classes, according to value, except that class three should be settling land and a minimum price per acre placed upon each class.[19] The minimum prices set by the law are shown in Table 39.

TABLE 39

MINIMUM PRICE SET ON EACH CLASS OF PUBLIC LAND BY THE LAW OF 1832

Class	Price per acre
I	$0.75
II	.60
III	.50
IV	.40
V	.30
VI	.20

The terms of payment were changed so that it was possible for a lumberman to purchase land and begin operations without any cash payment. It was provided that the land should be paid for in five annual payments, with interest; that the state should have a lien on all timber cut until the land was paid for; that no timber should be cut without a permit from the land agent; and that the title to the land should not be conveyed until the last payment was made. Since the date of the first payment was not designated, it was possible for a lumberman to buy land, make the first winter's cut, and then, out of the proceeds of the sale of that cut, make the first annual payment.[20]

The ease of the terms of sale contributed to the development of a great speculation in Maine lands. Hugh McCulloch, Secretary of the Treasury in the administrations of Presidents

[19] *Resolves of Maine 1832*, ch. 119.
[20] *Ibid.*

Lincoln, Johnson and Arthur, gives vivid description of conditions in the early Thirties: [21]

The wildest speculation that has ever prevailed in any part of the United States was in the timber lands of Maine. In 1832 . . . it became known to people in Massachusetts that a good deal of money was being made by a few investors in the Maine timber lands. . . . The lands were offered for sale by the State at very low prices and those who bought early and judiciously did make what were then considered large fortunes by their investments. It was not long before reports of their gains went out from the neighborhood to which they were confined and, as is usual with such reports, they were magnified as they were repeated until almost everybody in New England who heard them was seized with the desire to speculate in Maine lands.

The desire to speculate became so strong and the excitement so great that a courier line was established between Boston and Bangor, by which orders first to buy and subsequently to sell, were rapidly transmitted, and for months little was talked about but Maine lands. Brokers' offices were opened in Bangor which were crowded from morning until night and frequently far into the night by buyers and sellers. All were jubilant, because all, whether buyers or sellers, were getting rich. Not one in fifty knew anything about the lands he was buying, nor did he care to know as long as he could sell at a profit. Lands bought one day were sold the next day at a large advance. Buyers in the morning were sellers at night. The lands were bought and sold over and over again, until lands which had been bought for a few cents an acre were sold for half as many dollars. As is always the case when speculation is rampant and inexperienced men become speculators, dishonesty was in the ascendant.

This great speculation came to a climax in 1835, when 230,146 acres were sold at an average price of $1.45 an acre. Cash and securities amounting to $335,478.62 were received from these sales. In 1833, the last previous year when information was available, only 70,987 acres were sold, the average

[21] Hugh McCulloch, *Men and Measures of Half a Century* (1888), p. 215.

price per acre having been forty-two cents. The depression began in Maine in the early part of 1836, and as a result, sales of timber land ceased. In describing the situation, the land agent,[22] at the end of 1836, said:

> The sales of public land the past season have been very small, and mostly confined to closing the old settling land contracts. Such has been the pecuniary embarrassments of the whole community, it was not thought advisable to put any on the market. None, therefore, has been sold except in settlers' lots.
>
> The wild spirit of speculation which so recently swept like a desolating pestilence over the whole country, turning industry and capital from their natural channels, has at length spent its fury, and men are beginning to return to their respective occupations.

Large sales of timber land were not resumed until 1844, when 147,673 acres were sold at an average price of $1.08 an acre. There was some demand for timber land in the early Forties but sales did not increase then because a law had been passed which provided that land could not be sold to one person in an amount greater than 700 acres and that it must be paid for in cash.[23] The land agent, in his annual report of 1843, said that little land could be sold under those terms and recommended the repeal of the law. In 1844, restrictions as to the quantity of land which could be sold were removed, and it was provided that the terms of payment should be one-quarter of the purchase price in cash and the remainder in three annual payments.[24]

Reference to Table 38 shows that the annual sales were large until 1854. By the end of 1853, the most valuable lands had been sold and consequently in following years, with some exceptions, sales were small. With the grant of 700,000 acres to the European and North American Railroad in 1868, practically all of Maine's timber land was gone. That which remained was in

---

22 *Annual Report of the Land Agent 1836*, p. 12.
23 *Public Laws of Maine 1842*, ch. 33.
24 *Ibid., 1844*, ch. 129.

small tracts scattered throughout the state. The final disposal of the remainder of the timber lands will be considered after the policy followed in the case of the settling lands is described.

In the case of land suitable for agriculture, the policy of encouraging settlement, rather than that of raising revenue, was followed from the beginning. Governor King, in his first message to the legislature, wrote as follows:

The lands belonging to the State will deserve your attention. Should a system be adopted for their management, calculated to prevent speculation, at the same time giving every encouragement to the real settler, the expectations of the best friends of Maine will be fully realized in an extended cultivation and an increased number of inhabitants.[25]

The first law regulating the sale of the public land, passed in 1824, made liberal provisions for the sale of land suitable for agriculture and for the encouragement of settlement. The law provided that the land agent should select those townships that were suitable for settlement and cause them to be surveyed into lots of one hundred acres each. The first forty settlers in a township were entitled to purchase a lot for thirty cents an acre. The remainder of the land in the township was to be sold at sixty cents an acre, but not more than five hundred acres were to be sold to any one person. If a person purchased more than three hundred acres, he was required to locate two settlers on the land and perform for each lot the same settling duties as were required for the purchase of single lots. The terms of payment were that one-half the purchase price should be paid in cash, and the other half in labor on the roads of the township. In addition to paying the purchase price for the land, the settler was required to live on the lot and, within four years, to build a house and to clear fifteen acres, ten of which to be laid down in grass. As an additional aid to settlement, it was provided that the best mill site and two hundred acres should be reserved

25 "Message of the Governor 1820," found in *Resolves of Maine 1820.*

and given to the person who should build the first saw and grist mill and offer bond that he would maintain and operate it for eight years.[26]

An analysis of the provisions of this law shows that the subject of settlement had been given careful consideration and that there was a desire to eliminate or alleviate the usual difficulties of settlement. The actual amount of money required was small, only fifteen dollars for one hundred acres; an attempt to provide roads was made by allowing settlers to pay part of the purchase price of the land by working on the township roads; by requiring settling duties the possibility of speculation in the lands was lessened and encouragement was given for the building and maintenance of a saw and grist mill.

In 1828, this policy of disposing of the settling land was abandoned, and the land agent was authorized to sell settling lands in any amounts to any one person at a price of not less than fifty cents an acre. The terms of payment were that one-fourth of the purchase price be paid in cash during the first five years and that the remaining amount be paid in three annual payments during the next three years.[27] In 1832, the law was changed so that settling lands could be sold to " such persons only as intend and will engage to settle and improve the same." [28]

In 1835, the settling duties provided by the act of 1824 were restored and the amount of land which could be sold to any one person was limited to four lots of 170 acres each. The price was fifty cents an acre and the terms of payment were that one-fourth was to be paid in cash and the remainder in three annual payments, the annual payments to be secured by notes with two or more sureties.

That this system of disposing of the settling lands was not successful is attested to by the land agent in his annual report for 1837. He said:

26 *Public Laws of Maine 1824*, ch. 280.
27 *Ibid., 1828*, ch. 313.
28 *Resolves of Maine 1832*, ch. 119.

However advantageous these terms may appear, their practical effect was anything but favorable to the growth and prosperity of the towns thus opened for sale and settlement. No sooner did a town commence settling than the want of mills and roads and schools was severely felt, and not infrequently caused the more enterprising, after a few years of privation, to leave and seek more commodious location. . . . If an agent had been invested with discretionary power to open roads, erect mills and supply such other aid as is furnished by proprietors, this effort might have been more successful.[29]

In 1838, the legislature, recognizing that more liberal terms were necessary for the promotion of the settlement of the public land, changed the terms of payment to one-fourth cash, to be paid within four years, and the balance to be paid by labor on the roads within three years. It was also provided that when twenty or less settlers gave bond that they would erect a saw and grist mill on a lot in the township, designated by the land agent, they should be given that lot free, also a deed to their own lots on the performance of the settling duties.[30] In 1842, that section of the law relating to saw and grist mills was repealed.[31]

No more changes in the law were made until 1850, when a more liberal policy was adopted. Since 1850 marked the beginning of a new policy, it will be interesting to obtain some idea of the success of the settling land policies up to that date. A statement by the land agent in 1848 throws light on this subject:

From the year 1838 to the year 1842, under the impulse given by these several enactments, about sixty thousand acres of settling land was conveyed, subject to the conditions of the settling law; but although very extensive sales were made during this time, the conditions failed to be complied with . . . and of the sixty thousand acres sold, less than seventeen thousand acres had been settled for.

29 *Annual Report of the Land Agent 1837*, p. 11.
30 *Public Laws of Maine 1838*, ch. 354.
31 *Ibid., 1842*, ch. 33.

Nothwithstanding these terms, liberal as they certainly are, the call for settling lands has diminished yearly from 1842 to the present time .. and in the past year there has been issued from this office but two certificates, each for a lot of one hundred and sixty acres. The truth is that the situation of these lands, so far to the north, their distance from market towns, the injury to the wheat crop by the weevil, the rot of the potato, all conspire to retard seriously the progress of their settlement. Let us hope that the two last will prove but temporary impediments and that these crops may hereafter reward the husbandman with their former abundance.[32]

In 1850, under the leadership of Governor Hubbard, the law was revised with the purpose in mind of giving a greater stimulus to settlement. It was provided that not more than 200 acres should be sold to any one person. The price was fifty cents an acre, to be paid for by labor on the roads in three years. The same settling duties were retained. The land agent was instructed to build roads in the settling townships as rapidly as they were needed. Agents were appointed in each township to aid the settlers in locating their land, supervise the performance of settling duties and road work.[33] No further changes were made in the settling land law.

In the next few years, roads were built into the settling townships as fast as they were needed and the public became better informed of the exceptionally fertile qualities of the Aroostook County soil, with the result that sales of land increased. Reference to Table 40 shows that from 1860 on, annual sales were large and regular. By 1878, the state's supply of settling land was exhausted and the land agent was able to say, "All the public lands of the state having been disposed of, no favors are now within the power of the state to grant for homesteads for settlers."[34]

[32] *Annual Report of the Land Agent 1848*, p. 6.
[33] *Public Laws 1850*, ch. 206.
[34] *Annual Report of the Land Agent 1878*.

Following the grant of land to the European and North American Railroad in 1868, the state had only a small amount of timber land remaining. In 1874, the legislature authorized the land agent, under the direction of the governor and council, to sell at public auction the remaining timber lands and such portion of the lands as had been designated as settling lands, but which were not suitable for settling.[35] The sale was held in

TABLE 40

SALE OF SETTLING LANDS IN MAINE, 1840-1878 *

Year	Number of acres	Year	Number of acres
1840	6,642	1865	10,876
1841	15,869	1866	9,408
1842	24,138	1867	7,434
1844	4,049	1868	11,167
1846	732	1869	11,189
1848	320	1870	14,211
1855	7,082	1871	43,572
1856	5,199	1872	18,736
1857	2,245	1873	14,188
1859	45,700	1874	23,489
1860	47,767	1875	14,616
1861	40,543	1876	13,054
1862	33,709	1877	10,833
1863	12,452	1878	21,382
1864	9,355		

* Annual reports of land agent.

Bangor in 1874. By this sale, the state parted with 118,034 acres for which it received $145,553. After this sale, there still remained some scattered lands, which were sold at public auction in 1875.[36] There now remained only a small amount of settling lands, which were disposed of by 1878.

Having treated the acquisition and disposition of the public lands, it remains to consider the revenue received from them.

35 *Resolves of Maine 1874*, ch. 319.
36 *Report of the Forest Commissioner 1908*, p. 92.

From 1820 to 1860, the land agent paid into the treasury $1,988,000. This was twenty-one per cent of the total receipts for that period. Between 1860 and 1870, the land agent paid into the treasury $284,000. After 1870, with the exception of the years 1874 and 1875, when the auctions mentioned above took place, the receipts were insignificant. The total receipts from the public land were not far from $2,500,000.[37]

Summarizing, it can be said that when Maine became a state, about half of the area of the state was public land; that only a relatively small portion of it passed directly from the state to the possession of actual settlers; that a relatively large portion went into the hands of large land owners at nominal prices and that in only one period (1820-1860) were the receipts from the sale of this land of any particular significance to the finances of the state government.

[37] The data in this paragraph were compiled from the annual reports of the treasurer.

CHAPTER X
THE TRUST FUNDS

THE State of Maine is custodian of several trust funds, two of which—the Lands Reserved for Public Uses Fund and the Permanent School Fund—are of considerable historical interest. In amount, these two funds comprise sixty-seven and one-half per cent of the total funds which the state holds. The history of these two funds will be treated first.

The Lands Reserved for Public Uses Fund had its origin in the early days of the statehood of Massachusetts. On July 9, 1784, the general court of Massachusetts passed a resolve instructing the committee for the sale of eastern lands, " in conveying each township . . . to appropriate two hundred acres for the use of the ministry, two hundred acres for the first settled minister, two hundred and eighty acres for the use of the grammar school, and two hundred acres for the future disposition of the general court." [1] On March 26, 1788, the general court ordered the committee to reserve in each township conveyed, " four lots of three hundred and twenty acres each; one for the use of the first settled minister, one for the use of the ministry, one for the use of the schools and one for the future appropriation of the general court." [2] In 1820, when Maine became a state, there were 53,000 acres of these lands which had been reserved, but which still remained in the care of the state because the townships in which they were located had not been settled.[3]

The act of separation contained two provisions which were of great importance for the future of the reserved lands. The first one reads as follows:

[1] *Annual Report of the Land Agent 1882*, p. 5.
[2] *Ibid.*
[3] " Report of the Joint Committee of Maine and Massachusetts," found in *Resolves of Maine 1821*, p. 77.

All grants of land . . . or grants of land not yet located, which have been made by the said commonwealth, before separation of the said district shall take place, and having or to have effect within the said district, shall continue in full force, after the said district shall become a State.[4]

This provision prevented the state of Maine, without the consent of Massachusetts, from appropriating the reserved lands to purposes other than those which were intended.

The second provision reads as follows:

In all grants hereafter to be made by either State, of unlocated land within the said district, the same reservations shall be made for the benefit of schools and of the ministry, as heretofore have been usual, in grants made by this commonwealth.[5]

This provision was important because it compelled both Massachusetts and Maine to continue the reserved land policy, and since the act of separation was considered as a contract between the two states, neither one could change it without the consent of the other. It was particularly advantageous to Maine because it compelled Massachusetts to reserve lands in those townships which were allotted to her by the act of separation.[6]

The first act for the regulation and disposal of the public land was passed by Maine in 1824. It provided that:

There shall be reserved in every township suitable for settlement one thousand acres of land, to average in quality and situation with the other land in such township, to be appropriated to such uses, for the exclusive benefit of such town, as the Legislature may hereafter direct.[7]

---

[4] Constitution of Maine, art. x, sec. 5. Found in *Revised Statutes of Maine 1841*.

[5] *Ibid*.

[6] The act of separation allotted one-half of the public land to Massachusetts, amounting to about 4,500,000 acres, or about one-quarter of the area of the state.

[7] *Public Laws of Maine 1824*, ch. 280.

This act did not conform to the requirement of the act of separation in two respects. In the first place, the act of separation required that there should be lands reserved in every township, while the act of 1824 required lands to be reserved only in townships suitable for settlement. This difficulty was remedied in the act of 1828, which read as follows: " There shall be reserved in every township, suitable for settlement, whether timberland or otherwise. . . ."[8] This act was evidently interpreted to mean that 1,000 acres should be reserved in every township, since that was the practice followed from this date.

That portion of the act of 1824 which reads, " for the exclusive benefit of such town, as the Legislature may hereafter direct," was not in conformity with the act of separation, because the Massachusetts statute provided specifically that specified portions of these lands should be reserved for schools and the ministry, and this statute was carried into the constitution of Maine by the act of separation. A careful examination of the laws passed from that day to this has failed to reveal any act passed by the legislature directing any use to which these lands should be put. The inference has been drawn from the phrase "for the exclusive use of that town" that when a township was incorporated, the reserved land should be turned over to that town, and this practice has been followed. There is nothing, even today, in the *Revised Statutes of Maine,* which directs that after a town comes into the possession of these reserved lands the income from them or the income from a fund created by the sale of them shall be used for school purposes, although this is the practice and is thought to be the law.[9]

In 1824, the legislature passed another act which is often cited as the authority by which the reserved lands were appropriated for school uses. The significant part of the act follows:

8 *Ibid., 1828,* ch. 393.
9 See *State v. Mullen,* 97 Maine 336.

That in all cases where lands have been reserved or granted for the use of the ministry, or the first settled minister in any town in this state, where the fee in such lands has not already become vested in some particular parish within such town, or in some individual, the fee and estate in such lands shall be, and is hereby declared to be vested in the inhabitants of such town, and not in any particular parish therein, for the support of the Gospel Ministry in such town forever. And in all cases where lands have been granted or reserved for the use of the schools in any town within this State, the fee in which is not already vested otherwise, the same shall be and is hereby declared to be vested in the inhabitants of such town, for the support of the schools therein forever.[10]

This act could have referred only to the lands which had been reserved by Massachusetts before separation, because the act of 1824 providing for the reservation of 1,000 acres says, " for such future uses, for the exclusive benefit of such town, as the Legislature may hereafter direct." The legislature had not then, or has not since, directed any use.

In 1831, the legislature passed an act requesting Massachusetts to agree to a modification of the act of separation, so that lands reserved for the first settled minister and for the ministry, or any funds arising from the sale of such lands, could be used for schools.[11] Massachusetts agreed to this,[12] and in 1832 the legislature of Maine passed the following act:

That the income from any fund, which has arisen, or which may arise, from the proceeds of the sale of lands reserved for the use of the ministry, or for the first settled minister, in any town in this State, and which fund, or the land from which it may arise, has not become vested in some particular parish within such town, or in some individual, is hereby required to be annually applied to the support of primary schools in such town.[13]

10 *Public Laws of Maine 1824*, ch. 254.
11 *Ibid., 1831*, ch. 391.
12 *Laws of Massachusetts 1831*, ch. 147.
13 *Public Laws of Maine 1832*, ch. 39.

This law did not apply to the lands reserved under the act of 1824 because the legislature had not directed the use to which these lands should be put.

In 1832, Maine and Massachusetts made an agreement that the undivided lands should be sold in common and that the practice of reserving lands in each township, which had been followed by Maine, should be followed in these joint sales.[14] Up to this time in the townships which Massachusetts had sold, four lots of 320 acres each had been reserved. Following 1832, the reserved lots in all townships were 1,000 acres.

The question may now be considered as to why the legislature of Maine has never passed a law specifically directing what the future use of the land should be, and why they have come to be considered as lands reserved for school purposes, even though there has been no specific legislative sanction for it. It should be recalled that the Massachusetts law of 1788 reserved 320 acres for the first settled minister, the ministry, and for the schools respectively, for the use of those parties in the particular town where the land was located. The act of separation, which was incorporated in the constitution of Maine, provided for the continuation of this policy. That this act was presumed to have established a contractual relationship between the two states is evidenced by the fact that when Maine desired to divert the ministerial lands to school uses in 1831, it was thought necessary to secure the consent of Massachusetts. It will be recalled that the first law passed by Maine regulating the public lands provided for the reservation of lands " for the exclusive benefit of such towns, as the legislature may hereafter direct." The question arises: Did the legislature of Maine have the constitutional power to direct the uses of these lands? If these acts—the Massachusetts Act of 1788, the Act of Separation, the Maine Act of 1824, and the Maine Resolve of 1832 to which Massachusetts agreed—are read together it is clear

---

14 *Resolves of Maine 1832*, ch. 119. For the policy of joint sales, see ch. ix, p. 221.

that the intent for the use of these lands was for school purposes in the towns in which they were located.

The key to the legal authority under which the reserved lands become vested in a town when it is incorporated and which compels the use of this land for school purposes, is clarified by a case which came before the supreme court of Maine in 1912. The decision reads in part:

By the Statutes of 1824, Chapter 280, as revised by the Statutes of 1828, Chapter 393, the State by general law enacted that there should be reserved in every township, suitable for settlement, whether timberland or otherwise, one thousand acres of land, to be appropriated to such public uses, for the exclusive benefit of such town, as the legislature should thereafter direct. By this legislation the State constituted itself a trustee, retaining as such, the legal title, but subjecting the land to such future public uses, for the benefit of the town, as the State itself might afterwards direct, until the town should be incorporated, when, under the Statute of Uses, the title would vest in the town.[15]

The court, by using the clause, "when, under the Statute of Uses, the title would vest in the town," recognized that there was no specific legislation vesting the title to this land in the towns or directing the uses of this land. By bringing in the Statute of Uses, the court established as law that which had long been custom and practice.[16]

The distinction between the reserved lands and the fund now known as the Reserved Land Fund should be emphasized at this point. The title to the 1,000 acres of reserved lands in each township is held by the state until a township is incorporated as a town. When a town is incorporated, the title to the land is conveyed to the town, and the town is compelled to create a school fund with it, the income from the land or from the fund created by the sale of the land, to be used for the support of the

15 *Mace v. Land and Lumber Company*, 112 Maine 420.

16 See *Words and Phrases, third series*, vol. vii, p. 152. Also see *Ohio and Colorado Smelting and Refining Company v. Barr*, 58 Colorado 116.

schools of that town. The fund known as the Reserved Land Fund has been created from money received from the sale of timber and grass on the reserved lands. The history of this fund will now be treated.

The first law authorizing the sale of timber and grass on the reserved lands, passed in 1846, provided:

The moneys arising from the sale of timber on the reserved lots in any unincorporated township, or from trespasses on such lots, and which have already been or may hereafter be paid into the treasury of the county where any such township is situated, shall constitute funds for school purposes, of which the income only shall be expended and applied.

The county commissioners in each county may invest such funds in the securities of any such county, or in the stocks of this State. ...

If there are no inhabitants on such township, the annual interest accruing from such investments shall be added to the principal of the fund; but if the inhabitants of any such township shall have become organized into a plantation, for election purposes or otherwise, and shall have organized one or more school districts according to law, the county commissioners shall cause the said annual interest to be paid yearly to the clerks of such plantations, and the same shall be applied to the support of schools in such district.[17]

In 1850, an act was passed transferring the management of the reserved lands to the land agent and requiring the county officials to pay to the state treasurer the money which had already accumulated. The land agent was instructed to sell permits to cut timber and grass on the reserved lands, the length of these permits to be from the time of sale until such time as the township should be organized into a plantation, or incorporated as a town. It was provided that the price of these permits should be " at the same rate per acre as the tract or township shall, or may have sold for," and that " the purchaser of the tract or township may elect to purchase such right; but

[17] *Public Laws of Maine 1846*, ch. 217.

in any case such party refuses to buy the right aforesaid, the land agent is authorized to sell the same to any other person." [18]

The state treasurer was required to open an account for each township and to keep a record of the amount due each township. Nothing was said in the act of 1850 about interest on these funds. Evidently it was not considered that the act of 1850 repealed that section of the act of 1846 which provided that the interest should be added to the funds, because in the revision of the statutes in 1857, there appeared the following: " The annual interest shall be added to the principal of such fund until the inhabitants of said township or tract are incorporated into a town or organized as a plantation." [19] This provision remained in the statutes until changed in 1917.[20]

No legislation of significance was passed between 1850 and 1917. In 1917, it was provided that this fund should be converted into two funds, one to be known as the Unorganized Township Fund and the other as the Organized Township Fund. The income from these two funds was to be used differently. The Organized Township Fund was composed of money which had accumulated to the credit of townships organized as plantations. The state agreed to pay interest at the rate of four per cent on these funds to plantations for the benefit of the schools.[21] This was substantially the practice which had been followed since 1846. In 1919 the rate of interest was increased to six per cent.[22]

The Unorganized Township Fund was to be composed of money which had accumulated to the credit of unorganized townships. It was provided that the income from this fund, instead of being added to the principal as had been done since 1846, should go to the state school equalization fund. The state agreed to pay interest at the rate of four per cent on this fund.[23]

18 *Ibid., 1850*, ch. 196.
19 *Revised Statutes of Maine 1857*, ch. 5, sec. 15.
20 *Ibid., 1916*, ch. viii, sec. 21; *Public Laws of Maine 1917*, ch. 261.
21 *Ibid.*   22 *Ibid., 1919*, ch. 15.
23 *Ibid., 1917*, ch. 261.

If the line of reasoning followed on page 206 is correct, the law establishing the Unorganized Township Fund is unconstitutional. The Massachusetts Law of 1788, which was carried into the Maine constitution by the act of separation, stated that the lands were to be reserved for the *exclusive benefit* of the towns in which they were located. The point upon which the constitutionality of this law depends may be presented by the following question: When a trust fund is created for the use of a specific party, this party to come into possession of this fund at some future time, when he shall have performed some particular act or some specific thing shall have happened, is the trustee of the fund entitled, without specific authority, to appropriate the income from this fund for his own use, or should it be added to the principal of the fund? Of course the answer is simple. The trustee is no more legally entitled to the income from the fund than a stranger would be. The case at issue is analogous to the question propounded. The state of Maine stands in the relation of trustee to these funds until such time as the township shall have been organized as a plantation or incorporated as a town. Nothing is said about the disposition of the income from this fund. The state is diverting the income from this fund to purposes other than the *exclusive use of such towns*. As the matter stands, at some future time the state may be asked to restore to this fund the income which it is now diverting. The present amount of the reserved lands fund is $834,512.06.[24]

The Permanent School Fund was created by an act passed by the legislature in 1828. Excerpts from this act will convey information concerning the origin of the fund and the regulations under which it was to be operated.

That the land agent, under the advice of the Governor and Council, be, and he hereby is authorized to sell at Public Auction or Private sale, whenever in their opinion the same can be done at a fair price, any number of townships already surveyed, and not

[24] *Report on The State Trust Funds*, Governor Gardiner, 1932.

otherwise appropriated, not exceeding in the whole twenty townships of land.

Be it further enacted, that the Treasurer of the State be directed to keep a separate account of all monies he may receive from the sales of said land . . . and the same shall constitute a permanent school fund to be reserved for the benefit of the primary schools. And said fund shall be put out at interest, in such manner as a future Legislature shall determine, and the interest annually distributed among the several towns and plantations in the State according to the number of scholars therein. . . . [25]

This law also provided that any money which might be received from the Massachusetts militia claim, in excess of what the state might owe at that time, should be added to the Permanent School Fund. When the claim was paid, however, the public debt exceeded the amount received and consequently nothing was added from this source.[26]

In 1834, the act of 1828 was amended so that it became mandatory for the land agent to sell twenty townships as soon as possible.[27] In the revision of the statutes in 1857, it was provided that the state in the future should pay interest on this fund at the rate of six per cent.[28] In 1857, a resolve was passed providing that in the future twenty per cent of all money received from the sale of public lands should be added to the Permanent School Fund.[29] The last addition to this fund was in 1864, when it was provided that the timber on ten townships should be sold and the proceeds of the sale added to the fund.[30] The amount of this fund in 1932 was $566,894.62.[31]

The Passamaquody Indian Fund is a fund which originated with the sale of timber and grass on Indian Township, and the

[25] *Public Laws of Maine 1828*, ch. 403.
[26] *Cf. supra*, p. 23.
[27] *Resolves of Maine 1834*, ch. 58.
[28] *Revised Statutes of Maine 1857*, ch. ii, sec. 73.
[29] *Resolves of Maine 1857*, ch. 72.
[30] *Ibid.*, *1864*, ch. 326; *1868*, ch. 253.
[31] *Report on the State Trust Funds*, Governor Gardiner, 1932.

sale of fishing permits on islands owned by the Passamaquody Indians. The fund amounted to $138,260.83 in 1932.

The Penobscot Indian Fund came from the sale, in 1833, of four townships of land belonging to the Indians. It was provided that the proceeds of the sale of these townships should be retained by the state and only the income from the fund, thus created, should be used for the benefit of the Indians. The amount of this fund was $88,092.44 in 1932.

The remainder of the trust funds were created by bequest. Their origin is not deemed of sufficient interest to warrant inclusion in this study. The names and amounts of the trust funds are presented in Table 41.[32]

Prior to 1917, the state had never segregated and invested any of the trust funds which it had received. As these funds had been received, they were used to meet current expenses and a liability was set up on the books of the state, upon which interest was paid as the conditions of the trusts or legislative enactment required. In recent years, these funds have been restored by the state.

The beginning of this restoration was the result of a political controversy, which arose in 1915 over what Governor Curtis, a Democrat, thought was an attempt by a Republican legislature to discredit his administration by making excessively large appropriations. The governor refused to allow the expenditure of many of the appropriations for buildings on the grounds of insufficient funds in the treasury. As a means of creating a condition in which there would be insufficient funds in the treasury, he interpreted that section of the revised statutes, which said that the reserved lands fund should " be held in the Treasury " to mean that it should actually be held in cash. He accumulated in the treasury cash equal to the amount of the reserved lands fund and credited it to that fund. By that procedure he created a condition whereby there was

[32] For a detailed explanation of the origin of the trust funds created by bequests, the reader is referred to "Report of the State Trust Funds" (1931) by Frank Cowan, which is now on file in the state treasurer's office.

TABLE 41
STATE TRUST FUNDS, 1932*

	Amount
Augusta State Hospital	$ 58,773.44
Bangor State Hospital	2,000.00
University of Maine	219,300.00
Central Maine Sanitorium	1,812.02
Western Maine Sanitorium	90,009.54
State Military and Naval Children's Home	23,730.02
State School for Girls	11,712.15
State School for Boys	1,300.00
Pownal State School	6,000.00
Jordan Forestry Fund	1,000.00
Houlton Academy	2,000.00
Foxcraft Academy	1,000.00
Hebron Academy	1,100.00
School District—Madison	1,000.00
Madawaska Training School	5,000.00
Maine School for Deaf	6,384.44
Penobscot Indian Fund	88,092.44
Passamoquody Indian Fund	138,260.38
Permanent School Fund	566,894.62
Lands Reserved for Public Uses	834,612.06
Total	$2,057,781.59

*Taken from *Report on State Trust Funds,* 1932, by Governor Gardiner.

insufficient free funds to pay for the building appropriations. Consequently when the next administration took office, it was necessary to make some disposition of this large amount of cash.[33]

As a result of this condition, an act was passed which created the Farm Lands Loan Commission, and provided that this money should be invested in farm mortgages, bonds of the United States, Maine and several other states, as well as bonds of municipalities of those states.[34]

[33] Information in this paragraph was obtained from the state auditor, Mr. Elbert D. Hayford.
[34] *Public Laws of Maine 1917,* ch. 303.

The next step in restoring the trust funds was taken in 1923. In that year, at the suggestion of Governor Baxtor, Mr. Elbert D. Hayford, the state auditor, drafted an act and caused it to be introduced into the legislature, providing that both the state and municipalities should restore and invest their trust funds. This act met great opposition, because it would have required both the state and municipalities to raise immediately large sums of money in order to restore their trust funds. The mayor of Portland stated that if this act were passed, his city would be compelled to raise $250,000 from taxation. A compromise was reached whereby all funds received in the future, either by the state or municipalities, should be invested.[35]

In 1929, an act was passed which provided that when in any one year there should be received more than $1,000,000 from the inheritance tax, this excess should be used to restore the trust funds. This money was to be allotted to the different funds and to be invested by the treasurer.[36] In 1930, some money was available for this purpose, while in 1932 sufficient was received to complete the restoration.[37]

These funds were invested in bonds of several states and municipalities and deposited in banks chartered by the state of Maine. Since 1931 there have been losses on the bonds and some of the banks in which there were deposits have failed. Because many of the banks are still in the process of liquidation and because at this time it is difficult or impossible to determine the worth of many of the bonds, the treasurer has not been able to determine the extent of the losses. These losses bring up the question of the liability of the state for them. It is an open question as to whether or not the state is legally liable. There is, however, a moral responsibility and it is probable that when the amount of the losses is determined, the state will replace them.

35 *Ibid., 1923*, ch. 222.
36 *Ibid., 1929*, ch. 273.
37 *Report on State Trust Funds*, by Governor Gardiner, 1932.

CHAPTER XI
FINANCIAL ADMINISTRATION

PREVIOUS chapters have dealt chiefly with the two main divisions of public finance, which are payment for services performed by the government and provision of funds with which to make these payments. Financial administration is that phase of government which ties these two together. It includes planning and executing, recording and verifying, collecting and paying and the custody of funds.[1] In a broad sense, financial administration includes everything which has anything to do with governmental finances and when thus construed it touches every detail of governmental operations. Consequently, the quality of financial administration which a government has is largely determined by the kind of administrative organization which has been created. Overlapping functions, bureaus and departments independent of executive control, and officials not responsible to the executive render impossible any adequate financial administration. In most American states the government has grown in a haphazard fashion. New departments and bureaus have been added as new functions have been assumed, without any attempt to create a unified or integrated governmental organization. As a result, when attempts have been made to reorganize and improve the financial administration of a state, it has been found necessary to change other phases of the state administration. Such changes usually involve increasing the power of the chief executive, unification and departmentalization of scattered administrative bureaus and establishing an effective system of financial control.

Maine was no exception to the general rule. For over a hundred years its administrative organization grew without any effective attempt to create an efficient administration, until in 1930 the National Institute of Public Administration was en-

[1] H. L. Lutz, *Public Finance* (New York, 1936), pp. 851-852.

THE TRUST FUNDS 215

gaged to make a study of the state government and present a plan for reorganization. The purpose of this chapter is to present a brief description of conditions which existed prior to 1930 and to explain the reforms which grew out of the recommendations of the institute.

The structure of the present state government originated with the constitution of 1819. That document created the offices of governor, secretary of state, treasurer, attorney general and the council. In the early Nineties an amendment to the constitution created the office of adjutant general. The governor is elected by popular vote for a term of two years. The other constitutional officers, with the exception of the adjutant general, who is appointed by the governor, are elected by the legislature for terms of two years.[2] Statutory offices and boards were added as the functions of government were increased, until in 1930 there were sixty-five of them in existence, about twenty of which were single officers. The ability of the government to function under such an administrative organization was well summarized by the institute in its study.

Viewed as a single structure, the administrative organization is a ramshackle one, consisting of many statutary leantos without proper constitutional foundation, not at all integrated in administration and largely lacking in coordination of functions. Besides, many antiquated methods are still followed, especially in the state's financial procedure. The state administration as a whole lacks unified direction and control; it has too many officials for a comparatively small state government and official responsibility is too easily shifted if not practically dissipated.[3]

Probably the most serious difficulty which the institute found with the state government and one which grew out of the whole administrative organization, was the limited scope of

[2] Originally the terms of office were for one year but in 1880, the constitution was amended to provide for two-year terms.
[3] *State Administrative Consolidation in Maine*, 1930, p. 8, National Institute of Public Administration.

the authority of the chief executive. Article V, section 1 of the constitution provides that " the supreme executive power of this state shall be vested in the Governor," but subsequent sections of this document place serious limitations on the exercise of this power. The curtailment of the governor's power did not end with the limitations set by the constitution. The whole plan of state administration, as established by legislative enactment, tended to place further limitations on the office of the chief executive and to cause it to be one of relative unimportance. In addition to the difficulties caused by the many independent and uncoordinated departments, boards and agencies, many of the powers which, according to the institute, should have been lodged with the governor, were given to the council, thereby weakening the office of chief executive.

The council, as previously stated, was composed of seven members elected by the legislature for terms of two years, provision being made for apportionment of membership among the several counties on the basis of population. The duties of the council, prior to 1930, as summarized by the institute, were as follows:

This body approves the selection of all state employees, fixes salary rates and increases, passes on trips to out-of-state conventions by state officials, confirms all appointments of notaries public, justices of the peace and other officials appointed by the governor. It passes on specifications and bids for road and other construction, approves contracts for state printing and binding, sits on the issuance of state bonds and distributes the fire insurance on state property. It approves the refunds of foreign inheritance tax receipts and the refunds of receipts erroneously paid on fish and game licenses. It sits on accident claims in the state highway and other departments; it approves pensions to state employees and others, as well as doles to state paupers. It holds hearings and passes on all pardons. It approves all warrants for payment by the state treasurer, all transfers between appropriations, all expenditures to be made from the contingent fund of $300,000 . . . [4]

[4] National Institute of Public Administration, *op. cit.*, p. 25.

FINANCIAL ADMINISTRATION 217

From the foregoing it appears that the authority of the governor was seriously limited by powers granted to the council and that many duties placed on that body were of such a nature that it could not efficiently perform them, this being particularly true concerning the approval of warrants for payment by the state treasurer.

Another weakness of the administrative system was the provision for keeping the accounts of the state and for auditing them. The office of state auditor was created in 1907 and the duties of maintaining central accounts, checking all claims for payment, preparing warrants for the approval of the governor and council and auditing all state accounts were assigned to it.[5] The institute found that no satisfactory system of central accounts had been established and that the auditing work left much to be desired.[6]

The institute also found that no satisfactory system of budgeting existed. A budget committee had been created in 1919 composed of the governor, governor-elect, the state auditor, the treasurer, a member of the house of representatives appointed by the speaker of the house and a member of the senate appointed by the president of the senate. The duty of this committee was to prepare a report for the next legislature containing a statement of appropriations and expenditures for the current biennium, an estimate of revenues and recommendations for appropriations for the next biennium.[7] The institute, believing that the budget should be prepared solely by the executive, did not approve of the existing law.

No central purchasing agency existed except an unofficial association, known as the State of Maine Purchasing Agents Association. Membership in this association and purchases through it were wholly voluntary. In 1929, only twenty-six per cent of the state's purchases were made through this association.

5 *Public Laws of Maine 1907*, ch. 147.
6 National Institute of Public Administration, *op. cit.*, pp. 50-54.
7 *Public Laws of Maine 1919*, ch. 102.

The administration of taxes was found to be scattered among several departments, property taxes being administered by the state board of assessors, the gasoline tax by the state auditor, the inheritance tax by the attorney general, motor vehicle licenses by the secretary of state and bank taxes and other excise taxes jointly by the state board of assessors and certain boards and commissions.

The institute in considering the problem of reorganization said:

We believe that nothing short of complete administrative reorganization should be undertaken. No halfway measures, no piecemeal readjustment will meet the present situation. Nothing less than a comprehensive, well balanced and properly integrated reorganization will suffice. Such a plan will require constitutional as well as statutory changes for its adoption.[8]

The reorganization plan proposed by the institute was designed "to center all executive responsibility in the governor through the establishment of a small number of administrative departments under his control and direction." It proposed to establish nine major departments as follows: (1) executive; (2) finance; (3) health and welfare; (4) agriculture; (5) highways; (6) corporations; (7) conservation; (8) labor and (9) education. Within these nine departments, all activities of the state were to be consolidated except the attorney general's office, the public utilities commission, the Port of Portland Authority, the University of Maine and the Maine Development Commission. No immediate change was contemplated in the status of these latter agencies. The office of state auditor was to be left elective and its activities restricted to conducting post-audits of the accounts of the state and its agencies. It was thought that by making the auditor elective he would be in a position to conduct independent audits free from executive influence and thus act as a check on the executive and the departments.

[8] National Institute of Public Administration, *op. cit.*, p. 8.

On the submittal of the report of the institute, Governor Gardiner, at whose instance the survey had been undertaken, appointed a citizens committee, representing different sections and interests of the state, to study the report and to make recommendations to the legislature. Mr. A. E. Buck, who had been a member of the institute staff making the survey, was employed to work with the committee and draft a bill for presentation to the legislature. The bill presented was passed and became a law in 1931.[9] Charts 1 and 2 show the organization of the government before and after the passage of this law.

While the reforms brought about by this law were substantial, they were not so extensive as the recommendations of the institute called for. No constitutional changes were made; the powers of the council limiting the authority of the governor remained nearly the same as before and there still remained numerous agencies not consolidated within the departments. Four new administrative departments, finance, health and welfare, sea and shore fisheries, and education were created and twenty-eight offices, bureaus, divisions, boards and agencies were abolished, the functions which they formerly performed being transferred to various departments. The office of state auditor was changed to that of a department of audit and its duties restricted to making post-audits of the accounts of the state government and all of its agencies.

In a government reorganization which seeks to center all executive responsibility in the hands of the governor, the establishing of an adequate department of finance is of paramount importance. It has been said that "the department of finance should be the right arm of the governor in managing the state's business."[10] Scattered financial agencies should be concentrated in one department under the direction of an official appointed by and responsible to the governor. Among the more important duties which should be given such a department are the keeping

[9] *Public Laws of Maine 1931*, ch. 216.
[10] National Institute of Public Administration, *op. cit.*, p. 51.

of central accounts which will give information quickly, facilities for preparation of the budget, purchasing of supplies and possibly tax administration.

The administrative code [11] established in the department of finance a bureau of accounts and control, the head of which is a new officer known as the state controller; a bureau of purchases, the head of which is known as the state purchasing agent; a bureau of taxation which is headed by the state assessor and a state budget officer. As head of the department of finance, a new officer was created known as the commissioner of finance, who is appointed by the governor with the approval of the council. The heads of the bureaus and employees are appointed by the commissioner of finance with the approval of the governor and council.

To the bureau of accounts and control was given authority to maintain a general system of accounts; to examine and approve all contracts which incur obligations against the state; to audit and approve all claims; to make monthly reports to the governor and state auditor on all receipts and expenditures of the state government; to make monthly reports to the governor, state auditor and departments on appropriations, allotments and encumberances; to establish such subsidiary accounts for the various departments and agencies as seem desirable and to examine the accounts of every department or agency receiving appropriations from the state.

The condition of the accounting system of the state prior to the enactment of the code is summarized by the controller as follows:

Each institution and department had had its own bookkeeping system for many years. . . . Each of these was a separate unit and there was little or no relation or control with the financial offices in the state house. It was necessary in ascertaining the balances and cost information to go to the various institutions and

[11] The law reorganizing the state government became popularly known as the "Administrative Code" and will be referred to hereafter as "the code."

CHART I
Organization of the State Government of Maine Prior to the Reorganization in 1931.*

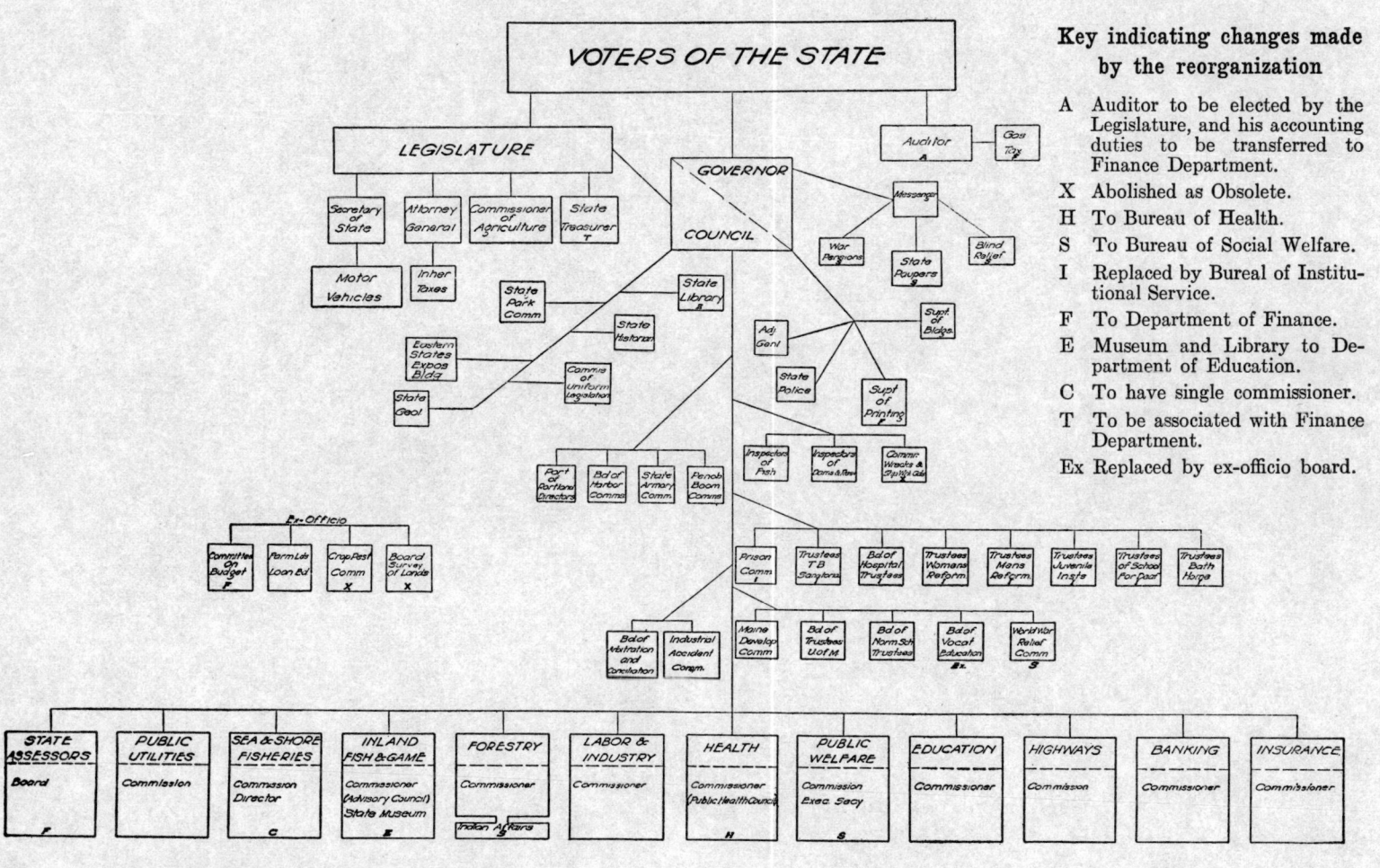

Key indicating changes made by the reorganization

A Auditor to be elected by the Legislature, and his accounting duties to be transferred to Finance Department.
X Abolished as Obsolete.
H To Bureau of Health.
S To Bureau of Social Welfare.
I Replaced by Bureal of Institutional Service.
F To Department of Finance.
E Museum and Library to Department of Education.
C To have single commissioner.
T To be associated with Finance Department.
Ex Replaced by ex-officio board.

* *Message of Governor Gardiner to the Legislature, 1931.*

CHART II
ORGANIZATION OF THE STATE GOVERNMENT OF MAINE AFTER THE REORGANIZATION IN 1931.*

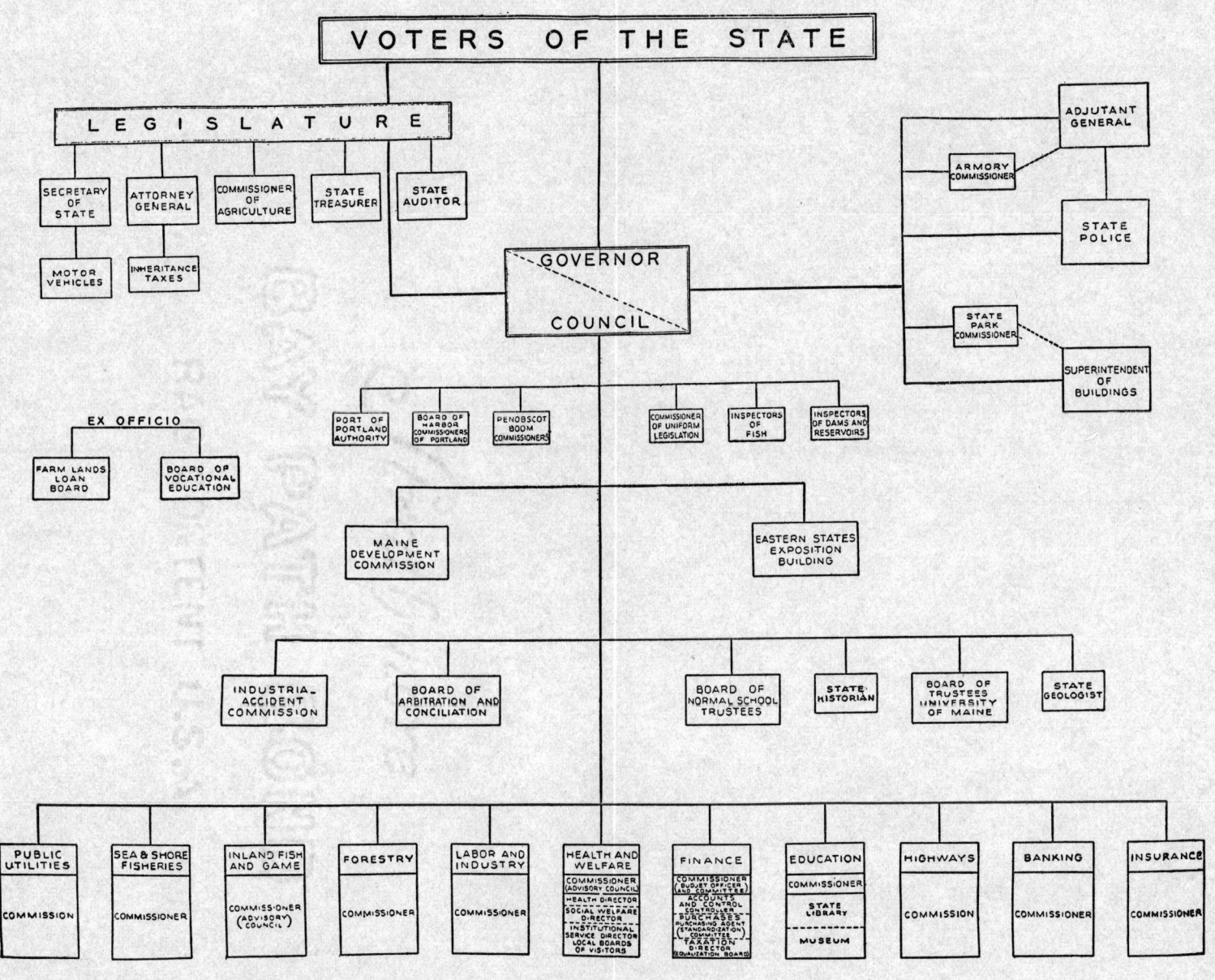

Message of Governor Gardiner to the Legislature, 1931.

FINANCIAL ADMINISTRATION 221

departments. . . . The results thus found took so much time to get that they were practically useless at the time they were finally secured as in most cases the current need had long since passed.[12]

A new system of accounting was installed which centralized practically all records in the bureau of accounts and control. The only accounts now being kept by the departments and institutions are inventory and voucher registers. The treasurer's office, which was not consolidated with the department of finance because of constitutional difficulties, now keeps only a cash book of receipts and disbursements. Because of the great amount of detail which was involved and the necessity of getting out reports quickly, the Hollerith machine system was installed. This system permits not only the keeping of records in great detail but also the supplying of information with great facility. Expenditure accounts may be classified as to function, object, fund or organization unit; it takes but a few minutes to ascertain the unexpended balance of any department or to make a summary report of the conditions of state finances; financial reports which formerly took months to prepare can now be made in a few days.[13] With such a system of accounting in effect, good control of the state finances is made possible.

Authorities generally agree that the power of preparing and executing the budget should be lodged with the chief executive.[14] An attempt was made to do this but, as will be seen later, without complete success. The office of state budget officer was created in the department of finance with authority to prepare a biennial budget; to examine and recommend quarterly work programs and allotments for each department and agency of the state government; to investigate duplication of work of

12 *Biennial Report of the Department of Finance 1934*, p. 16.

13 Information concerning accounting was obtained from the *Biennial Report of the Department of Finance 1934* and from the state controller, William A. Runnells.

14 A. E. Buck, *The Budget in Governments of Today* (New York, 1934), ch. 3.

departments and other agencies; to study the organization and administration of departments and to make recommendations for improvements; and to prepare any financial data which the governor and legislature might require.

The scope and form of the budget is prescribed with considerable exactness. It is required that the budget shall present a complete financial plan for each fiscal year of the ensuing biennium, which shall set forth all proposed expenditures, all interest and debt charges and an estimate of revenue. The budget must be set up in three parts, part one consisting of a message by the governor outlining the financial policy of the state government for the next biennium and presenting a general budget summary in such manner as to show the balanced relations between proposed expenditures and anticipated revenues, contrasted with corresponding figures for the last complete fiscal year and the fiscal year in progress. Part two must contain the detailed budget estimates both of expenditures and revenues. Part three must be an appropriation bill embracing the recommendations made in the first two parts of the budget. Appropriations for operation and maintenance of the departments and agencies must be in lump sum; for the acquisition of property they may be itemized in such manner as the governor may direct.

As procedure for preparation of the budget, each department and agency of the state government is required to present to the state budget officer on or before November 1 of the even numbered years, on forms prescribed by him, estimates of their expenditure requirements for each year of the next biennium, compared with corresponding figures for the last complete fiscal year and the current fiscal year. These expenditure estimates must be classified so as to set forth the data by funds, organization units, character and object, or in any other manner which the budget officer may require. These estimates must be reviewed by the governor and the governor-elect, with the assistance of the state budget officer and such changes made as seem desirable. A legislative advisory committee is also provided, consisting of a representative and a senator, and a legislator chosen by these two. The representative is appointed by the speaker of the house and the senator by the president of the senate. Their function is advisory but the governor is under no legal obligation to consult them. After the estimates have been revised, the budget officer is required to prepare the budget document, which must be presented to the legislature by the governor not later than the fourth week of the regular legislative session.

The first step in the execution of the budget is the preparation of work programs and allotments. It is required that not later than June 1 of each year, each department and agency shall present to the department of finance a work program for the ensuing fiscal year, such program to include a statement of all appropriations made and requested allotments for expenditures by quarters for the fiscal year. The governor and council, with the assistance of the state budget officer, must review these requests and make such changes as seem advisable before approving them. After approval by the governor and council, the state budget officer is required to transmit copies of the work programs and allotments to each department or agency concerned, and also to the state controller, who is given authority to authorize all expenditures on the basis of such allotments. Work programs and allotments may be revised at the end of each quarter with the approval of the governor and council. In order to provide some degree of flexibility, the governor and council may require each agency or department, when making the original allotments, to set up a reserve, the exact amount of which is determined by the governor and council. At any time during the year, this reserve may be returned to the original appropriation to which it belongs or it may be transferred to the allotment of any other department or agency. Any unexpended or unencumbered allotment at the end of each quarter is credited to the reserve set up for the fiscal year.

As procedure for making disbursements, it was provided that the state controller should examine and authorize the payment of all claims against the state and that such authorization be in the form of a warrant drawn in favor of the payee, which shall become a check on a designated bank when countersigned by the state treasurer. This procedure is of questionable constitutionality, because the constitution provides that " no money shall be drawn from the treasury but by warrant of the Governor and Council." It is possible, however, that the courts might decide that approval of work plans and allotments by the governor and council fulfill constitutional requirements.

The budgetary procedure established by the code is along lines generally recognized as sound [15] except for the division of authority between the governor and council in the execution of the budget. The council, as evidenced by events in the two administrations from 1932 to 1936, through its power of approving appointments, work programs and allotments, is able to force the governor to retain officials and to make appointments not satisfactory to him and is also able to dictate to a considerable extent departmental work programs and allotments.

To the bureau of purchases, established in the department of finance, was given authority to purchase all supplies, material and equipment needed by the state government; to establish and enforce standard specifications for all supplies, material and equipment; to purchase or contract for all telephone, telegraph, postal and electric light and power service for state departments and agencies; to lease all grounds, buildings, office or other space required by the state; to give general care and supervision to central storerooms operated by the state government; to transfer to or between state departments and agencies or sell supplies which are surplus or unused; to make an inventory of state property and keep it current and to establish a central mailing room for the state departments located at the capitol. Under this authority a system was established which it is

[15] National Institute of Public Administration, *op. cit.*, ch. iii.

FINANCIAL ADMINISTRATION 225

claimed saved fifteen per cent on state purchases in the biennium July 1, 1932 to June 30, 1934 and thirty per cent in the biennium July 1, 1934 to June 30, 1936.[16] It is also claimed that by control of storerooms of the departments and institutions much waste and loss has been prevented. The purchase of liquor for the state liquor stores by the state liquor commission is a notable exception to the centralization of state purchasing. These purchases amounted to $3,320,341.75 in 1936. The state purchasing agent recommends that the buying of liquor be done through the bureau of purchases.[17]

Although the institute recommended that all tax administration be concentrated in a bureau of taxation in the department of finance, this recommendation was only partly realized in the code. A bureau of taxation was created in the department of finance as recommended, but only the administration of the property tax and the gasoline tax was transferred to it. Later the administration of the retail store license tax was given to it.[18] The state board of assessors was abolished and its duties transferred to the division of property taxes in the bureau of taxation. The office of state assessor was created, the duties of which are to be head of the bureau of taxation and chairman of a new board of equalization. This new board consists of the state assessor and two part time members, the part time members to serve only as required by the state assessor and to be paid on a per diem basis. Administration of other taxes remained, as before, scattered among the different departments.

The location of tax administration in the department of finance may appear logical but plans which appear logical on paper may not always work out well. Such seems to have been the case regarding tax administration in Maine. Although the institute recommends that tax administration be placed in a

---

16 *Biennial Report of the Department of Finance 1934*, pp. 13-15; *1936*, p. 14.

17 *Ibid.*, *1936*, p. 14.

18 *Public Laws of Maine 1933*, ch. 260.

department of finance, other authorities are by no means agreed that this is the best plan.[19] Professor H. L. Lutz, who has made a study of taxation in Maine, condemns the location of tax administration in the department of finance and the lack of any real tax administration reform in the reorganization of 1931. In support of his position, he has the following to say:

The position taken here in respect to the bureau of taxation is that the relatively minor place to which it was assigned by the reorganization act of 1931 has had a bad psychological effect. The bureau has been treated by everyone as a minor bureau because of its minor position. So far as the act of 1931 goes, tax administration is a less important matter than budgeting, purchasing or accounting. Of the 30 sections in Article II of this act (the department of finance article), only three sections at the end of the article relate to tax administration, and one of these is taken up with establishing a relatively useless state board of equalization. The result has been that state tax administration in Maine has been neglected, both from the standpoint of its financial support and from that of recognition of its fundamental importance to the state.
. . . Maine has never had an adequately developed state tax administration, and when the opportunity of improving the situation was presented, at the time the state reorganization scheme was being planned, nothing was done to lift the tax administration to its proper level.[20]

Professor Lutz then went on to recommend that a department of tax administration be created with the administration of all taxes concentrated in it and that adequate powers and funds be given to it. With the views and recommendations of Professor Lutz, this writer agrees.

A department of audit was created which was required to perform a post audit of all accounts and other financial records of the state government or any department or agency thereof;

19 *Proceedings of the National Tax Association 1925*, pp. 263-288; H. L. Lutz, *Public Finance*, ch. xxxv.
20 H. L. Lutz, *The System of Taxation in Maine 1934*, pp. 80-81.

to install accounting systems and to perform audits for cities, towns and villages when requested to do so by them; to prepare and publish an annual report setting forth the essential facts concerning its audit of the department of finance and other departments and agencies of the state government sixty days after the close of each fiscal year. It is also provided that the head of this department shall be known as the state auditor and that he shall be elected by the legislature for a term of four years. The purpose of making the auditor elective by the legislature was to free him of executive control in order that he might make an independent audit of the departments and institutions responsible to the executive. This purpose has not been achieved, however, because of limited appropriations granted. Each year the auditor has said in his annual reports, " As stated in previous reports, the present force in this office is available for only a small part of the auditing which the law requires." [21] No audit has been made of the department of finance since its creation. The department of audit has devoted its time to the auditing of special funds such as trust funds, agencies receiving money such as normal schools and the accounts of a relatively small number of cities and towns. While the auditing which has been done is desirable, the really important work is that of auditing the central accounts that are kept in the bureau of accounts and control. With only three auditors [22] it should be obvious that the department of audit can do nothing in auditing such an extensive system of accounts. Through budgetary control the executive, intentionally or unintentionally, has been able to prevent an independent audit of departments and institutions under his control as effectively as he would have been able to do had the appointment of the state auditor been left in his hands. A possible remedy for this situation would be to take requests for appropriations for the department of audit out of

21 *Annual Report of the Department of Audit 1935*, p. 2.
22 *Ibid., 1934*, p. 2.

the budget and make financial relations direct between the state auditor and the legislature, as has been done for the judiciary.

In summarizing, it may be said that substantial progress has been made in consolidating and coordinating departments and agencies of the state government, although much remains to be done; a good system of budgeting has been established but executive control of the execution of the budget has not been achieved; a modern and satisfactory system of accounting has been created; no adequate facilities for tax administration exist; and provisions for auditing would be satisfactory if sufficient appropriations were granted.

BIBLIOGRAPHY

GENERAL WORKS

Abbott, John S., *History of Maine*, Portland, 1892.
Bartlett, E. H., "Local Government in Penobscot County," *University of Maine Studies*, second series, no. 21.
Blakey, R. G., *Taxation in Minnesota*, Minneapolis, 1932.
Brush, Edward H., *Rufus King and His Times*, New York, 1926.
Buck, A. E., *The Budget in Governments of Today*, New York, 1934.
———, *Public Budgeting*, New York, 1929.
Burrage, Henry S., *Maine in the Northeastern Boundary Dispute*, Portland, 1919.
Cleveland, F. A. and Buck, A. E., *The Budget and Responsible Government*, New York, 1920.
Coe, H. B. (editor), *Maine: Resources, Attractions and Its People*, 5 vols., New York, 1928.
Coleman, J. K., *State Administration in South Carolina*, New York, 1935.
Conwell, R. H., *Life and Public Services of James G. Blaine*, Augusta, 1884.
Davis, Daniel, "Proceedings of the Two Conventions Held in Portland to Consider the Expedience of a Separate Government in Maine," *Massachusetts Historical Society Collections*, first series.
Dingley, Edward H., *Life and Times of Nelson Dingley*, Kalamazoo, 1902.
Dingley, Nelson, *Autobiography of Nelson Dingley*, Lewiston, 1874.
Dodge, M. A., *Biography of James G. Blaine*, Norwich, 1895.
Fessenden, Francis, *Life and Public Services of William Pitt Fessenden*, Boston, 1907.
Greenleaf, Moses, *Survey of Maine*, Portland, 1829.
Hamlin, Charles E., *Life and Times of Hannibal Hamlin*, Cambridge, 1899.
Hamlin, Cyrus, *My Life and Times*, Boston, 1893.
Hatch, L. C., *Maine, A History*, 4 vols., New York, 1919.
Hormel, O. C., "Maine Towns," *Bowdoin College Municipal Research Series*, no. 9, 1932.
Hasse, Adelaide, *Index to Economic Material in the Documents of Maine*, Washington, 1907.
McCall, Samuel W., *Life of Thomas B. Reed*, Boston, 1914.
McDonald, William, *The Government of Maine, Its History and Administration*, New York, 1902.
McCulloch, Hugh, *Men and Measures of Half a Century*, New York, 1888.
National Industrial Conference Board, *Cost of Government*, New York, 1934.
Proceedings of the Fifteenth National Tax Conference, 1922.
Proceedings of the Twenty-Third National Tax Conference, 1930.
Pattangall, W. R., *Maine's Hall of Fame*, Augusta, 1916.
Ramsdell, H. J., *Life and Public Services of James G. Blaine*, Philadelphia, 1884.

Report of the New York State Commission for the Revision of the Tax Laws, Albany, 1932.
Stanward, Edward, " The Separation of Maine from Massachusetts," *Proceedings of the Massachusetts Historical Society*, series iii, vol. i, pp. 125-165.
Stanward, Edward, *James Gilespie Blaine*, Boston, 1905.
Staples, Arthur G., *The Letters of John Fairchild*, Lewiston, 1922.
Stetson, W. W., *History and Civil Government of Maine*, New York, 1898.
Sullivan, James, *History of the District of Maine*, New York, 1795.
Williamson, Charles E., *Life of Abner Coburn*, Bangor, 1885.
Williamson, Joseph, *Bibliography of Maine*, 2 vols., Portland, 1896.
Williamson, W. D., *History of Maine*, Hallowell, 1832.
Willoughby, W. F., *The Principles of Public Administration*, New York, 1927.
Words and Phrases, third series, vol. 7, St. Paul, 1929.

Official Documents of Maine

SERIAL

Annual Report of the Adjutant General, 1832-1936.
Annual Report of the Secretary of Agriculture, 1859-1936.
Annual Report of the State Board of Assessors, 1891-1931.
Annual Report of the Attorney General, 1859-1936.
Annual Report of the State Auditor, 1907-1936.
Annual Report of the Treasurer, 1827-1936.
Banking:
  Annual Report of the Bank Commissioners, 1829-1867.
  Annual Report of the Bank and Insurance Commissioner, 1868-1869.
  Annual Report of the Bank Examiner, 1870-1871.
  Annual Report of the Condition of Savings Banks, 1872-1904.
  Maine Bank Report, 1905-1936.
Biennial Report of the Budget Committee, 1917-1936.
Collected Documents:
  Public and Legislative Documents, 1828-1867.
  Public Documents, 1868-1934.
Biennial Report of the Department of Finance, 1932-1936.
Report of the Forest Commissioner, 1891-1933.
Industrial and Labor Statistics of Maine, 1883-1886.
Annual Report of the Insurance Commissioner, 1870-1936.
Annual Report of the Land Agent, 1832-1892.
Laws:
  Public Laws of Maine, 1820-1936.
  Private and Special Laws of Maine, 1820-1936.
  Resolves of Maine, 1820-1936.
Legislative Documents:
  Public and Legislative Documents, 1828-1867.

Legislative Documents, 1868-1899 and 1931-1936.
Legislative Record, 1903-1936.
Senate Bills and Senate Documents, 1901-1929.
House Bills and Documents, 1901-1929.
Maine Senate Journal, 1854-1936.
Maine House Journal, 1855-1936.
Messages of the governors to the legislature, 1824-1934.
Maine School Report, 1854-1936.

NON-SERIAL

Farm Taxation in Maine, Bulletin 336, Agricultural Experiment Station, University of Maine.
Annual Reports of cities and towns, 1903 and 1932.
Annual Reports of counties, 1903 and 1932.
Financing of the Public Schools in Maine, 1934, "Report of the Maine School Finance Commission."
"Forests of Maine," *Maine Forestry Bulletin*, no. 8.
"Report of the Joint Commission of Maine and Massachusetts," found in *Resolves of Maine*, 1821.
Report of the Special Tax Commission of Maine, 1889.
Report on the State Trust Funds, Frank Cowan, 1931.
Report on the State Trust Funds, Governor Gardiner, 1932.
State Administrative Consolidation in Maine, National Institute of Public Administration, 1930.
The System of Taxation in Maine, H. L. Lutz, 1934.

FEDERAL DOCUMENTS

Bureau of the Census:
  Financial Statistics of State and Local Governments, 1932.
  Census of Population, 1930.
  Statistical Abstract, 1933.
Interstate Commerce Commission:
  Statistics of Railways in the United States.

INDEX

Accounts, Bureau of, 224-225
Administration, Budget, 221-224; Bureau of Accounts, 224-225; Bureau of Purchases, 224-225; criticism of administration, 215-218; Department of Audit, 226-227; Department of Finance, 220; financial administration, 214; proposal for reorganization, 218-219; reorganization, 218-220; tax administration, 218, 225-226
Agriculture, Department of, 92-93
Aid to soldiers' families, 52
Assessment of property, 108-113, 122-123
Assessors, State Board of, abolished, 126-127; authority over local assessments, 125-126; criticism of, 134-136; created, 123; duties, 123-124; qualifications of members, 125
Audit, Department of, 226-227

Banks, national, taxation of, 139-144, 151-153
Banks, saving, number and deposits of, 148; taxation of, 66-67, 147-151
Banks, state commercial, charter of, 27; number and capital of, 140; purchase of stock by state, 27; receipts from tax ceased, 44; taxation of, 19, 137-139
Banking, venture of state into, 27
Banks, general comments on taxation of, 151-154
Bartlet, E. H., cited, 107
Bridges, Kennebec, 102; Waldow-Hancock, 103
Budget, preparation and execution of, 221-224
Budgeting, no satisfactory system of, 217
Burrage, H. S., cited, 187
Buck, A. E., cited, 219

Capitol, of the state, building of, 25-26
Charities and Correction, Department of, 87
Children, care of dependent, 87-88
Cities, chartering, 108
Civil War, aid to families of soldiers, 52; beginning of, 42; condition militia, 46-47; enlistment bounties, 47-52; enlistment of first ten regiments of militia, 46-47; protection of the coast, 47; reorganization of militia, 47
Conservation and development, 91-92
Constitution, amended to provide uniform taxation of property, 122; provisions concerning taxation, 109
Corporations, double taxation of, 119-120; franchise tax, 72, 82-83
Counties, development of, 107-108; functions of, 107-108
Courts of common sessions, establishment of, 24
Court, supreme judicial, establishment of, 23
Cowan, Frank, cited, 211

Debt, of the state government, 28-29, 33, 53-56, 60-65, 74-77, 99-104

Education, support of, 41, 59; also see schools
Enlistment bounties, 46-52
Express companies, taxation of, 57, 182-183
Equalization, State Board of, created, 126-127
Expenditures, 22-27, 31, 35-39, 40-41, 43-53, 57-60, 67-70, 72-74, 79-81, 83-95

Farm Lands Loan Commission, 212
Finance, Department of, 220
Forestry District, creation of, 74; increased rate of tax, 93
Forests, taxation of growing forests, 127-128
Functions of government, division between state and local, 22

Gasoline, taxation of, 83
Government, units of, 107, 108
Greenleaf, Moses, cited, 184-185

Health and Welfare, history of, 86
Highways, early building and maintenance, 22; first state highway law, 73; history of state highway department, 88-91
Hospitals, aid to, 88

233

INDEX

Indians, Penobscot, annuity, 18; treaty with, 18
Inland Fish and Game Department, 93
Insane asylum, building of, 26
Insurance companies, taxation of, 57, 154-158
Internal improvements, board created, 27
Lotteries, 19-22
Lutz, H. L., cited, 132, 214, 226

Maine, District of, separated from Massachusetts, 15-18
McCulloch, Hugh, cited, 193
Militia, condition of in the year 1861, 46-47; enlistment of the first ten regiments; expense of maintaining, 22
Mothers, aid to, 87
Municipal bounty debts assumed by the state, 55
Municipalities, forms of, 108; functions of government performed, 108

National Institute of Public Administration, cited, 215, 216, 217, 218, 219, 224
Northeastern Boundary Dispute, 17, 37, 39

Organization of state government before 1931, 219; after 1931, 220; proposals for reform of, 218

Pier, Maine State, 101-102
Plantations, description of, 108-109
Polls and estates, procedure of levying tax on, 113
Prison, recommendation for building, 24
Property, assessment of, 108-113, 122-123
Property taxation, assessment of, 109-113, 122-123; certain manufacturer's property exempt, 119-120; constitution amended to provide uniform taxation, 121; collection of taxes, 113; double taxation, 119-120; exemption, 117-120; intangibles escape taxation, 124-125; interests in timber and improvements on public lands made taxable, 120; jurisdiction for tax purposes, 118-119; levies, 129; Maine adopts Massachusetts' tax laws, 107; personal property defined, 116-117; real estate defined, 116; recommended improvements, 132-137; rates, 128-130; revision of tax laws, 116-117; studies of property taxation in Maine, 133-134; revision of tax laws, 116-117; yield of property taxes, 120-121
Purchasing, no central agency, 217-218
Purchases, Bureau of, 224-225
Public Lands, amount of, 17, 184; disposal of timber land, 188-196; disposal of settling land, 195-199; division between Maine and Massachusetts, 18, 187; grants, 188-189; Northeastern Boundary Dispute, 185-187; purchase of public lands owned by Massachusetts, 39, 187; public land sale, 20; sales by Massachusetts before 1820, 184-185; settling duties, 195-196; speculation in, 193; receipts from sales became negligible, 44; remaining lands sold at auction, 199-200; revenue received, 199-200

Railroads, chartering and growth of, 159-160
Railroads, regulation of, 159
Railroads, subsidy to European and North American, 45, 160
Railroads, taxation of, excise tax, 167; franchise tax, 161-167; "gross-net" tax, 169-177; property tax, 160; special provisions in charters, 160-161
Reform school for boys, building of, 41
Reformatories for men and women, establishment of, 93
Revenues, 21-22, 31-32, 39-40, 43, 56-57, 66-68, 71-72, 78, 80, 82-83, 96

Sanitariums, tubercular, 87
Script, issuance of, 53
Schools, common, appropriation of savings bank tax to, 59; common school fund, 23; support of, 70-73, 84-86
Schools, free high, 59
Sea Shoe and Fisheries Department, 93
Sinking fund of 1865, created, 55; discontinued, 62
Sinking fund of 1868, created, 57; discontinued, 64

INDEX

Soldiers, allotments, 52; aid to families, 52
Stanward, Edward, cited, 16
Subsidies to farmers, 37
Subsidy to European and North American Railroad, 45

Taxation, banks national, 139-144, 151-153; banks saving, 66-67, 147-151; banks state commercial, 19, 27, 44, 137-139; banks general comment, 151-153; express companies, 57, 182-183; forestry district, 74; forests, 127-128; gasoline, 83; insurance, 57, 154-158; polls and estates, 113; property, see property taxation; raidroads, 160-177; telephone and telegraph companies, 57, 177-182; trust and banking companies, 145-147
Tax administration, 218, 225-226
Taxation, Bureau, created, 126-127
Tax Commission, appointed 1889, 122-123

Taxes, delinquent, 114-115
Taxes for religious purposes, 115
Tax, local for highways, 115
Taxation, shift of burden from property to business, 121
Telephone and telegraph companies, taxation of, 57, 177-182
Towns, government of, 108
Township, description of, 108-109
Trust and banking companies, charter of, 144-145; number and assets, 146; taxation of, 145-147
Trust funds, Investment of, 213; Passamaquody Indian, 210-211; Penobscot Indian, 211; Permanent School, 209-210; Reserved Lands, 201-209; Restoration of, 211-213
Tubercular sanitariums, establishment of, 87

War of 1812, claim of Massachusetts on Federal Government, 18, 23
Williamson, W. D., cited, 19, 109